MW01199464

The
Almightier

ALSO BY PAUL VIGNA

The Age of Cryptocurrency
by Paul Vigna and Michael J. Casey

Guts: The Anatomy of The Walking Dead

The Truth Machine
by Michael J. Casey and Paul Vigna

The
Almightier

HOW MONEY BECAME GOD,

GREED BECAME VIRTUE,

AND DEBT BECAME SIN

Paul Vigna

ST. MARTIN'S PRESS
NEW YORK

First published in the United States by St. Martin's Press, an imprint of St. Martin's Publishing Group

EU Representative: Macmillan Publishers Ireland Ltd, 1st Floor, The Liffey Trust Centre, 117 -126 Sheriff Street Upper, Dublin 1, DO1 YC43

THE ALMIGHTIER. Copyright © 2025 by Paul Vigna. All rights reserved. Printed in the United States of America. For information, address St. Martin's Publishing Group, 120 Broadway, New York, NY 10271.

www.stmartins.com

The Library of Congress Cataloging-in-Publication Data is available upon request.

ISBN 978-1-250-34328-4 (hardcover)
ISBN 978-1-250-34329-1 (ebook)

The publisher of this book does not authorize the use or reproduction of any part of this book in any manner for the purpose of training artificial intelligence technologies or systems. The publisher of this book expressly reserves this book from the Text and Data Mining exception in accordance with Article 4(3) of the European Union Digital Single Market Directive 2019/790.

Our books may be purchased in bulk for specialty retail/wholesale, literacy, corporate/premium, educational, and subscription box use. Please contact MacmillanSpecialMarkets@macmillan.com.

First Edition: 2025

10 9 8 7 6 5 4 3 2 1

To Jeanne-Michele

She is Avarice, through whose influence money is deified in men's minds, and the dignity of divine worship is extended to a coin.

—Alain of Lille, *De planctu Naturae*, twelfth century

CONTENTS

INTRODUCTION

The Catechism of Cash

In 1933, the United States was at the nadir of economic depression. It had been three painful years since the Crash of 1929. Millions were out of work and there weren't any jobs to be had. People lost their homes. Hunger marches and riots became common across the country. Okies migrated in dilapidated cars to California, looking for jobs that weren't there. The government had few programs in place to help its citizens and it didn't have the money to do so, either; gold hoarding by banks and the ultrawealthy meant there wasn't enough currency circulating for everybody else. Soup kitchens sprung up in cities and towns across the nation. The grim mood was summed up by one of the most popular songs of 1932: "Once I built a tower up to the sun, brick and rivet and lime. Once I built a tower, now it's done; brother, can you spare a dime?"

There was one doozy of a job opening that year: president of the United States. Digging the country out of the mess it was in was going to be a gargantuan task, but there was one man who was up for it, who seemed even eager for it. Franklin Delano Roosevelt attacked this job with gusto. In his inaugural address, he famously declared that "the only thing we have to fear is fear itself." His administration was open to any and all ideas, and over the years would implement some absolutely radical policies. They passed new securities laws. They created a jobs program. They created programs that would rescue people from poverty and despair. Some of these initiatives are still with us today. But Roosevelt's plan to keep America from utter ruin had one more critical component. He had to rebuild the people's faith. Less than ten days after his inauguration, on March 12, 1933, FDR conducted the first of his national radio broadcasts, called "fireside chats." And in the midst of the worst economic collapse in the nation's history, the topic he chose was an apt one: money and the monetary system.

Roosevelt explained how banks work, and noted that the collapse was mainly due to a loss of confidence in the soundness of those banks. He talked about the things he would do to restore the system and people's confidence in it, zeroing in on the most important part of the entire endeavor. "There is an element in the readjustment of our financial system more important than currency, more important than gold, and that is the confidence of the people themselves," he said. "Confidence and courage are the essentials of success in carrying out our plan. You people must have faith; you must not be stampeded by rumors or guesses. Let us unite in banishing fear. We have provided the machinery to restore our financial system; and it is up to you to support and make it work. It is your problem no less than it is mine. Together we cannot fail."

Confidence and faith may seem like odd words to use when talking about money, but FDR was right to focus on them. Every time a monetary system collapses, or there is runaway inflation—Weimar Germany in the 1920s, Russia in the Bolshevik Revolution, Zimbabwe in the late twentieth century, Argentina today—the common denominator is that the people lose faith in their money. But why should their faith matter? Because money, to be blunt, isn't real. It has no objective existence of its own. Money doesn't grow on trees, or anywhere else for that matter. It doesn't *grow* at all. "It is not nature but law that gives it existence," Aristotle said more than two thousand years ago. The Greek word for money, *nomisma,* was derived from their word for law, *nomos.* Money was nothing more than a collectively agreed-upon system. Much more recently, the philosopher John Searle argued that money exists because of a "collective intentionality," which occurs when a group of people agree on a set of beliefs about something.[1] In other words, money has value because—and only because—we believe it has value. Monetary systems don't work because of the intrinsic value of gold, or dollar bills, or bitcoins. They work because of our faith in them. And infusing money with faith has resulted in a world where money is the bedrock of our entire society, the thing around which everything else is built.

It's not going too far to say the world revolves around money. Five thousand years ago, people's primary motivation in life was to please imaginary gods in the hopes of securing their favor while alive and everlasting peace after they died. Today the primary motivation is to make money. Money brings food and shelter, it brings security. Money brings comfort and peace of mind. Money can literally buy you life: wealthy people live longer, healthier lives than poorer people.[2] No, money doesn't buy everything, but it buys enough. I've gone through times in my life when I've had lots of money and times when I've had no money, and I can say pretty conclusively that life is *much* easier when you have money. How many of you tie your self-worth to your salary? Actually, forget that, it doesn't matter what you tie your self-worth to. *Society* ties your self-worth to your salary. That's what your salary is. Money is its own morality, its own value system. Some of you may disagree with that, and that is noble and admirable, but it's naïve. Don't kid yourself. Money is the prime mover in our world. How that came to be has largely been buried under the strata of history. I want to dig up that history and examine it, because I believe a lot of today's seemingly intractable problems are related to our misguided faith in money (my aim is to examine primarily American attitudes toward money rather than global, so the road I'm tracing here goes from the US through Europe and back to Mesopotamia).

At its most basic level, money is an accounting system, a way for a society to keep track of its stuff. That allows it to perform several useful functions. Money is a way to buy things, it's a way to standardize the value of different types of things (the value of everything from Italian ices to mansions can be expressed in dollar terms), and it's a way for people to warehouse their wealth. When it's working well it's a pretty handy thing to have. It's not surprising that soon after money appeared in the historical record, human society began to flourish and expand at an unprecedented rate. The problem doesn't start with money itself. The problem starts when we start believing that a simple tool is somehow something more. Before we can fix any of the really big society-level problems, we need to untangle that knot.

FDR did, ultimately, restore people's faith—in the banks, in money, in the government, in the whole thing—despite the considerable pain they were going through. He convinced them to have faith again, and once they did, he went ahead and killed the gold standard (because he needed to print more money) and implemented a "fiat" standard; everybody was okay with it because the particular details of a monetary system aren't as important as faith in the system itself. The infrastructure around our money is designed to reinforce this faith. Our currency is crammed with arcane symbols and regal images of past leaders designed to impress upon us a certain sense of majesty, permanence, and power. The New York Stock Exchange and the Federal Reserve's headquarters in Washington, DC, the Eccles Building, are basilicas of money, designed in the grand classical style. I'd wager every town in America has a local bank designed in the same way, with columns and marble and vaulted ceilings to emphasize the weight and importance of their endeavor: managing your money. They are churches of money. In fact, seen from this vantage point, the most important job of central bankers is to calibrate their monetary system in a way that maintains these beliefs. They are money shamans. You might at this point be thinking that money sounds like a religion. You'd be wrong. Money isn't *like* a religion. Money *is* a religion.

Money is a product of ancient temples dedicated to long-forgotten gods. The oldest records of money come from the temple in the Mesopotamian city of Uruk, where temple officials employed a system to keep tabs on the city's possessions: barley and grains, land, livestock. They needed a way to track all the commodities getting paid as tribute into the temple and going back out for the next planting season. These scribes came up with a system of standardized weights that allowed them to measure things more precisely. The standardized measurement they called a shekel, which became a unit of account, a means of exchange, and a store of value. This system was both useful and powerful. It created an efficiency that hadn't previously existed. Money was a key invention that helped create the rise of the first powerful city-states in history, massive walled communities that transformed human society.

But this new technology had a dark side. Money became not just a record of debts but a source of power and wealth in itself—and people quickly developed a taste for it. Long before the collapse of Lehman Brothers in 2008, or the Crash of 1929, or before Cortés slaughtered the Aztecs for their gold, people schemed up ways to make money. The ancient Greeks came up with a word for this tendency: *philargyros*, which meant "money-loving." Over the centuries, the word morphed across languages. In Latin, it was *avaritia* (the root word for avarice). In German, *habsüchtig*. In Old English, it was *grædig*, and in modern English, it became *greed*. Plato, in the *Republic*, said *philargyros* was the conduit through which man's honor was destroyed. St. Paul echoed that, writing that "the love of money is the root of all evil." The Romans had laws against usury. When the Christian ascetic Evagrius Ponticus made his list of deadly sins—he started with eight, later cut down to seven—greed was number two. Despite those condemnations, greed flourished, often in the shadows, more recently out in the open. Greed would be the conduit through which men practiced their money religion, a discipline that has continued right through to today. When the corporate raider Gordon Gekko, in 1987's *Wall Street,* said "greed, for lack of a better word, is good," he was echoing a sentiment that had driven people for thousands of years.

Money proved so popular and desirable in the ancient world that it eventually broke loose from the temple. Private creditors built up lending networks that made them rich and powerful while holding countless people as debtors. Those who couldn't repay had their farms seized or got sold into indentured servitude. The kings resented having their subjects' lives destroyed over debt, if for no other reason than it took away productive assets from the temple. For thousands of years there was a competition between the kings, the temple, and the creditors. Over the last five-hundred-odd years, this balance of power shifted dramatically. In Europe, the pope's authority was contested by Martin Luther. The English Civil War questioned the divine right of kings to rule as absolute monarchs. Then the American Revolution shattered that concept, and every scientific advance since Copernicus has further chipped away at religion's primacy. Nations that had previously been based around the religion-fed authority of kings and popes swapped them out and rebuilt their governments on the authority of the citizens themselves.

In the second half of the twentieth century, religion retreated further from the center of society than it had ever been before. "Despite little pockets of success, the religious life seems to have gone into irreversible decline, with almost all religious orders, for either sex, dwindling," a writer named A. N. Wilson wrote in 2018 in the *Catholic Herald*.[3] In 1944, 98 percent of Americans believed in God, according to Gallup. By 2022, that number had fallen to 81 percent.[4] A *Wall Street Journal* survey in 2023 concluded that religious faith, along with patriotism, having children, and other traditional values, was becoming less important in people's lives.[5] Obviously most Americans still believe in a religion, that isn't the point. The point is that religion has less authority than it's ever had before.

Throughout it all, though, money retained its seemingly celestial legitimacy. The popes certainly embraced their own love of money, but even Protestant leaders like John Calvin and Martin Luther, who were outspokenly critical of the Catholic Church's excesses, didn't denounce money itself. Calvin argued persuasively that money was actually a tangible sign of God's favor; people who had money had it because God *wanted* them to have it. Christianity's embrace of money as a sign of God's favor became the underappreciated, underlying, driving force behind Europe's rise out of the Middle Ages, its explosion across the oceans, and the conquest of the Americas. This ethic of the Protestants is the cornerstone of American culture.

There was one thing people told the *Journal* that they valued more, even as their belief in God was fading: money. As the supreme authority of religion faded from the proverbial town square, something that had a very similar quality and feel to it slipped into the vacuum: money, which had begun in ancient temples and carried the imprimatur of the almighty. We swapped worship of a deity with the pursuit of wealth as the central thing around which our society revolves. We are all parishioners inside an opaque religion. Nobody teaches it to us. Nobody explains its precepts. Nobody recites its catechism. But everybody knows it instinctively.

The big problem with all this is that money isn't good at being a religion. It wasn't built to be one and it doesn't have any of the redeeming qualities of one. Money doesn't provide any ecclesiastical, existential, or metaphysical answers. It doesn't tell you why or for what reason you're here or what you're supposed to do while you are. Money is silent on values. Christianity, Islam, Judaism, Buddhism, Taoism all have texts and traditions that try to explain human nature and outline models for good behavior. Money has nothing and offers nothing. If the world doesn't make sense to you anymore, it might just be because the collective we, over the course of centuries, have put an amoral contrivance on a pedestal and made obtaining it our highest virtue. We'll need to deconstruct that entire belief system before we can realistically hope to tackle the whole rigged system of inequality, political corruption, global warming, and even racism.

Now is a critical time to look at faith and money and try

and understand it, because the old systems are breaking down and we can't replace them with new systems built on the old faiths. The foundation of our entire global economy, going back to ancient Mesopotamia, rests on concepts like the "law" of supply and demand that are in turn based on fundamental "truths" like the scarcity of resources—material goods like food and land. "Economics is the study of how men and society choose, with or without the use of money, to employ scarce productive resources to produce various commodities over time and distribute them for consumption," the economist Paul Samuelson wrote in *Economics: An Introductory Analysis,* a classic of Econ 101 courses. Scarcity is a core tenet of the faith.

That made sense, once upon a time. Virtually every society, certainly in the ancient world, was one major calamity away from disappearing. Drought, crop failure, plague, earthquake, fires, floods—people lived at the mercy of the planet. So it made sense that they appealed in desperation to the gods they assumed actually existed and could intervene on their behalf; when we started building a discipline called economics, it absorbed those old beliefs. We don't live in that world anymore, though. We are not at the mercy of nature. If we wanted to, today, as a global society, we could produce enough food, energy, and shelter, and provide healthcare and education, for every person on the planet.

That's not hyperbole. The world as a whole already produces more than one and a half times enough food for everyone on the planet,[6] and there are ways to grow more. We have enough aluminum, steel, cement, polysilicon, fiberglass, copper, silver, and other materials we'd need to power the entire world with *renewable* energy, to say nothing of conventional energy.[7] Solar panels covering just 1 percent of the Sahara Desert could generate enough electricity to power the entire world.[8] That one surprised me, too. All empirical evidence concludes that building more houses makes housing more affordable, not less.[9] There are roughly 150 million homeless people in the world. There are roughly 2.3 billion homes in the world.[10] The block here isn't fundamental, it is an industry incentivized to keep supply low and prices high. The internet makes access to information virtually free for everybody. Universal healthcare is already a reality in most advanced nations. Access to healthcare in even the remotest parts of the world would involve building new infrastructure, but the biggest roadblock there is affordability, not access or ability.

Everything it would take to provide the basic needs for our entire global population of eight billion people already exists. Every person in the world could have the basic foundations of a decent life provided for them. Our economics has not even remotely begun to grapple with this new reality. How many more Bill Gateses and Albert Einsteins and Miles Davises are out there who could flourish with access to education or healthcare or decent food? It should be self-evident to say that we would all be better off collectively if each of us had a chance to live in a stable home and pursue our dreams. For some reason, though, that is not self-evident at all.

"The final victory of man's machines over nature's materials is the next logical process of evolution," the economist Simon Patten wrote. In the Old World, some would die of famine while others had more food than they could eat. The laws of scarcity resulted in a constant competition for resources. Powerful countries would colonize others and plunder their riches. The strong preyed upon the weak, capitalized off their labor, and left them bereft and broken at the end of their productive lives. Children were exploited. None of these things are necessary any longer,

Patten said. The main problem, he argued, is that the new, postscarcity reality has not yet sunk in for most people. We are already living in a new world, but we don't realize it. "The changes wrought by that process are so recent that the effects of old conditions have not disappeared," he wrote. "They persist in a revolutionized order of things which has not yet definitively reconstructed the traditions and orthodox modes of thought. Mental habits continue long after the economic conditions which fashioned them have disappeared, and popular beliefs reflect the passing age of nature's deficit, while the actions of men who hold those beliefs are chiefly governed by the new age of surplus in which they live. The economic revolution is here, but the intellectual revolution that will rouse men to its stupendous meaning has not done its work."

As Patten says, our minds have not caught up to our means. But it's even worse than Patten thought; after all, the words I just quoted are from a book he published in . . . 1907.[11] The old beliefs he talked about have in fact persisted far, far longer than he could have ever imagined. The intellectual revolution he advocated for never happened. The economic conditions changed, but we didn't change our thinking to match them. Our "modern" monetary system reflects a world that doesn't exist anymore, and that system still doubles as the primary incentive in our culture. This is keeping us from taking that next step as a society that Patten talked about more than a century ago. We are and have been at the point where we can make sure every person, everywhere, really does have the security of life, liberty, and the pursuit of happiness. It is entirely within our power to make that world happen.

Remember what I said about Aristotle explaining that money got its power from the law? I left out the second half of that quote: "It is not nature but a law that gives it existence, *and it is in our power to change it and make it useless.*" In the coming chapters, you'll learn that the main thing that's kept us from changing our economics to match our conditions is a fundamental misunderstanding about what money actually is and how we've come to value it the way we do. Our retrograde ideas about money are preventing us from pursuing a better world that is right in front of us. We'll never grow past this until we understand where those attitudes came from and how they evolved.

PART I

Avarice, sometimes, is beneficial.

—Poggio Bracciolini, *De avaritia*, 1428

I

IN GOD WE TRUST

In the beginning . . . there wasn't any money. There was the temple, and there were temple officials. A lot of stuff passed through the temple and in and out of the temple officials' control: wheat, barley, cows, goats—the things that constituted real wealth in the ancient world. Temple officials needed a way to keep track of all this wealth, so they devised a system of standardized measurements that became "money," which came with the moral authority and imprimatur of the kings. Once there was money, there were lenders, and with the lenders came debt. The kings chased grandeur and magnificence through the accumulation of wealth, but the lenders were similarly entranced by the love of money, and fought for millennia with the temple and with kings over control of this system.

A little more than five thousand years ago, a man named Kushim tallied the supplies of ingredients for making beer.[1] He counted twenty-nine thousand measures of barley, which had come into a storehouse over a period of thirty-seven months. He gave barley to three different officials, recorded the amount given to each one, and noted the total amount he'd handed out. We know almost nothing about Kushim—we don't even know for sure whether that was his name or his job title—but we know a lot about the supplies he controlled, because he meticulously recorded everything on clay tablets. These tablets are among the oldest evidence of writing and accounting, and the system they illustrate is essentially still in use today. We call it money.

Kushim lived and worked in Uruk, a walled city in ancient Mesopotamia (in modern-day Iraq) situated on the wide flat plain between the Euphrates and Tigris Rivers. Uruk was the New York of its day—a major cosmopolitan, economic, and cultural center, with fifty to eighty thousand people living inside the city (the number changed over the eons) in an area comprising a little more than two square miles, and tens of thousands more outside the city walls.[2] It was the largest city in the world, the most powerful of the ancient kingdoms, and like most ancient kingdoms it was often in conflict with its neighbors. In most respects, though, life in ancient Mesopotamia wasn't all that different from today:[3] some people lived in the city, some lived in the countryside. The family was the basic unit around which society was organized. People worked as farmers, fishermen, tavern keepers (the Mesopotamians invented bars not long after they invented beer), accountants, priests, bankers, merchants, goldsmiths, and soldiers, among other professions. After the day was done, they kicked back in the pub and listened to music (musician was an occupation, too). Uruk was a major power from around 3500 BCE to 2000 BCE, and was occupied until the Muslims overran the area in the seventh century CE and the city was abandoned.

There was one way in which Uruk—and indeed every city of the ancient world—was significantly different from modern cities. It was built around a massive, towering temple, dedicated to the sun god Anu.[4] No other building was remotely as large. Travelers could see the temple from well beyond the city walls. It was likely the largest building in the world at that time. The temple was the physical and spiritual center of life in Uruk, an arrangement that was standard in ancient cities. But these were not states in the way we think of them today; in fact, "the state" as we understand it didn't exist. The entire point of the city and the empire wasn't so much to create a good environment for *people* but to create a good environment for *the gods,* who took care of the people. The gods created the Earth and everything it contained, and the people were working in tandem with and in service to them.[5] All resources went into the temple for the gods' approval, and were parceled back out to the people to grow the next season's worth of crops. Increasing wealth, which was generally measured in land and physical commodities, and expanding the empire were taken as tangible signs that the gods approved of the ruler, and by extension the kingdom. The king was regarded either as the gods' hand-picked representative on earth or at times as the gods' offspring; either way, he was seen as essentially a god on Earth, and religious worship extended to him, too. The entire city and every aspect of daily life revolved around the single-minded goal of pleasing the gods in order to obtain their favor. The temple was as central to society as the palace. It would be like the White House and the National Cathedral sharing power, or Buckingham Palace and St. Paul's. You can trace the authority of leaders throughout history—from the sort of "absolute monarch" who ruled for millennia until the English Civil War and American and French revolutions to the people today pushing the idea of the "unitary executive"—back to this weird power-sharing arrangement between a man and a myth. And, very interestingly, money's authority can also be traced right back to this point. It was in the temple where the accountants worked, the records were stored, and the wealth was calculated. Money, power, and religion have been lashed to each other from the start, each one amplifying and reinforcing the others.

While "money" existed in the ancient world, in the beginning it was likely very different from money as we now think of it (I say likely because there is still a lot about the ancient world we do not, and may not ever, know.)[6] Lots of things were used as money: barley and other grains, silver, gold, tin, even livestock. But back then, "money" was more of an abstract concept that represented wealth rather than wealth itself. The average Mesopotamian didn't carry around money; they may never have touched anything specifically called "money" at all. Coins didn't come into use until the first millennium BCE, and paper money centuries after that. Instead, they had tabs. You'd run up a tab at the ale house, for instance, and then settle it at harvest time, most of the time using grain, or sometimes silver.[7] Debts to the temple or private creditors were paid with possessions like crops or livestock or even with one's own freedom; indentured servitude was a common aspect of life in the ancient world.

The temple was key to the monetary systems of the ancient world.[8] The temples were economic engines. They were major landowners, and controlled vast fields of crops and animals, which in those times were the real sources of wealth. All state business and much private business went through the temple. A vibrant temple and a wealthy kingdom were signs of the gods' approval. In cities from Uruk to Jerusalem the temple was the ultimate financial intermediary. Temple scribes like Kushim were specially trained and entrusted with all manner of record-keeping—regarding temple business, but also private contracts, land ownership, debt and credit arrangements, and commodities storage. Of course, the temple was the arbiter if legal disputes arose from those records. Debt records often listed the temple scribes as the creditors; in which case, the people understood that essentially their debts were owed to the gods themselves. In that sense, the business of debt and credit in ancient Mesopotamia was the realm of deities. "In God We Trust" is a saying for us, but it was literal to the Mesopotamians. They entrusted their gods with everything they owned. It was all for the glory of the supernatural beings they thought controlled their lives; in this sense, failure to repay a debt was a sin against the very nature of the universe, and the debtor's punishment therefore deserved. Money and morality have been intertwined from the start.

THE FIRST SHEKEL

We don't know exactly when money was invented. It seems to predate the written word. The first things ever written in fact were records of debts recorded by temple accountants like Kushim. It's very likely that the invention of writing itself was a *result* of the advancement of money, a need to keep tabs on who owed what to whom. The late anthropologist David Graeber argued in his book *Debt* that money wasn't an evolution from a barter system but an evolution from a credit system. The Mesopotamians used a system of debt and credit to facilitate trade and agriculture and industry, and they needed a way to track it all, and what resulted was money. The oldest records come from Uruk and Mesopotamia, but that doesn't necessarily mean money was invented there. It's not very likely that we somehow managed to recover the very first record of the very first instance of money. It's not likely we will ever know. Now, the standard explanation of how money was created, handed down from Aristotle, has been that it evolved out of barter.

This story was accepted uncritically for millennia. Adam Smith cited it, and another merchant we'll discuss in a couple of chapters, Benedetto Cotrugli, also repeated it in a fifteenth-century book he wrote. It is the prevailing theory even today. But there's a good chance it's wrong, if Graeber is right. And he very well might be; after all, Graeber had access to a wealth of information recovered from more than a century's worth of archeology that Aristotle likely did not.

In the city-states of Mesopotamia, there was a system of measuring items like barley against standardized weights of silver, the basic unit of which was called a shekel. "Wages" would be paid in a certain shekel's worth of barley or some other grain. It seemed to have been as much about allocating resources as anything else. True wealth and power was represented by land and possessions. "Money" was just the record-keeping system, notations marked onto big clay slates recording who got paid what, and who had exchanged what with whomever, and who owed and who was owed on either side of that exchange. The debts of the common people were mainly taxes and fees owed, paid in grain or some other commodity, to the local temple or royal treasury. Laws evolved to support enough balance in society—these were after all still rigidly hierarchal nations—such that the society itself could grow and prosper. Money quickly became central to the functioning of the city. Of the 282 rules in the Code of Hammurabi, the oldest existing set of laws in the world, dating back nearly four thousand years, more than a hundred of them mention money (I counted). In that code, it set limits on interest rates: 33 percent on grain and 20 percent on silver.[9] Most temple loans were for small amounts, a sign that they were mainly taken by poor farmers who needed support until the next harvest. The temple was the equivalent of today's financial system.

Speaking of interest, it was from out of this temple

monetary system that we got a financial instrument that is today the engine of the global financial system: the interest-bearing loan. At some point clever people realized you could leverage the temple's record-keeping system. If the state said you owned such and such, you could use that as a possession to borrow against, and soon you had loans. Then they got super clever and invented something even more ingenious than the loan: compound interest. They realized if you paid back a loan with some predetermined additional payment—the interest—at fixed intervals that over time the creditor would be earning interest on the interest. Money, in essence, gave birth to more money. That was an *extremely* alluring concept to the person doing the lending. Soon enough, loans and lenders and interest rates were a thing. With that came commercial debt and creditors, the forerunners of modern banking, long before J. P. Morgan or the Rothschilds or the Medici, before mortgage loans or letters of credit or branch banking. The temples made loans, but so did private creditors. These moneymaking enterprises were family-run businesses, and the families became fantastically wealthy and powerful. In these debt-based societies, they noticed something else about their economic system: thanks to compound interest, those debts had a persistent habit of multiplying.[10] The debt grew and grew. It destroyed farmers, it ruined families. People lost their homes and their land to pay debts. People were sold into bondage to pay debts.

Cities traded with each other, and the world's first merchants emerged, and the monetary system steadily became more complex and ingrained, especially the practice of lending. This came to be called usury, and to say it was controversial would be an understatement. Philosophers and moralizers assailed it. Kings and rulers didn't appreciate that it usurped their own control over money via the temple. It seemed to weaken the state itself. The private creditors rolled up those debts and their families grew wealthier and more powerful at the expense of the health of the state. The balance sought by those laws got warped. A farmer laid low by debt and sold into bondage, after all, was no longer a productive member of society. The families and the kings clashed for centuries over the legality of usury, with the lives and livelihoods of ordinary people hanging in the balance. The parallels to our current world should be obvious. Then, like now, debt was a major source of friction in society. The Mesopotamians developed a novel law to restore balance.

Sometime around the year 2400 BCE, a king named Enmetena, who ruled a powerful city east of Uruk called Lagash, conquered a neighboring city called Umma.[11] After he occupied the new city he made a declaration: he wiped out all personal debts. Farmers were released from their debts to creditors. People who'd been sold into bondage to cover debts were freed and returned to their homes. "He restored the child to its mother, and the mother to her child. He cancelled interest," the declaration read. Enmetena wiped the proverbial slate clean. It's not clear that Enmetena's declaration was the first of its kind, but it is the oldest for which we have a record, and the practice was still common well into the sixth century BCE, when the Persian king Cyrus freed the Israelites and other indentured servants after he conquered neighboring Babylon. The original name for this freedom- and balance-restoring law translates to "return to mother" (thus that language winding up in Enmetena's declaration itself). In Sumerian, the word was *amargi*.

The *amargi* was magnanimous, but it was also practical. A society buried in debt was not a productive one. Farmers would lose their farms, and thus the ability to grow crops. Able-bodied men sold as bondservants to wealthy creditors could not then be conscripted into the army. A declaration of *amargi* allowed a community to start over. Farmers could go back to their land and start working again, feeding themselves and their families. They could pay the next round of taxes and serve in the military when needed. Temples could be rebuilt when needed, and thus the financial infrastructure to support the local economy could be reestablished. These *amargi* were a safety valve for society; they prevented the buildup of debt from destroying the state, and they restored a sense of balance that allowed the society to grow to its potential (if the gods approved, of course). "Even in the normal course of economic life, social balance required writing off debt arrears to the palace, temples or other creditors so as to maintain a free population of families able to provide for their own basic needs," the economist Michael Hudson wrote.[12]

The practice spread across the ancient world. In the fifth century BCE, a Persian Jew named Nehemiah was sent to Jerusalem, which had been conquered and largely destroyed by the Babylonians in 586 BC.[13] Nehemiah's job was to rebuild the city, both physically and spiritually. While he was erecting new walls and fighting off the Israelites' enemies, he was also trying to restore a just and balanced economy based on the laws of Moses. Nehemiah found that the local Jews were practicing usury, charging each other interest, which in earlier Jewish law had been banned (throughout history, as we'll see, usury has been both illegal and widely practiced, and Jews have been widely scapegoated for it). As a result, people had lost their farms, their families, and their freedom to creditors. "I urge you," Nehemiah said, "cease from this practice of usury. Please restore to them, even this day, their fields, their vineyards, their olive groves and their houses, along with a hundredth part of the money, the grain, the wine, and the oil that you had exacted from them" (Nehemiah 5:10–11). What Nehemiah was arguing for was essentially an *amargi*. The Israelites codified the concept in the book of Leviticus, which stipulated that every fifty years would be a "trumpet-blast of liberty." Lands lost over debts were restored. Bondservants were freed. When the books of the Torah were translated into Latin by the Christians, the word used to describe this was *iobeleus*. In English, it's *jubilee*.

These debt-cancelling declarations were a necessary counter to the seemingly insatiable growth of the private creditors, but there's a sort of pretzel logic to all this. If money is a product of the king/gods, then it can only be a good thing. But in practice, money clearly creates a lot of pain, so much pain that those same kings have to impose limits on it. But why should you limit anything that is celestial? Around and around, and we've basically been having this same debate for about five thousand years. Money's value is wrapped up in the moral authority of religion, or of a king like Hammurabi (or, to put it in today's terms, the federal government of the United States), who speaks on Earth for the gods, declaring what is just or unjust. Improper uses of money, therefore, weren't just immoral, they were literally going against the gods. But money itself can't be bad because it comes from the gods, so pursuing it can't be bad, so people kept doing it and the authorities kept swatting them down, even as those same authorities declared both the power to create the thing and the power to decide how much of it is a good thing. Of course, the problem here is that quite obviously money didn't come from the sun god or any other god. It was just something people invented to help them do a job. And yet none of these moral hang-ups surrounding money have gone anywhere in the millennia between then and now. It's no wonder there are such moral undertones to cash and credit and debt and such fierce debates about it.

By Aristotle's time, in the fourth century BCE, money more closely resembled what we use today. Money had morphed over the millennia (to get a sense of the passage of time we're talking about here, the age of Kushim the temple official was further away from the age of Aristotle than the age of Aristotle is to today) and wasn't just a way to compare dissimilar things. Coins were in common usage across the Near East and Mediterranean empires, and represented wealth in and of themselves. A kingdom called Lydia in modern-day Turkey minted the first coins sometime in the seventh century BCE. The coins were made of an alloy called electrum and had a standardized size and value. This was an innovation that was very popular and became one of the main sources of the kingdom's wealth.[14] The expansion of coinage across regions and kingdoms and city-states only amplified people's lust for it and the degree to which having it reinforced the desires of others for the same thing.

At the upper levels of society, there was an attitude that Aristotle called "magnificence"; keep it in mind, this concept will become important to us in a couple of chapters. Magnificence, Aristotle wrote, "means suitable expenditure on a grand scale."[15] What he's talking about here is the kind of large-scale public works projects that were built by kings and other nobles. The pyramids in Egypt, or temples all over Greece, the kinds of things only powerful people could do back then. "The motive of the magnificent man in incurring this expense will be honor." This person is a connoisseur, one who spends huge sums but *exactly* the right sums for *exactly* the right works. The spending is a physical sign of his high character. The whole goal is to show greatness, and excellence, and the scale is so large it is only for people with great wealth to begin with. "A poor man cannot be magnificent," he states bluntly.[16] In other words, the pursuit of magnificence is mainly a game for the rich and the nobles. It is not something for commoners.

The rise of hard money and stored wealth raised other complicated questions. What did this new thing actually represent? From where did it derive its power? To what degree was the pursuit of it a help or hindrance to society? What was an acceptable level of *philargyros*? What we think of today as "economics" was to those Greeks a question of managing a household. Wealth was an extension of how well you took care of your family. Did they have a home? Food? Did you have enough land to grow crops and raise animals? Were you self-sustaining? All of that was true wealth in the ancient world. Was the pursuit of money, which could certainly add to one's household wealth, therefore an acceptable practice? These are essentially the same kinds of questions we wrestle with today. The Greeks also spent a lot of time arguing about them.

Aristotle said that money was not a natural phenomenon. It was an illusion that people convinced themselves was real. It was man-made, and got its power from the law. In ancient Greek, *nomos* was the word for law and *nomisma* was the word for money.[17] The latter was derived from the former. Because of this, money's use was acceptable only if it was attached to some natural social dynamic. Trade represents a basic demand for goods and interaction that binds society together, he said. So money as a representation of that demand is just. On the other hand, the "art of moneymaking," as Aristotle called it, was treated by the philosopher with contempt. Money, he argued, not being real, could not reproduce on its own, so the entire concept of interest, a process by which money appears to beget more money, was unnatural. Like many through the ages, he assailed usury. "The most hated sort, and with the greatest reason, is usury, which makes a gain out of money itself, and not from the natural use of it," he wrote. Moreover, he argued, nobody should put up with such a perversion. "It is in our power to change it and make it useless."[18] He was blunt on the topic of greed. "The greedy man does good to no one, not even to himself."[19]

Over the course of eons and cultures, Aristotle's position on greed had a lot of support. I've found no moral framework in which greed was considered good. Every religion roundly condemns it. In Hinduism, greed is one of the six enemies of the mind, something to be overcome. In Buddhism, greed is one of the "three poisons," along with hatred and delusion. The Koran predicts a long stay in hell for people who value money above God. In Christianity, St. Paul called greed the "root of all evil." People who freely and cheerfully give their money away, the Koran says, "are the truthful; these are the righteous." The idea that greed is a bad, dark impulse indulged in only by bad, dark people is deeply embedded in our most revered moral tales and religious texts. And yet greed endures.

It seems odd to me that Aristotle tried to thread a needle between greed and magnificence. To argue that the former was bad but the latter was good he had to ignore the plain reality that people could not pursue the latter without implicitly or explicitly deploying the former. And in a large way, the rest of this book is really about this contradiction in Aristotle's worldview and how over the intervening 2,400 years the culture completely flipped the script on the philosopher. If you just look around, you will see that greed today is embraced to one degree or another by everyone, and I do mean everyone. Not just crazy bitcoiners, corporate raiders, avaricious Ponzi schemers, or billionaires. The "pursuit of wealth"—which is the habit that gave birth to the word *greed* in the first place—is today inarguably seen as a good thing. We all want money, seemingly instinctively. We have built a culture that requires money in order to do just about anything. The water you use in your morning shower, for which you pay your local government. The food you eat at breakfast, which you bought from a store. The clothes you wear, the home or apartment you live in, the car, the public transit, the internet, the books you buy (and thank you!), the movies you watch, the music you listen to, the coffee you drink, the vacations you go on. On and on and on. You cannot operate in modern society without money, whether it's physical bills, credit or debit cards, or digital payments. Money is in the middle of just about everything we do, every day. You need it just to live. So I'm defining greed here very broadly. In our own way, we are all striving for Aristotle's magnificence and deploying our greed to get it. Gordon Gekko's "greed is good" speech explains capitalism as it actually operates, not as the textbooks tell you it operates. Capitalism didn't create greed. Greed created capitalism.

OF KINGS AND CREDIT

Despite Aristotle's condemnation, neither debt nor usury disappeared. Attempts to check the power of the creditors generally failed, and even the most godlike kings couldn't kill greed. The creditor families—think of them as the forefathers of the Medici, the Morgans, and the Rothschilds—grew in power over the centuries, leading to a situation where a debtor might owe both the palace and the private creditor. That situation did not sit well with the kings, since grains and crops paid to satisfy private debts were not sent to the temple—people ruined by debt could not do anything to increase the wealth of the kingdom. That led to a very long game of cat-and-mouse between rulers and creditors. The king would declare an *amargi,* the creditors would look for a loophole to evade it. The king would issue ever more detailed instructions closing the loopholes, the creditors would come up with new loopholes around the closed loopholes. For more than a thousand years there was a persistent friction across the Middle East, Greece, and Rome between rulers and the growing power and greed of private families that controlled land and people. Usury, and commerce in general, were seen as so distasteful that Roman law forbade nobles from engaging in it (these laws were completely disregarded, a fact that will soon become very notable to this story). In Greece, there were popular rulers who used debt relief as a tool. They were bitterly opposed by the creditors, who felt these princes lacked the authority to forgive debt, and tagged these rulers *tyrannos*.[20] In Latin, the word was *tyrannus*. In English, it's *tyrant*. Let's look at one tyrant.

A Spartan king named Agis came to power in 244 BCE; the Spartans had a system of co-kings, and Agis's counterpart was named Leonidas. Agis was young, only about twenty, and apparently idealistic. Sparta as a kingdom had become pretty powerful and rich—this was after they'd knocked off the Athenians—and the wealthy reveled in it. The entire city had come under the sway of *philargyros*. "The love of money made its way into Sparta," the historian Plutarch wrote in his biography of Agis, "and brought avarice and meanness in its train."[21] Ancient laws had been twisted such that land, which used to be handed down strictly along family lines, could be acquired by anyone. Soon the majority of the city's wealth was concentrated into the hands of just a few families. "The rest of the people were poor and miserable." This upset Agis. He proposed laws to redistribute the land and to cancel debt. Agis saw it as restoring the original laws of the kingdom handed down by Lacedaemon (Plutarch interchangeably calls these people Spartans and Lacedaemons). As he came from a wealthy family himself, Agis had to first convince his mother, Agesistrata, and grandmother, Archidamia, to support him. They did, and began agitating among other wealthy families to also support him. It goes without saying, of course, that the "poor and miserable" of Sparta supported him. In fact, according to Plutarch, Agis's plan was wildly popular among the common folk. This created a problem for the rest of Sparta's wealthy families, and for the other king, Leonidas, who sided with the city's wealthy and powerful but feared the wrath of the commoners.

Agis publicly declared that he would give up all his land and wealth to support the reforms; as he was one of the richest Lacedaemons, this made a very big impression. His mother and grandmother did the same, as did the other families they'd won to their side (Plutarch doesn't specify exactly how many were on board). At one point, Agis literally gathered up all the physical records of all the debts (called *claria*) owed by all the Spartans, piled them up in the public marketplace, and burned them. "When the fire began to burn, the moneylenders and other creditors walked off in great distress," Plutarch wrote. I'll bet! The people rejoiced and immediately began demanding Agis implement the other part of the reform, the land redistribution. Before he could do it, though, he was forced to leave the city to go fight one of Sparta's enemies. While he was gone, Leonidas, city officials called *ephors*, and the wealthy families that opposed Agis conspired against him. They arrested him upon his return from the war, tried him (Plutarch doesn't say exactly what he was charged with), and had him executed. For good measure they hung Agesistrata and Archidamia, too, and then publicly dragged their bodies out of the city. It sure sent a message.

A king had tried to implement an *amargi* and the creditor class rose up and literally killed him for it. "It is certain that

Agis was the first king of Lacedaemon to be put to death by the ephors, and that he suffered only for engaging in an enterprise that was truly glorious and worthy of Sparta," Plutarch wrote. That was just about the end of that. The long-standing conflict between rulers and creditors was resolved in the creditors' favor. Laws were put in place that codified usury's position and limited the power of the tyrants. Eventually what you end up with is a system that looks a lot like what we have today. Money is issued on the authority of a king (today it's mainly governments), the temple handles most of the record-keeping and logistics (today that's the central bank), while the private market operates on its own. Everybody was part of the system, but no one party controlled it. And of course the *amargi* disappeared. There was one last major attempt in the ancient world to stem this tide, to curtail the greed of the creditors. The attempt itself failed but the person behind it had a profound effect on world history. You know the story but not in quite the way you're about to hear it.

2

THE LAST JUBILEE

The Romans may have created a high culture that exceeded the Greeks and Mesopotamians in size and grandeur, but its citizens were just as susceptible to the base lure of avarice as were citizens of prior empires. In 33 CE, the empire nearly collapsed from a financial panic created by the greed of its own ruling families. The crisis consumed the banks of Rome and spread to the Senate floor itself, but it was sparked by unlikely events in the outermost provinces. And in one dusty corner of the empire, at the exact same time that Rome's debts were threatening to destroy the empire, an itinerant preacher went from town to town proclaiming an era of the iobeleus—debt forgiveness.

One day, somewhere around the year 30 CE, in Roman-occupied Nazareth, the local Israelites were holding their regular synagogue services. Among the crowd that day was a young Nazarene named Yeshua who'd left town some years prior and whose reputation as a teacher of the Word had grown.[1] He'd been preaching in other towns, drawing crowds, and causing a commotion. The local authorities wanted to hear for themselves what this man had to say, so Yeshua was invited to address the congregation.

He got up in front of the crowd and read from a scroll containing the teachings of the prophet Isaiah. "The Spirit of the Lord is on me," Yeshua said, "because he has anointed me to preach good news to the poor. He has sent me to proclaim liberty to the captives and recovery of sight to the blind, to release the oppressed, to proclaim the year of the Lord's favor."[2] The particular passage from Isaiah includes a quote from Leviticus. The line that Isaiah was quoting was Leviticus 25:10–13, which says this:

> Consecrate the fiftieth year and proclaim liberty through-out the land to all its inhabitants. It shall be a jubilee for you; each of you is to return to your family property and to your own clan. The fiftieth year shall be a jubilee for you; do not sow and do not reap what grows of itself or harvest the untended vines. For it is a jubilee and is to be holy for you; eat only what is taken directly from the fields. In this Year of Jubilee everyone is to return to their own property.

This was the *iobeleus,* the Hebrew version of the Meso-potamian *amargi.* The year of the Lord's favor was a trumpet blast of freedom, a time when debts were abolished. The people were flabbergasted. They'd known Yeshua—the son of a carpenter named Joseph—from his childhood. They could not believe what they were hearing. By calling out a year of the Lord's favor, he was essentially saying that there should be an *amargi,* and there were at least two radical things about that. One was that the proclamation was being made at all. It had likely been a long time since anybody had observed one—the *amargi* and the *iobeleus* had faded as a social tool; nobody really used them anymore. The other was that Yeshua had the audacity to assume he had the authority to declare it. Debt cancellation was a power wielded only by kings of old, and this young man clearly was no king. But he persisted in his crusade, and he created a lot of followers who believed in his vision, and a lot of enemies who wanted him gone. In a way, both eventually got what they wanted. Over the years, his story would get told and retold. It would be translated into Greek, where his name became *Joshua*. It would be translated into Latin, where his name became *Iesus*. It would be translated into Old English, where his name became *Haeland*. In modern English, his name is *Jesus*. And he wasn't preaching in a vacuum, either. A cataclysm had hit Rome that made Yeshua's words both timely and exceptionally incendiary.

While Yeshua was traveling around the Levant pushing for his *iobeleus*, three ships from the Alexandrian merchant Seuthes and Son were sailing north on the Red Sea.[3] Their cargo holds were filled with ostrich feathers, spices, ivory, and other exotic goods from the Far East. Shippers like Seuthes would collect merchandise from China and India, sail it across the Indian Ocean and up the Red Sea, and carry it over land to Alexandria, the port city at the mouth of the Nile famous for its massive lighthouse and library. From there, they loaded the goods onto other ships bound for Rome and Europe. Goods went west and north, hard currency went south and east. Business empires were built on the trade. However, this particular voyage for Seuthes and Son was a disaster. A hurricane hit the Red Sea. The ships and their cargos sunk. It was a total loss, and it bankrupted the firm. At roughly the same time, Phoenician workers at an inking concern called Malchus in the eastern Mediterranean city of Tyre revolted.[4] We don't know the details of the revolt, or the nature of the workers' complaints. What we do know is that the uprising drove Malchus out of business as well. As it happened, both firms were clients of a Rome-based creditor called Maximus and Vibo. They must have been big clients, because the two bankruptcies threatened Maximus and Vibo's solvency to the point where it had to (literally) close its doors to prevent customers from overwhelming the firm with demands for their money; in other words, a bank run, quite possibly the first in recorded history.

Banking had become big business in the capital. Despite laws prohibiting it, many Roman nobles practiced usury, using other, non-noble, people as their fronts. It had in fact become such a popular moneymaker that it was crowding out owning land and farming as the preferred business of Rome's elite, and it revived all the old antagonisms. "A powerful host of accusers fell with sudden fury on the class which systematically increased its wealth by usury," the historian Tacitus wrote.[5] An old law was renewed, which forced Rome's elite to put most of their wealth into land. The idea was to both tamp down on usury and support Italian agriculture. After that, interest on loans was capped at 10 percent. Then cut in half. Then compound interest itself was banned. Still, Tacitus related, usury continued. One praetor brought the issue to the Senate, only to discover that every single one of them was guilty of the crime. The Emperor Tiberius gave everybody eighteen months to get into compliance with the law.

That sparked a mad frenzy to call in debts, get paid, and turn around and buy land. Creditors sued debtors for payment, debtors sued creditors for usury, the courts clogged, and everybody hoarded whatever money they had. Debtors who were forced to pay their debts often had to sell land to raise money. A glut of property hit the market, and prices plummeted. The scheme to raise the value of property ironically ended up tanking it. When Maximus and Vibo shut its doors, though, it catalyzed a situation into a crisis. Now there were fears about bank collapses, sparking a string of bank runs in Byzantium, Carthage, Corinth, and Lyons. Banks in Rome shut down. It was a complete credit freeze and from the floor of the Senate in the Forum to the most distant territories it shook the most powerful empire the world had ever seen.

The year was 33 CE. And in a far-off province, that rabble-rousing Hebrew radical Yeshua, whom we call Jesus, was demanding debt relief and the return of a long-forgotten law that abolished debt. His crusade and Rome's crisis crashed headlong into each other. This, then, is the rarely discussed context of the ministry of Jesus Christ, and I think it paints his story in a very different light.

If you're not a Christian, it's hard to say anything conclusive about the life of Yeshua (because the story I'm telling is about a man and not a messiah, I'm going to stick with his original name).[6] There is very little objective evidence. Absolutely nothing about him from his own lifetime remains. He didn't write anything down, at least nothing that's survived, and there is scant evidence of him elsewhere. Decades later, a Jewish historian named Josephus mentioned him.[7] A century later, Tacitus made a quick reference to him.[8] That's it, outside of the Gospels. Now the Gospels are of course the best source for information about his life, but objectively speaking they aren't completely reliable. For one thing, they are all secondhand. None of the writers actually knew Yeshua; they are recounting stories handed down. The Gospel of John is ostensibly written by the disciple John, but nobody really believes that (this isn't considered heretical; even my edition of the Bible discounts it). They don't agree with each other, either. They tell different stories, or different versions of the same stories. None of the Gospels that have come down to us are even original; the earliest versions of them are copies of the originals, none of which have ever been found. Lastly, they are not objective histories. They are not trying to tell the full story of Yeshua's life. They are trying to make the case that he was the messiah. But even if you discount every single miraculous thing attributed to Yeshua in the Gospels—and most of the Gospel stories are miracle stories—and the messiah complex elements of the stories, there is *still* another story in there. It's about a man who saw an injustice, demanded it be addressed, attacked the very heart of the injustice, and had a solution. We can all learn something from that story.

I do not believe Jesus is God, even though I was raised Roman Catholic. I suppose we should get that out of the way up front. I don't believe in any god. I think of course that Yeshua himself believed in God, very much so, and that he had a radical interpretation of God's law. And his followers believed in him so passionately that at some point they came to see him as the prophesied messiah. Yet I still believe in the man and in the moral philosophy he preached, which is why I care about this story, and why I see it as central to this entire tale of money and morality. The "good news" Yeshua announced that day in the temple was about restoring a tool to rebalance society by erasing debts. The most famous man in the history of the Western world, maybe even in the entire world, was agitating for debt forgiveness, in the middle of a financial crisis. And the Romans killed him for it. I know it's hard to shake off two thousand years of Christian dogma and canon, but if you can look at this story with fresh eyes, I think you'll see that the things Yeshua was saying back then still have currency today.

How likely is it that Yeshua was preaching during Rome's financial crisis? Well, the timelines match up. Tacitus puts the financial crisis at 33 CE. The Gospels say Jesus Christ was executed during the administration of Pontius Pilate, who ruled from 26 to 36 CE. All four Gospels agree that Jesus was arrested during a Passover celebration. John alone says the crucifixion occurred before Passover, the others say it was the Sunday after. Passover always begins at sundown on the fourteenth day of the month of Nisan on the Jewish calendar, and the month itself is aligned so that the first full day of Passover, the fifteenth, occurs on a Sunday and coincides with the full moon. Moreover, the Gospels mention the moon turning to blood, which could be a reference to an eclipse. Scholars have tried to line up all those criteria (even Sir Isaac Newton gave it a go) and see if there is a date that matches all of them.[9] There is: Friday, April 3, 33 CE. That would mean the pinnacle of Yeshua's crusade—when he chased the moneychangers out of the temple in Jerusalem during the Passover celebration, followed by his arrest and execution—took place in the same year as Rome's financial crisis. It is entirely possible Yeshua was proclaiming—no, *demanding*—a debt jubilee at the exact same time that Rome was going through a debt crisis. They didn't teach us that in catechism class.

The Gospels are hazy on the dates, but it appears he started preaching only a few years before his execution. We don't know what the inciting incident was. Maybe he saw how debt wrecked a relative or friend. Maybe he himself was in debt. Maybe he was sued for payment of debt by a creditor, couldn't pay, saw the injustice of it all, and went on an extended rant that drove him across Galilee. Maybe he left his wife and children at home, which would explain why they never appear in the Gospels. What the Gospels do tell us is that at some point in his adulthood, Yeshua started preaching with a frenzy, going from town to town and riling people up everywhere he went. Like Nehemiah centuries before, he was trying to restore the old laws. Yet Yeshua wasn't a royal or temple official. He was just some local carpenter. It was audacious for him to claim the power of a king and demand a debt jubilee. He must have been wildly dynamic, the very picture of an Old Testament fire-and-brimstone preacher. His name spread far and wide, people came from miles around to see him. They hung on his every word. Like I said, he never wrote anything down, so we have no idea if the things attributed to him are really his own words, but it's reasonable to assume that the words in the Gospels are his in essence if not in exactitude. He traveled fairly extensively, living the life of a vagabond, attracting crowds everywhere he went, staying in the country or lodging with well-wishers. He was locally famous.

Not everybody was so open to his message, though. His sermon that day in Nazareth at the temple did not go over well, as Luke related. While the elders were sitting there, talking about how special it was that Joseph's son had grown into this eloquent speaker, Joseph's son was getting mad. He had just said something important, and they were talking about *him*. They heard him, but they didn't hear what he *said*. They weren't really listening. Of course, it's understandable. What he said must have sounded nuts. Who is this peasant to demand debts be erased? But Yeshua had no time for their dithering. He antagonized them. He told them that next they'd ask him to repeat the speeches he'd made in other towns, as if he were some entertainer. "No prophet is accepted in his hometown," he sneered, and told stories about different prophets who weren't welcomed in their hometown. And the hometown crowd got *pissed*. They drove him out of the synagogue, out of the town, and took him to a high hill. They were going to throw him over it, Luke said. They were going to kill him right there. But Yeshua "passed through the crowd and went on his way,"

Luke said. Maybe someone defended him. Maybe they all cooled off, and decided against it. Maybe he got loose and ran. Luke might have chalked it up to a miracle, but it was a foreshadowing of things to come. It wouldn't be the last time Yeshua angered the authorities.

He didn't just talk about debt, of course, but nothing else he preached was any less demanding. The moral philosophy of Yeshua must have been just as polarizing to the people who heard it as his demand for debt relief. The two were in fact connected, and that is something you should sit and think about. Yeshua's morality centered on an absolute, radical regard for and love of every other human being. Yeshua defended lepers and prostitutes. He counted himself among the most undesirable people in Judea. He cited the Golden Rule, "do unto others as you would have them do unto you," and it dovetailed so seamlessly with his philosophy that I always assumed he coined it. But the Golden Rule can in fact be found across ancient cultures from Greece to Egypt to India at least as far back as 2000 BCE. You can almost look at it as the first universal law, which makes a lot of sense. How else could people live together? Don't do anything to somebody you wouldn't want them doing to you. It is the basis of civics. It's the rule that was the underlying framework for civil society itself. Would you yourself want to be sold into slavery? Would you yourself want to lose your possessions, your livelihood, your family? Would you want to have your entire life ruined over a debt, a notation somewhere on somebody's little record book? Of course you wouldn't. This is the key to Yeshua's entire worldview and crusade. This, he argues, is God's law. To treat each other as you would a brother or sister, or yourself. To forgive debts that are so onerous they destroy lives.

In the parable of the sheep and the goats, Yeshua told a story about townspeople who took him in though he was a stranger. They gave him food when he was hungry and drink when he was thirsty, they clothed him and cared for him when he was sick. These people, he said, shall inherit the kingdom of God. But the people themselves didn't know what he was talking about. They asked him, when did we do that? Yeshua replied: "Truly I tell you, whatever you did for one of the least of these brothers and sisters of mine, you did for me." Then he admonished the unrighteous. They all did the opposite. They didn't feed him, or clothe him, or take him in, or look after him when he was sick. And they protested. When did we refuse to do these things for you? "Truly I tell you, whatever you did not do for one of the least of these, you did not do for me," he said. The meaning is clear. All men and women are part of one whole. Whatever you do to any one of them, no matter how important or insignificant a person, you are doing to God Himself.

Yeshua's theology was a challenge, then and now. One time a wealthy man asked Yeshua how he could have eternal life. Yeshua told this man to follow the commandments. The man said he had done that. Yeshua told him to sell everything and give it to the poor. "At these words his face fell and he went away in deep distress, for he was very rich." As the man walked away, dejected, Yeshua pointed him out to his followers and told them "a camel could more easily squeeze through the eye of a needle than a rich man get into the kingdom of God." Yeshua wasn't just talking about these things in private, or in sermons. He personally confronted and directly attacked the entire economic system at its source: the temple in Jerusalem.

OCCUPY THE TEMPLE

In 33 CE, Yeshua and his followers made the pilgrimage to Jerusalem for Passover. This was a far cry from the little villages of Galilee; Jerusalem was the center of the Jewish world, and the temple, much like its counterparts throughout the ancient world, was the center of economic, religious, and political life. King Herod had undertaken a massive project to rebuild and expand the temple. It took decades and fortunes to do it (the Gospels claim it took forty-six years). Herod's Temple, as it would come to be called, was a commanding structure. The entire complex covered about thirty-six acres defined by high walls, and in the middle, tall enough to be seen for miles, was the stone temple itself, similar in plan and grandeur to the temple in Uruk. The sheer size and majesty of it was a testament to the god in whose name it had been built, but also to the largess of Herod. Just like in Mesopotamia, shows of wealth were considered a sign that the local king had the favor of the almighty. (The Western Wall in modern Jerusalem, also called the Wailing Wall, is all that remains today of Herod's Temple. It was destroyed when the Romans sacked Jerusalem in 70 CE. Muslims took over the region in the seventh century; the Al-Aqsa mosque is built on top of the spot where Herod's Temple stood and the Western Wall was incorporated into the mosque.)

The temple would have been a dynamic place at any time, but especially during Passover. Hundreds of thousands of Jews made the pilgrimage to Jerusalem and the temple, jamming the city. Men stationed at the gates collected tithes and taxes and other items that were deposited there, recorded the deposits, and issued receipts. Inside the walls was a vast open courtyard. All manner of business took place inside those walls.[10] There were officials that witnessed oaths to seal business contracts or enterprises. Some officials adjudicated disputes, sometimes turning to prophecy or even a proverbial roll of the die to ascertain the Almighty's favor. They charged for the service, and almost certainly charged more than they should have sometimes. As far back as the eighth century BCE, the prophet Micah complained that temple officials overcharged and took bribes. "Her leaders judge for a bribe, her priests teach for a price, and her prophets practice divination for money."[11]

The temple was also a marketplace filled with stalls. Some were selling cattle, sheep, and doves (the doves were used in sacrifices). Other stalls were for the moneylenders. This holy place should have been the very physical manifestation of everything Yeshua had been talking about. This was where the edicts about the *iobeleus* should be coming from. Instead, they were making loans! Charging interest, taking advantage of the poor, and perpetuating the imbalance that made life so hard on the very people the temple was supposed to be helping. To Yeshua, it was a complete perversion. And it ticked. Him. Off.

He took cords of rope and bound them into this crazy superwhip. He ran into the temple, brandishing this weapon, and chased everybody out. The moneylenders, the merchants, the livestock, the temple scribes and officials. He kicked over the tables and threw the money everywhere. He single-handedly upended the economic center of the Israelites. "My house shall be a house of prayer, but you have made it a den of thieves," the Gospels tell us he said. You can imagine he probably said a few other things as well. To top it all off, after this act of wild vandalism and destruction, Yeshua sat down in the temple in the middle of the mess he made . . . and he started teaching! No wonder he made such an impression on people. Temple officials ran to the local Romans, but nobody had the courage to actually go into the temple and try to remove him. They were afraid they'd get torn to shreds by his followers.

A lot is happening at this point. Yeshua destroyed the economic life of Jerusalem. He had driven away the moneychangers and merchants. And that's not all. The throngs of pilgrims there for Passover were in the temple with him. They collectively took it over. And it seems from the Gospels that Yeshua and his followers remained there for days. This isn't just an incident. This is a full-scale rebellion. This is Occupy Wall Street two thousand years ago. You can imagine what those pilgrims did with the money and record books they found tossed around the temple. The money, gone. The records, destroyed. They got their *iobeleus*. Debts were obliterated. God's law was implemented. Balance was restored. Yeshua wasn't just a preacher anymore. He took over the temple like a conqueror, like a king. And people began to revere and worship him as such. In a short time, they'd come to see him as a god, too.

A god roaming around the hinterlands agitating the locals was not something the local Roman governor, Pontius Pilate, was about to tolerate. The worker revolt to the north in Tyre had been one of the sparks of the financial crisis. Now a vagabond carpenter in Jerusalem had started another revolt. Where might this disease spread next? This needed to be stopped, immediately, and somebody needed to be made into an example. It was obvious who that should be. Since the authorities couldn't drag Yeshua out of the temple, though, they found another way: they bribed one of his followers. Judas Iscariot agreed to ID him to the cops one night after they'd all left the temple. He infamously got thirty pieces of silver for his troubles.

Pilate is portrayed in the Gospels as a noble guy who couldn't find any crime Yeshua committed that demanded execution. Herod purportedly couldn't find a crime, either. Yeshua was sent back and forth between the two, neither of whom knew what to do with him. That's how the Gospels relate the story, but that doesn't make sense; he had clearly committed any number of crimes. Pilate famously "washing his hands" of the whole affair is almost certainly something added by later writers with an agenda. What does make sense is that Yeshua's demands for debt relief reached a climax that Passover in the temple in Jerusalem, the empire was in the middle of a debt crisis, people were revolting, and those revolts needed to be stamped out. The Romans were notoriously violent and merciless. Why would one of them suddenly go soft for this random agitator? No, Pilate condemned him to death, went home, had a huge dinner, and probably didn't think about it again.

And here is where I tell you that I can't prove that one single word of my account of Yeshua's story is accurate. All of it is conjecture, based on my interpretation of the scattered evidence that exists. What I do believe, though, is that my story of Yeshua makes sense within the larger context of how money, debt, and the creditor class were developing in the ancient world (and I think it makes more sense than the Catholic interpretation, but that's a debate for another day). Money sent a very basic, obvious signal to people (it still does today): it signifies power, and the more you have of it, the more powerful you appear. "Money" as we understand it today was still relatively new in Yeshua's time; the pursuit of it, the quest for Aristotle's magnificence, stood in contrast to even older beliefs and creeds. It was a big friction. I think Yeshua really thought the patterns of people's attitudes toward money could be changed. He stood opposed to that signal and believed it went against what he saw to be God's law. He tried to change the tide of history. I think also there is a message in the things he said that is just as essential today as it was when he first said it. *Do unto others what you would have them do unto you. Whatsoever you do to the least among these you do also to me. Forgive us our debts as we forgive our debtors. Liberty to captives. Release the oppressed.* Yeshua tried with all his might to get his message across. He was willing to give his life for it. And in 33 CE, he did.

Crucifixion was an incredibly violent, painful method of execution.[12] The victim's arms were nailed to the cross at the lower forearms. The feet were nailed to the cross with the nail being driven through their Achilles tendon. The Romans discovered that in order to simply draw in a breath, the victim would have to raise and lower his body, pushing up on his nailed feet and pulling with his nailed arms. So they'd break the victim's legs, to prevent him from being able to do even that. It was actually a small mercy: the victim now could not breathe and so died sooner.

Up on his cross, tortured and dying, Yeshua was given one final indignity. They put a crown of thorns on his head and hung a sign, written in Hebrew, Greek, and Latin, on the cross above the man who claimed to have a power that had died with the sovereigns of a bygone era: "Yeshua of Nazareth, king of the Jews." After Leonidas and the ephors executed Agis—and his mother and his grandmother—and after Pilate and the Romans executed Yeshua, nobody talked any more about *amargi* or jubilees.

3

EVERYTHING IS DONE FOR MONEY

We shift now from the ancient world to Europe in the years around and after the Black Death (1347–49), the deadly bubonic plague that wiped out anywhere from a third to half of Europe. The plague killed so many workers that the entire feudal economic system also broke down; the workers who were left found themselves for the first time with actual leverage and started to demand better conditions and wages. Moreover, the plague left such deep psychological scars that Europeans started to open their minds to new ideas. One of those ideas came from an influential writer, Poggio Bracciolini, a man who was chief secretary to multiple popes and close friends with the powerful Cosimo de' Medici. Bracciolini wrote a treatise asking a question that reflected the opinion of many of Europe's merchants and bankers, but one that risked the church's wrath: What if greed was actually good?

The Roman financial crisis of 33 CE was solved ultimately in a way that would be familiar to us today: Tiberius opened up his royal treasury, flooded the market with a hundred million sesterces, and gave everybody more time to settle their affairs. Yeshua's followers, meanwhile, fled Jerusalem. They spread out across the Levant and beyond and kept talking up his ministry, though they focused less on *his* beliefs and more on *their* belief that he was God incarnate and the world was coming to an end. In the ensuing centuries, Christianity rose as a force across the Roman Empire, and the followers of Christ carried with them their founder's disdain for usury. St. Jerome, St. Aquinas, and others argued that lending for any gain was a sin. Despite all the seeming antagonism against greed and usury, both survived the ages. Usury had long ago been codified into Roman law, even if the amount one could charge would change over time—the old Roman laws capped interest at roughly 8 percent, but it was raised to 12 percent in the first century BCE. In the sixth century CE the emperor Justinian created tiered limits: 6 percent on ordinary loans, 8 percent for banks, 12 percent for maritime loans.[1] Usury could be shamed, but it could not be eradicated.

Slowly Europe sank into a millennium-long funk, starting roughly after Emperor Constantine (c. 272–337 CE) moved the empire's capital from Rome to the ancient Greek city of Byzantium at the entrance to the Black Sea, renaming it Constantinople. He also made Christianity the state religion, but with the capital of the empire now in the east, Rome's influence waned. It was sacked in 420. For the next three-odd centuries, European cities and principalities as well as the eastern regions centered around Constantinople were all ostensibly still "Rome." The Europeans pledged allegiance to a series of "kings of Rome," feigned fealty to the emperor in Constantinople, and fought with each other for supremacy at home as a plethora of kings and nations ebbed and flowed across Europe (a full list of large and small kingdoms, fiefdoms, territories, and cities would probably run a page or two; there were a lot of them). The Franks spread westward, taking over large and small regions and spreading their dominion among a number of kings and dynasties.

In the eighth century one of these Frankish kings, Charlemagne, was dubbed Emperor of the Roman Empire, which did two things. One, it attempted to unify the Europeans once again under one banner. Two, it more or less definitively split "Rome" between the Europeans and Constantinople. Charlemagne's attempt to revive the empire was relatively successful—his Holy Roman Empire would stand until the beginning of the nineteenth century—but the continent remained pretty splintered, and the city of Rome itself slowly sank into ruin and decay. There was still an official bishop of Rome, the head of the church, and he had direct control over a small clutch of land in the middle of the Italian peninsula, the Papal States, and indirect influence over the rest of Europe through the church. It was a very strange setup, to be honest.

The Roman bishop was still something of a player in the continent's politics and exercised a lot of power through the church structure. He appointed cardinals and bishops and gave them their territories to run.[2] These regional magistrates collected taxes and other forms of revenue from the local parishes, which collected it from the local population. A percentage of everything got kicked back and up to the bishop of Rome.[3] Honestly it was a bit like a mob syndicate. Local church officials had a lot of power over an uneducated, highly superstitious populace, and the ability to soak up a lot of the collective wealth of the people. Before long, being a church official actually became one of the most lucrative jobs in Europe. The church may have railed against greed, but greed had burrowed its way into the minds of priests, bishops, cardinals, and popes. For centuries the main complaint against the church really boiled down to the greed of its officials and the abuses of the people because of it.

The church wasn't in the habit of censuring its own officials, but it did officially maintain a ban on usury and kept up a persistent damnation of anything smacking of it or commerce at all (though over time actual charges of usury became rare).[4] To the church, merchants were held in lower esteem than even the most derelict, impoverished pauper; after all, the meek at least would inherit the Earth.[5] The penalty for practicing usury was severe: excommunication, denial of a Christian burial, and condemnation to spend eternity in hell, a place as real to medieval Europeans as London or Paris. Usurers learned to keep a low profile, to never flaunt their wealth, to operate either in the shadows or under the rubric of another business. The royals, the nobles, and the rich jockeyed for power and money, whether inside or outside the church. Greed was only for the ruling classes.

Trade was diminished but not dead. The commercial revolution that would explode across Europe in the fifteenth century had started percolating as early as the tenth century. While minds might have been closed during the "Dark Ages," the roads out were open, and some people trekked across them. Trade routes flourished across the Middle East and Asia. Marco Polo, the son of a merchant family, famously made it all the way to the court of Kublai Khan in China and reported back to Europe everything he'd discovered. Travels like these exposed Europe to new ideas, which it desperately needed. Importantly, the rapidly spreading religion of Islam did not condemn commerce. On the contrary, the new doctrine of Mohammed (who like Yeshua five centuries before him started out as a dynamic, wandering preacher of the Word of God) held that honest merchants deserved a place in heaven.[6] Independent city-states emerged in Florence, Venice, Milan, and elsewhere that picked up the trail from Marco Polo and other travelers. They were organized as republics—Florentines referred to their city as a commune—and open to commerce. It seems like the exposure to different cultures had an effect on the Europeans.

Still, what really cleared the way for attitudes about greed to change and change permanently was one of the worst natural disasters in the history of mankind: the Black Death. In the mid-1300s, the bubonic plague swept across Europe. Nobody knows exactly how many people died. Some estimate a quarter of the population. Some say half. It absolutely destroyed Europe. It was the end of the world, *The Walking Dead* but with a real virus instead of fake zombies. Economic life collapsed. Fields went fallow. Famine crept across the Continent. Rich and poor alike were as liable to be killed. Under the intense strains, the bonds of civil society frayed and shattered. So many people died that there weren't enough peasants to do all the work. The feudal system around which European society was based shattered. It never came back.

Living in the shadow of oblivion, people started to imagine the outlandish. They became obsessed with any world that wasn't their own shattered one. Survivors turned to the chivalrous traditions of Europe. Tales of brave knights on exotic journeys of honor and adventure with fair maidens waiting in fairy-tale castles became very popular; the entire chivalrous tradition is really a response to the Black Death. Elsewhere, a group of writers and thinkers became obsessed with the philosophers and works of ancient Rome and Greece, fanning out across the continent in search of old manuscripts, learning to write in the ancient languages, and trying to revive the lost splendor of the empire.[7]

RETRO ROMANS

September 15, 1428, was a warm late-summer day, and Poggio Bracciolini was in a small town southeast of Rome called Ferentino.[8] Bracciolini worked in the Vatican's administrative staff, the Curia. The church wasn't his first love, though. His first love was the ancient, nearly forgotten world all around him, the ruins and old manuscripts of ancient Rome that were strewn across Europe, abandoned and misunderstood, columns marked in a language virtually nobody spoke anymore. That's what had brought him to Ferentino. At the city's highest point, overlooking the green valley, there was a stone acropolis and fortifications that were more than a thousand years old. To Bracciolini, they might as well have been made of gold. He worked for hours, carefully studying and examining the ruins, pulling away brambles and overgrowth, examining every part of the old walls, looking at the worn inscriptions. Nobody in Ferentino understood what they said. They were in ancient Greek, once the official language of the empire and largely a lost language in Italy by Bracciolini's time. Bracciolini understood the words, though. He was one of the few who did.

Bracciolini was part of a group of Italians who all had one thing in common: a thirst to uncover the glories of ancient Rome and Greece, to relearn what their ancestors in antiquity had already discovered. These were not musty lecturers delivering stilted knowledge to bored students. These guys were radicals. They were searching for *pre-Christian* knowledge, for an understanding of the world that was outside what was prescribed by the Bible. That could only happen because Europe had been profoundly shaken by the successive waves of plague. It became an obsession, an attempt to revive not just the language but *everything* about the ancient world that had been lost. The language, the plays, the poems, the treatises, the philosophy, the style and form, all of it. Apart from an obsessive love of ancient Greece and Rome, though, they didn't agree on a single thing, and fought with each other constantly. Bracciolini, a brilliant thinker with a biting wit and a fierce temper, was once so incensed with another writer that he tried to have the man killed (he gave up on the idea and wrote a blistering critique instead).[9]

Bracciolini, nearly fifty years old with wavy dark hair and a widow's peak, was not exactly a young man but a vibrant one. He slowly, methodically took the time to uncover all the inscriptions he could find and write them down, while people walked by on their way to and from their daily work. A stranger transcribing the unknown words drew attention from curiosity seekers. Two young women came and watched him as he toiled away, offering him prayers and applauding him as he worked. Bracciolini was not a monk; a confirmed bachelor at this point in his life, he had nevertheless fathered a number of children out of wedlock, and he definitely liked having the girls around him. "Their good looks and applause did me a lot of good," he wrote in a letter to his friend Niccolò Niccoli, who apparently admonished Bracciolini for it (Niccoli's letters have not survived, Bracciolini's have, so we have only one side of the debate). "You are certainly a fool and thoroughly unkind," Bracciolini wrote back. "Perhaps you are a Stoic," he wrote, in a pointed harangue. "I would prefer whenever I am writing inscriptions to have young girls with nice figures standing near me."[10] And Niccoli was one of his close friends! At around the same time, Bracciolini was working on something else: his own version of a dialogue, a literary form popular in ancient Rome. Bracciolini was inspired by the old writers, and wanted to recapture the form because it was from that past, and he was obsessed with it. What he wrote, though, would become a pivot around which history turned.

Bracciolini was born[11] in 1380 in a little hamlet called Terranuova (today it is called Terranuova Bracciolini, in honor of the town's favorite son) outside Arezzo, part of the Republic of Florence, in the decades after the first wave of plague washed over Europe. He was educated in Arezzo and moved to Florence itself when he was twenty to study notarial arts—what we would today call being a secretary—and Latin literature. In 1403, he went to Rome and got a job in the Papal Curia, which would become his life's occupation. He was a secretary and copyist to seven popes, during and after the tumult of the Great Schism, when there were competing factions within the church—there were two and sometimes even three men claiming to be the true pope.

You've probably never heard of Bracciolini; I know I hadn't before I started researching this book. He's a fascinating character, and I guarantee there is at least one thing about him you do know: his handwriting. Bracciolini was a noted copyist. It was one of the reasons he became the chief secretary to popes; he personally wrote all their correspondences. He was so good at this, in fact, that he essentially developed an entirely new style of writing, which became the basis for a font we all know well: italics.[12] He had other notable interests that also left their mark. One was collecting jokes. Really. He collected jokes and published what was probably the first book of jokes in history. What he is best remembered for, though, is his passion for searching for and finding old Greek and Roman manuscripts.

Bracciolini and his friend Niccoli were part of a small cadre, but they were the most ambitious and became the two most famous "book hunters," scouring monasteries and private libraries across Europe. They'd borrow or buy old manuscripts, make copies, share them among friends, and later sell them—always looking to do so at a profit. As a member of the pope's bureaucracy at a time when the papacy was often on the move—both because Rome had fallen into ruins and because his bosses were under siege from the other popes and even from other regions at war with the Papal States—Bracciolini had the opportunity to travel all over the continent, and he scoured every monastery and bookshelf he could find looking for original manuscripts from the nearly lost worlds of the old Romans and Greeks. He was responsible for much of Europe's rediscovery of these old works. His most significant find was the only existing copy of a poem by the first-century Roman poet Lucretius called *De rerum natura* (*On the Nature of Things*). The poem at one point included references to atoms, a concept that had been completely forgotten on the Continent. Thus, Bracciolini's discovery of Lucretius's work reintroduced Europe to the concept of atoms. This discovery, it has been argued, was the spark for the scientific revolution that would follow in the sixteenth and seventeenth centuries.[13]

In the late 1420s, Bracciolini wrote a dialogue that portrayed an imaginary debate among four people—real contemporaries of his, though the debate is fictional—he called *De avaritia*, "On Avarice." It was a work that attacked what he saw as hypocrisy in society at large and in the church in particular. The work was so potentially incendiary for Bracciolini—remember, he worked for the pope directly—that he didn't even try to publish it publicly at first, instead sharing handwritten copies with his friends. Eventually, two versions of the text were published and distributed. *De avaritia* struck a nerve in a changing world—versions of it were still being published a century later. And Bracciolini wrote this dialogue at a time *just* before Europe's transformation into the world's dominant power. You wouldn't be crazy to think those two things are connected.

"AVARICE, SOMETIMES, IS BENEFICIAL"

In Bracciolini's time, the church's official stance was that greed was a sin. There were entire orders of the faithful, called mendicants, dedicated to avoiding the sin of avarice. These mendicants took a vow of poverty. They would go from town to town, preach the word, and beg for their supper. And of course the church itself was based on the scriptures of Jesus, who'd had plenty to say on the subject. But the church was also a political force, maybe *primarily* a political force. The pope at this time commanded an army, and used it. Being pope was potentially very lucrative; they had bankers for the church, and bankers for their own personal accounts. Several of the banking families of Florence made a nice business providing services to popes. Indeed, based on Bracciolini's writing, money appeared to be the primary motivation for joining the order. And those impoverished mendicants? They could not personally, individually own anything. But, conveniently, the *orders themselves* could own things. The mendicants owned land and property collectively and were actually very wealthy. All of this wealth wrapped up in the church of Christ was a hypocrisy that did not sit well with Bracciolini.

The fact that Bracciolini grew up in and around Florence probably affected his opinions on the issue of wealth and greed. In his time, Florence was one of the most important cities in Europe. Founded by Julius Caesar as a home for military veterans, the city sat at the intersection of the main road leading north from Rome and the Arno River, which fed into the Ligurian Sea. It was a perfect location for commerce. In the two centuries before Bracciolini's birth, Florence had developed into a major industrial hub with a flourishing trade, particularly in wool. The city probably had a population of about 120,000 by the 1300s. It was a republic, with a representative government and guilds that represented the various industries. *Commerce* was not a dirty word in Florence. *Greed* probably wasn't either. And the city's elite had a habit of using their wealth to support public works. Many of Florence's most notable achievements in art and architecture, things you can go see today, were a result of this ethos. Still, bankers had to be wary about getting called out by the church for practicing usury. Most just hid their moneylending operations behind some factory or merchant business.

There was a friction, though, between mercantile Florence and the official church position, and the former was starting to affect the latter. This could be seen in a theme that started showing up in preachers' sermons: the concept of turning your life into a quest for "magnificence."[14] This stemmed from an idea Aristotle talked about that I mentioned in chapter 1, and Florentine clergymen worked to transform it into a modern concept. A preacher named Antoninus sought to mesh this theory of magnificence with Florence's wealthy elites, and with Christian dogma. He defined it succinctly: "Magnificence . . . is spending a great deal of money responsibly, so that, 'for the honor of God or the good of the republic, churches and the like may be built.'"[15] The works Florence's elites were supporting, the churches, the hospitals, the homes for the poor, these were the physical manifestations of the quest for magnificence.

It wasn't just about personal ambition, he argued. It was *moral.* Magnificence was a virtue. The wealthy Florentine merchant who supported the construction of public works through his liberality—his liberal spending—wasn't just avaricious or selfish, he was in his own way doing God's work. "The purpose of magnificence is to make something that is great, but what pertains to the person of an individual is not something great when considered in relation to the things of God or the community at large. It is these that the magnificent man should envisage," Antoninus said. He also wrote guides for other preachers to help them develop their own sermons. Magnificence figured prominently in those guides. Antoninus sought to find an acceptable mean between miserliness and greed, a space where the wealthy merchant could pursue his own business and give something back to society, pay his dues as it were, and be a morally upstanding member of the community. To Antoninus, that happy medium was liberality. Florence's citizens should work hard, should strive to make money, and should give back generously and liberally. This was a theme he hit on for *decades,* up to and after he became the archbishop of Florence in 1446, and it should be noted that in his own lifetime only the Bible itself was published more frequently than Antoninus's works. His words were very influential.

Bracciolini's *De avaritia,* completed around 1430, also reflects the changing attitudes coming out of Florence, and in some ways is a better explanation of how we see money today than Antoninus's fine line. *De avaritia* is a dialogue, a fictional conversation between four real people, friends of Bracciolini's in the Papal Curia. In it he details the argument that greed is good, that people giving in to their own greed inadvertently make society better as a whole—more than five hundred years before Oliver Stone put those words into the mouth of his famous fictional corporate raider. More than three hundred years before Adam Smith would make essentially the same case with his famous "invisible hand" metaphor. Centuries before the Calvinists also worked the same rationale into their religion, giving money a place of worship and eventually leading to what we today call the Protestant Work Ethic. The entire evolution of the idea that greed is good, an idea that gives birth to capitalism itself, starts with *De avaritia*.

Given just how prescient *De avaritia* is about the attitudes we would develop toward money, morals, and greed, it's surprising the work isn't more widely known. Or known at all. I covered markets and economics for twenty-five years, and I never once heard Bracciolini or his work referenced. For an English-language speaker, it is almost impossible to find a copy of *De avaritia*. I first saw a reference to it in an article online, I forget which one, and was wildly excited by the idea of it. But I couldn't find the work itself. I Googled it, and found nothing. With most old literature, it's easy enough to find an online edition. Somebody, somewhere, has usually uploaded some version. I couldn't find one for *De avaritia*. I looked on Amazon, but they didn't have a copy available for sale. I looked on other booksellers' websites. Nothing. This work of Bracciolini's was almost as hard to find as Lucretius's poem moldering away in that monk's abbey. I was having such a hard time finding a copy of *De avaritia*, I honestly started to wonder if it existed at all. Maybe it was some wild medieval conspiracy theory.

There were enough references to *De avaritia* to convince me it was real, but I still couldn't find a copy of it. The closest I got was finding a PhD student's thesis from 1972 that had a detailed breakdown of the text. Eventually, I came across some college libraries that had copies of the old Latin texts, and even had them scanned so you could look at them and read them online. But they were in, you know, Latin. Finally, I listened to an episode of the *History of Philosophy Without Any Gaps* podcast (episode 354, "Greed Is Good") that included a list of suggested readings on its website, and in that list it mentioned an English translation of *De avaritia* within a book called *The Earthly Republic*, a collection of writings by Bracciolini and his contemporaries published in 1978. That book was available in bookstores. It is the only English-language translation that exists, as far as I know. After weeks of searching, I finally had a copy of Bracciolini's obscure work in my hands. It was worth the wait. The story is kind of amazing to read. Every page has some quote or thought that reflects on us today. This debate between the people in *De avaritia* is one that could happen today, on a podcast or social media site or something, and it would be as relevant right now as it was six hundred years ago. It shows in a very vibrant way how our attitudes and society have been shaped by things that happened centuries ago, and we're not aware of it at all.

De avaritia is set up as a talk among some of Bracciolini's friends after a dinner hosted by a guy named Bartolomeo da Montepulciano. His guests were Antonio Loschi and Cencio Romano. Once the debate's begun, a fourth person enters, Andrea of Constantinople. Now, remember, the Black Death had changed everything. Half the continent's population died, the survivors endured a literal end-times apocalypse, the feudal system failed, and society had to be stitched back together. It was a time to take a hard look at everything, and greed was one of the things that was up for re-evaluation. It seems by the time Bracciolini wrote *De avaritia*, the change had already begun. At one point in the dialogue, Antonio notes that "desire for money has grown, so that avarice is not considered a vice but a virtue; the richer a man is the more he is honored." I think Bracciolini wrote this because he saw something important happening in society and wanted to reflect it. Millennia worth of people railing against greed and the evils of money was about to change course. *De avaritia* is almost like the fault line for greed in society. Before it, greed was the root of all evil. After it, people start thinking that greed maybe isn't so bad after all.

Bracciolini had to tread lightly here. He was, after all, working for the pope. So even if he was sympathetic to the pro-avarice crowd—and we actually don't know for sure that he was—he still couldn't write openly pro-avarice things. He'd have to couch them. So, of the four people he has speak, three make extensive, detailed, emphatic arguments against avarice being *anything* other than the uber-evil it historically had been. Only one of them, Antonio, makes the case in favor of avarice, and even then, another one, Cencio, makes the odd comment that he doesn't think Antonio even believes what he's saying but is only repeating what he's heard from the pro-avarice crowd out in the world. (The inside joke here, completely lost on anybody outside Bracciolini's circle of friends, was that apparently Antonio was a very generous, non-greedy man and Cencio was a well-known miser; Bracciolini was having a laugh at their expense.) It's entirely possible that was Bracciolini's way of writing an out for himself into his work should he be accused of heresy.

Bartolomeo gets the ball rolling with a long diatribe against avarice. He calls lust and greed "the two cruelest plagues to infect the human race," and then reasons that lust is actually just an offshoot of greed, so really it's greed itself that is the core problem. Bartolomeo just goes on and on describing the failings of the avaricious man, how destructive he is to himself and those around him, and to the general welfare of society. This, we can reason, is the general perception of greed among the upper classes in Europe. Finally, he lays it out: "The avaricious man should himself be destroyed and be outlawed. He is useless to the city and ruinous to the state. If we were all to imitate him, we would have no city at all." The others one after the other all deliver long, long speeches bashing the hell out of avarice.

Then, Antonio speaks, and this is where we can see the

strand of thought that would over the centuries become an overpowering force in our world. "Avarice, sometimes, is beneficial," Antonio says. He says that every single thing people do for work, every professional undertaking, is done for money. He rattles off a long list of occupations, even priests. In fact, not only do priests work for money, he says, they work as priests *because* they expect to have the least amount of work to do in order to get the most money. They are the worst hypocrites, he says. If all those people were to stop working for money, Antonio says, society itself would come to a grinding halt. "Everything is done for money, that is, because of avarice."

In fact, he says, avarice itself is what gives rise to civilization in the first place. What is avarice except the desire for more than just the bare necessities? If nobody wanted any more than the bare necessities, everybody would be a subsistence farmer living on their own. There'd be no brotherhood of man, there'd be no reason for anybody to work with or help anybody else or form any kinds of societal bonds. Charity would disappear. For one thing, nobody would have anything to spare for anybody else; they wouldn't be able to help each other. There'd also be no way to prepare for the future, and to build up any kind of storage or defense against calamity.

Forget about the great cities or the small towns. They wouldn't exist. There'd be no churches, or art, or commerce. We need avarice, he says. We need it to build our world. "If you think that the avaricious ought to be censured, then the whole world should be censured, and all mankind should change its ways and adopt other rules for living." The rich should not be condemned for their wealth, he says, but celebrated for it. For it is they, he says, who actually have something to give to the needy, the indigent. It's they who are in a position to help cities build their great works, the big halls and churches. "It is a custom established by common use and practiced from the very beginning of the world that we strive more for our own good than that of the community," Antonio says.

Bracciolini wasn't the only one making the case for greed at this time. Another writer named Francesco Filelfo argued in a 1440 dialogue called *On Exile* that wealth and poverty wasn't good or bad, that it depended upon the use. This is another work that wasn't translated into English until quite recently, 2013. Why these works never made it into English sooner is puzzling, but it certainly helps explain why they are virtually unknown today. Yet another influential writer, Leonardo Bruni, also wrote works that exalted the lifestyles of rich Florentines. Leon Battista Alberti praised the city's wealthy for their "great and noble deeds."

These arguments in favor of avarice, which very likely reflected the prevailing ethos of at least Florence and probably some of the other mercantile-driven republics of Italy, loosened the historic malice toward greed. They gave people an excuse to be greedy. Greed was the tool that gave the banker and the merchant license to pursue unlimited profits. Greed gave the conquistador the justification to slash and maim and murder his way through the Americas. Greed gave the European colonizer the warrant to enslave entire nations of people. Greed was unleashed by Bracciolini's novel line of reasoning, and it's greed that created capitalism. Greed has been baked into capitalism from the very beginning, and capitalism in turn became a shield to cover and justify our greed. It's a line of reasoning that you can clearly trace right through the centuries, which is exactly what I am going to do in the coming chapters.

Still, the change didn't happen overnight. Bankers and

merchants couldn't just act unapologetically greedy. Antoninus and Bracciolini seemed to draw the line in different places. Antoninus said "liberality" was good, "avarice" was bad. In his dialogue, Bracciolini sandwiched his new ethos of beneficial greed between some hardcore avarice bashers but basically said unvarnished avarice was good, *so long as it* produced good things on a societal level. So bankers and businessmen needed to *show* that their greedy works were good for society and not just themselves. They needed to be able to justify themselves in God's and the church's eyes. They did this by creating a new way of doing business, taking their exorbitant wealth and spending it on all manner of public works, churches, monasteries, art, funding just about anything they could get their hands on. One person in particular seized upon this new ethos of greed as a public good and used it to build an empire that so dominated Europe that his family's name is still synonymous with money and power. He used the new ethos to make himself one of the richest and most powerful men in Europe, a king in all but name: Cosimo de' Medici.

4

THE MAGNIFICENT MAN

The Medici were one of the great families of Europe, bankers who became rulers and popes over the course of generations. It can seem like the Medicis invented banking, even though they didn't. Nor did they invent lending, or letters of credit, or double-entry bookkeeping. What they did do was embrace the ethos of beneficial avarice, the one detailed by Bracciolini. And nobody used it to greater effect than the "Pater Patriae," the Father of the Country: Cosimo de' Medici. That's where our focus now turns.

In 1414 the then twenty-five-year-old Cosimo di Giovanni de' Medici traveled north across the Alps to the German city of Konstanz, on the shores of Lake Constance, to attend one of the Catholic Church's myriad councils. This one (the Council of Konstanz, naturally) was called to deal with a gnarly problem: the church had three popes. One in Rome, another in Avignon, and a third in Pisa. That was two too many, and the council's goal was to figure out a way to get two of them to step down without a literal holy war. It did this by bringing in people from all over Europe to talk, and they talked *a lot* (the council lasted for years). Cosimo went to represent both Florence and the family bank on behalf of its client, John XXIII, the pope in Rome. His father, Giovanni, wanted Cosimo there to get a sense of which way the council was leaning, and whether their client would come out on top (he didn't, and today this John does not appear in the *Annuario Pontificio*, the official church record; he was reclassified as an antipope). But also, and more importantly, Cosimo's presence at the Council had been *requested*. The church leaders wanted Cosimo there to take the measure of *him*. Cosimo was sent to Konstanz "to allay the ill-feeling against him," wrote his friend the bookseller Vespasiano da Bisticci.[1]

By the time he was twenty-five years old, Cosimo de' Medici was already famous. His family was well-known inside and outside of their home city of Florence. Giovanni had built the Medici Bank into a successful business that counted among its customers the Roman pope. Great things were expected of the son, who was one of those people who had an unmistakable aura. The book on Cosimo was that he was ambitious and avaricious, a serious young man who was whip-smart and cunning. Everybody knew Cosimo would be a big shot. Nobody could have predicted, though, just how big of a big shot he would actually become.

If you're familiar with the Medici name, it is largely because of Cosimo. For five generations, the Medici men essentially ran Florence, and for hundreds of years after that the family clung to power in various guises. But no member of the family had a light that shone as brightly as Cosimo's. When Giovanni Medici died in 1429, he left a small but profitable business to Cosimo. By the time Cosimo de' Medici died in 1464, the bank and the Medici family had been transformed into a continental power. He had a thirty-year run as Florence's de facto dictator, "a king in all but name," according to Pope Pius II. He was like Jamie Dimon with an army. And he was largely beloved; they called him the *Pater Patriae,* the father of the country. No single person before or since—not even today's captains of industry—embodied Bracciolini's ethos of beneficial greed as fully or as successfully as Cosimo de' Medici. He transformed banking, he transformed Florence, and he transformed Europe, which in turn transformed the world.

Cosimo was close friends with Bracciolini, and both were part of the circle of aristocrats that was obsessed with ancient Greece and Rome. Cosimo was an energetic supporter of Bracciolini's many trips around Europe looking for old texts. Both were part of the entourage that went with John XXIII to Konstanz; Cosimo as his banker, Bracciolini as his secretary. When Bracciolini sent his first drafts of *De avaritia* to Florence for his friends to read, he sent it with Cosimo's brother Lorenzo. I don't know when exactly Cosimo first read *De avaritia*, but it was almost certainly around this time. Bracciolini and Cosimo traveled together while the two were in northern Europe after John XXIII was de-poped, and they traveled together when both were in Rome, where the Medici family had a branch and where Cosimo lived for a few years in the 1420s (and fathered an illegitimate child with a mistress). Together, the banker and the manuscript hunter would explore the Roman ruins, the old gates and the crumbling temples, going to Rome's old port, Ostia, for instance, reading the Latin and Greek inscriptions. They made for an interesting pair, the banker and the writer.

Cosimo's tale is not a rags-to-riches story. He came from one of Florence's leading families. The Medici were successful bankers. Giovanni worked in a distant cousin's bank and started his own in 1397.[2] Cosimo was born two years later. Giovanni and his second cousin, Salvestro, had both been part of Florence's convoluted government; the city-state was a nominally republican independent state, with complex layers of representation that ostensibly kept any one person or faction from dominating. Of course, in practice, one wealthy family or another was usually either in control of the government or scheming to take control, to exile or kill their enemies. Both Medici men had served as head of the governing council, the Signoria, but Giovanni advised his two sons to stay as far away from politics as possible.

That, however, would not be the way Cosimo conducted his life. "There is not the same pattern for everything at all times and for all men," Bracciolini had once told his friend, and it was a comment he reminded Cosimo of after his father died.[3] Cosimo was his own man, Bracciolini was telling him. He didn't have to do things the way his father did.

THE MEDICI BANK

Florence in the time of the Medici and Bracciolini was a world of contradictions and change. Most of Italy was split up into city-states and kingdoms, which were all both independent and nominally part of the Holy Roman Empire, and all, ecclesiastically speaking, under the influence of the pope and church—and not even the same pope, depending upon where one lived. During Cosimo's lifetime, Florence was a key point in a centuries-long fight between two factions, the Guelfs—mainly comprising merchants loyal to the pope in Rome—and the Ghibelline, feudal aristocrats loyal to the Holy Roman Emperor in Germany. Literally, the church and the state were in conflict. The result was that everybody had two or even three rulers, and each of them had his own separate set of laws, which were routinely flouted. There were rules against usury, yet there were banks all over Europe. There were rules that dictated exactly who could wear what, the "sumptuary" laws, yet everybody found a way to make a button not a button and so not a violation of the rules. There were rules designed to keep people in their place—plebs were plebs, nobles were nobles, priests were priests—and yet wealthy merchants and workers alike chafed under them. Everybody paid taxes, and everybody tried to avoid paying taxes. The specter of eternal damnation was very real, yet everybody it seems was a sinner, and everybody was a serial repenter.

Cosimo came of age within that miasma. He had a topnotch tutor, and learned Greek and Latin. He was a serious young man who didn't waste his time on frivolities, according to da Bisticci, but he was also a polymath. He could talk literature with men of letters, theology with theologians, philosophy with philosophers, agriculture with farmers, architecture with architects, obviously banking with bankers, and music, painting, and sculpture with musicians, painters, and sculptors. He was a trustee of the Studio Fiorentino, the city university that nurtured Bracciolini and other writers and thinkers. He even learned chess from the best player of the era.

The Medici Bank was like countless other banks across Italy and Europe, and indeed the Western world. They were small compared to modern banks, family-owned, and trying to steer clear of the church and its never-ending holy war on usury. In Florence in those days, there were three different kinds of "banks" that all were members of the bankers' guild: pawnshops, which were considered banks back then; moneylenders that worked from tables in the open markets of the city, a distant descendent of the moneylenders that worked in the temples that so incensed Jesus Christ; and the *banchi grossi,* or great banks, which had actual offices and did their business indoors.[4] The Medici Bank was the third kind.

How do you avoid charges of usury when you are a usurer? The Medici partnership's founding charter stated the business was involved not in banking but in exchange and merchandise, "with the help of God and good fortune."[5] They owned two wool factories and would later add a silk factory to their portfolio. This wasn't unusual. Textiles were a huge business in Florence. But the textile businesses were a cover to hide the fact that they were bankers engaged in usury. When Cosimo took over the business in 1420, it had four branches, in Florence, Rome, Naples, and Venice. This setup gave the Medici a footprint in four of Italy's five main powers; the only place they didn't have a branch was in Milan. Over his forty years of running the family business, Cosimo expanded to Geneva and Basel in Switzerland, Bruges in Belgium, Avignon in modern France, and London; in Italy, he added branches in Ancona, Pisa, and eventually even Milan. Since Florence, Milan, Venice, Rome, and Naples were all separate kingdoms, that put the Medici Bank in nine European territories. It was a truly multinational bank.

Like his father before him, Cosimo was the principal owner of his empire, but it was set up as what today we'd call a holding company.[6] This was done so that if one branch failed, its losses were contained. Each branch of the Medici Bank was its own partnership, a separate legal entity, with its own capital and own accounting books. Its employees were not merely workers but partners who got a share of the profits. The Medici family themselves owned at least 50 percent of every partnership. The bank branches were ostensibly trading houses, not banks as we think of them today. The Medici partnerships financed trade in wool, cloth, silk, alum, dyestuffs, spices, olive oil, and citrus fruits. Sometimes they traded on commission, sometimes they entered partnerships with other merchants. But ultimately they were really banks.

Beyond financing commodities and trade, they did also kind-of sort-of make loans, but given the church's ban on usury they were not *called* loans, or structured like loans are today. They made a business of trading what were called bills of exchange.[7] Essentially the transaction was just an exchange of money, one currency for another. The contract was the bill of exchange, which had a timed element to it. The customer promised to trade the bill back to the bank after a certain set amount of time, often in another city, say three months later in London, or Milan, or wherever, to another branch of the Medici Bank. The Medici, and all the banking families, made their money on this business by very deftly managing interest rates. Every bill of exchange was calibrated to play off an exchange rate that would ultimately result in the customer repaying more than in the original exchange. It wasn't an exact science and the banker could and did lose money on some of these deals. But in general, the odds favored the house. There was another kind of transaction called a "dry exchange," in which the bank essentially made a straight-up loan masked as an exchange. Their balance sheets were set up to hide not only the dry-exchange business but even the fact of how they were actually making money. Everyone involved understood these transactions were really loans; the Medici were charging extra for the service and turning a profit from it—in a word, usury. We'll talk more in the next chapter about how the bank's accounting books themselves were structured to tell a story about a morally upright business enterprise, and the profound impact that had.

The partnership structure was a new way to build an enterprise, and it saved the Medici Bank from the bank runs and collapses that its competitors suffered from time to time. (Although in the long run this structure wouldn't save the Medici Bank, either. It collapsed in 1494 under the stewardship of Cosimo's great-grandson, Piero "the Fatuous," after the French invaded Florence.) Cosimo learned from other Florentine banks that operated under one roof; banks run by his rivals the Peruzzi and Bardi failed when problems at one branch took down the entire partnership. The Medici business proper in Florence had no operations of its own. It didn't actually do anything except own other companies. This model had a number of advantages. It controlled risk—if one branch melted down, the others were legally insulated. It also diffused the responsibility among the ownership groups—at least, every ownership group save the Medici.

Cosimo used all these tools, including the ethos of beneficial greed that Bracciolini wrote about, to turn his bank into a leviathan, a wildly profitable and ever-expanding business through which he burnished both his image and his grip on Florence. It was the model for every bank—hell, every business—that would come after it for six hundred years, and Cosimo himself became the model for every businessman that would come after him, too. You don't have to look far to see it. Blackstone's Stephen Schwarzman donated $100 million to the New York Public Library[8] (and got his name put on every entrance of the main branch on Fifth Avenue, the super-famous one).[9] Leon Cooperman donated $100 million to a hospital in New Jersey to build a (very nice, I've been in it) new wing.[10] The town I grew up in in New Jersey is one of the hundreds around the country with a library financed by Andrew Carnegie. And that's just off the top of my head, thinking about things around me. Meanwhile, the website Open Secrets has about a hundred entries for political donations from Cooperman;[11] it has about thirteen hundred for Schwarzman.[12] Then there is George Soros. Forbes estimated that he has given away more than three times his current (as of 2023) net worth;[13] he was also the biggest US political donor in 2022.[14] Forbes noted that about seventy of the four hundred people on its famous wealth list have pledged to give away more than half their net worth before they die (though Soros was the only one who had so far hit the mark). Two hundred and sixty billionaires, including Elon Musk, Jeff Bezos, Mark Zuckerberg, and Carl Icahn, have given away less than 5 percent of their wealth, but at least some of the ultrawealthy are following a "Gospel of Wealth" espoused by Andrew Carnegie a century ago (something I'll talk about later), which itself is an iteration of Cosimo's ethos. I'm not criticizing or praising any of this, just pointing out that these modern captains of industry and finance are following a model that was perfected by Cosimo de' Medici.

There have been myriad books written about the Medici and Cosimo analyzing their fortunes and empire, looking at their business practices and trying to figure out how they did it. What they have all missed is Cosimo's ability to leverage Bracciolini's ideas. Through Cosimo de' Medici, the idea that greed is good would find its first and best champion.

THE COMMONER KING

Bracciolini's *De avaritia* almost perfectly laid out exactly the kind of world Cosimo de' Medici would build. While the ruling classes looked at avarice as an iniquity, the ruled classes saw it as something else, a fact Bracciolini points out. "I don't doubt that if one were to seek the opinion of the common people that they would judge very differently from us," Antonio says in *De avaritia*.[15] Everybody, he says, by their very nature wants more than they need, and it's a good thing, too. Without it, nothing would get built. There wouldn't be any hospitals or public buildings, or churches, or even society itself. "You soon would see what total confusion would result if we wanted only enough to provide for ourselves."[16] When people are greedy, he argues, they end up providing not just for themselves but for the community as well. Because of the excess of their wealth, there are storehouses of food for the poor, there is aid for the "sick and wretched."[17] And because these wealthy give back to their communities (either through their own works or by taxes), society at large is able to protect against those things as well. "I say it has brought about great good."[18] The wealthy, he says, should be praised and courted. We should be happy to have them:

> It seems to be preferable to have many avaricious men whom we can depend on in times of difficulty like a stronghold or a citadel. Not only do they support us with money but also with advice, wisdom, protection, and authority. We have seen many who were considered avaricious consulted on state policy and counsel. In no way have the avaricious been harmful. I might add that they have often brought great ornament and embellishment to their cities. Not counting antiquity, how many magnificent houses, distinguished villas, churches, colonnades, and hospitals have been constructed in our own time with the money of the avaricious? Without these ornaments our cities would be deprived of their largest and most beautiful monuments.

Cosimo de' Medici became that avaricious man a city could depend on in times of difficulty. For thirty years, he was Florence's stronghold and citadel. In some ways, his entire life was the epitome of Bracciolini's argument. Cosimo was wealthy, he was powerful, he was consulted on all matters involving the governance of Florence. And he spent his money liberally and lavishly, enriching himself, endearing himself to his fellow citizens, and leaving behind a wealth of public works that still exist today.

The concept of public works was cemented before

Cosimo de' Medici, but the financing usually went through guilds or the city government. The most spectacular public work was the dome on the Florence Cathedral, an octagonal structure topped with the iconic red-clay tiles of the city. Construction on the church began in 1294, but for more than a century the ambition of adding a dome remained unrealized. It was too wide a space, and nobody in Europe had the technical knowledge to pull it off. In 1418, the city fathers, who at the time included Giovanni de' Medici, held an open competition, and gave a contract to Filippo Brunelleschi. His innovation—something he considered so valuable that he kept it secret even from the commission that awarded him the contract—was to build a dome within the dome, one supporting the other. It was radical, it worked, and the dome then and today is still the most prominent of Florence's myriad architectural gems. One person who took a particular interest in Brunelleschi was Cosimo de' Medici. Over the years they would execute a number of projects together and Brunelleschi would become one of Europe's most important architects. The two men's careers fed off each other. Every marvel the architect designed also reflected on his patron.

Cosimo wielded a combination of money, politics, religion, and business. He used money liberally to curry favor with people across the spectrum, turned key people into allies and passionate defenders, and used their support to build an empire. You have to really sit back and admire the skill and chutzpah it took to pull this off, to keep track over the years and decades of his business and allies and alliances and power. There's a reason that Medici became the template for every businessman to follow. He was really good at this. He had an impressive string of fans and an impressive string of haters. Everybody in Florence had a hot take on Cosimo de' Medici. Where Giovanni had been reluctant to get involved in politics, Cosimo seemed eager. He never sought public office himself but used his wealth and influence to basically pick who did occupy public offices. He put people in power. He got laws changed. He took part in Florence's myriad battles with her enemies and turned some, like the Duchy of Milan, into nominal allies. Cosimo never personally fought in a battle—indeed, all the Medici men for generations were notorious for their poor health—but he used the bank's money and power as lethally as any cannon.

That he did all this is fascinating in itself. He wasn't a noble, or a king. He wasn't a pope. He didn't start off with an army, or huge landholdings. He didn't command serfs. It seems like he instinctively grasped how to use both his vast wealth and the ethos of beneficial greed to his advantage. And this, I think, is the biggest impact of the work of Bracciolini and career of Cosimo: It's not necessarily that they made greed acceptable. It is that they made greed acceptable for *commoners*, for the *popolo minute,* the little people. Greed, as Bracciolini noted, is an ingrained human emotion. And for most of human history, it was tamped down—except among the ruling classes. The Roman elite were notoriously avaricious. Kings, dukes, even churchmen were allowed to be greedy. But it was off-limits to the peasantry. What Bracciolini and Cosimo together did was to make the idea of greed acceptable for everybody. And once that constraint was removed, you saw an absolute explosion of ambition in Europe.

The true brilliance of the Medici Bank and Cosimo's network of influence was illustrated in 1433 when his chief rival, Rinaldo degli Albizzi, conspired to have him exiled from Florence. Cosimo was summoned by the city council, and imprisoned on September 7. They held him in jail for nearly a month, with the intention of cutting him off from his personal wealth and his family business, destroying his credit and the bank, and bankrupting him, as he explained in his diary, before sending him to Venice (where the Medici luckily had a branch), presumably for life.[19] "But in this they failed," Cosimo wrote, "for we lost no credit, and many foreign merchants and gentlemen offered to us, and even sent to Venice, large sums of money." Two things helped Cosimo thwart this plan. One was his personal reputation abroad. The other was the banking network he'd created outside Florence.

It's hard for the modern mind to understand just how severe a penalty exile was. Back then, most people had all their wealth tied up in possessions—land, houses, heirlooms, and maybe some physical money. Virtually none of that went with you when you went into exile. You took only what you could carry. Exile was like having your entire life stripped away. But not for Cosimo. Not only was his reputation good—at Venice he was received like an ambassador, he wrote—but his *credit* was good. Because of the branch banking system, the monetary wealth held by Cosimo in Florence was still an asset to him in Venice. The branch banking system made money virtual as well as physical, and that ended up giving money all kinds of valuable uses it didn't have before. This helped not only Cosimo, but the bank's clients as well. You didn't have to lug physical money around anymore, so long as you had an account at a Medici bank. Your wealth might be stored in Florence, or Rome, but your credit was good everywhere. This was one of the secrets of the Medicis' success, and one of the reasons why they are to this day one of the most famous banking families in history. They made money mobile.

Cosimo was so popular in Florence that after only one

year his exile was canceled and he was back, and in complete control of the city. He was rich and, as his early return showed, powerful. He began a lifelong program of building up his native city, and also providing vaunting displays of his wealth and power. In 1434, fresh off his victory over the Albizzi, he commissioned a new project from his friend, the artist Donatello. This would be a mic-drop project, something that would stamp both men. The project was a life-size bronze statue of the Bible's David. Donatello's David broke every mold that then existed. First off, it was a free-standing bronze statue. There hadn't been one of those in Europe for a thousand years; the knowledge had fled the continent, but Donatello had relearned the old techniques. Most scandalously, this David was completely naked. He had only a hat on his head, a sword in his hand, and boots on his feet, one of which was on the severed head of the giant Goliath. Celebrating the human form, showing nudity, those were things that nobody did in Europe at the time. And given that Donatello was a closeted but generally known homosexual—something that was illegal in Florence at the time—it made the statue a bit more controversial. In fact, the entire thing would've gotten Donatello in trouble if not for Cosimo's support. The *Pater Patriae* didn't just commission the statue. He built a pedestal for it in his courtyard in the Medici home and stuck the statue on top. Everybody who came to visit—and Cosimo's house was as important a building as any in Florence, an unofficial palace for the city's unofficial king—saw the statue. Cosimo putting that statue in such a prominent place was practically daring anybody to come after him, or Donatello, or any of his allies for that matter. The statue wasn't just a master work of art. It was a major fuck you to Cosimo's detractors. If you want to see it today, it's in Florence's Museo Nazionale del Bargello, not far from the Medici home where it was first put on a pedestal.

Cosimo also maintained his obsession with old manuscripts. He spent copiously on them, often through his dedicated book hunters Bracciolini and Niccolò Niccoli as well as through other intermediaries and even his own branch bank managers, who had standing orders to buy books. Bracciolini and Niccoli had a lively letter-writing habit between the two of them, which usually focused on their quests for books, and most of the letters mention Cosimo in some capacity. The banker was always either reading, reviewing, collecting, or more often financing these trips across the continent. When Niccolò died in 1437, his collection of more than eight hundred volumes was left with Cosimo. The religious books went to a convent at San Marco in Florence; the rest he kept for his private study at his home in Careggi, which he opened to anybody who wanted to come by and look at them. He later moved the collection to the Medici palace in the city. This study became the model for the modern library. (Today, this collection is kept at the Laurentian Library, a building that was once the cloister of San Lorenzo church. Cosimo and Niccolò's collection has been there since 1532.)

The San Marco convent in Florence is a great example of how Cosimo used the ethos of beneficial greed to help cement his reputation, both with the general public, with the church, and with himself. Built in the 1200s, the convent by Cosimo's time was in very poor shape, and newly occupied by a group of Dominicans. He financed a rebuilding of the convent, supporting it with money, putting the Medici family's personal architect, Michelozzo, onto the project, and hiring an artist, Fra Angelico, to decorate it with murals. Michelozzo designed a simple but impressive complex, with white plaster walls and plenty of columns holding up buttressed, arched ceilings. Cosimo himself even had a small cell for his personal retreats. The reconstruction went on for years and cost Cosimo an estimated forty thousand ducats, and he continued to financially support the convent after the reconstruction was complete. While the convent was nominally for the Dominicans, it also housed a "public" library, centered around Niccolò's collection, used by Florence's educated elites. Everybody knew who had put it there. That helped Cosimo publicly, but it wasn't the only reason he supported it. Da Bisticci tells a story about San Marco: At one point, Cosimo was stricken with a crisis of conscience, da Bisticci wrote, centered around his money and the way he earned it. Most people would go to their local church for confession, but Cosimo had higher connections: he went right to the pope. It must have been an interesting conversation, the pope's banker talking to the pope about whether or not his actions would get him into heaven. The pope was, apparently, sympathetic. "He remarked to Cosimo that, if he was bent on unburdening his soul, he might build a monastery," da Bisticci wrote. Thus Cosimo's support of San Marco not only buttressed his public image, but it balanced his purportedly sinful career against the kinds of good works that would result in an afterlife spent in heaven. Who wouldn't believe a pope who told them that?

While Cosimo was working out his guilt and angling for eternity, he became a regular economic stimulus program. Da Bisticci said that he spent at least fifteen to eighteen thousand florins every year on public works. He financed churches and chapels and homes and libraries and monasteries. He personally oversaw the construction of an ostentatious tomb for John XXIII. He employed multitudes, and if a contractor should find that he'd misjudged the work and was going to lose money on the project, Cosimo would pay extra to ensure he turned a profit. Cosimo perfected the use of greed and money as tools. He wielded them aggressively. His largesse was, according to the theory, the result of his greed. That gave him the cover for getting filthy rich and incredibly powerful. In the end, the Medicis' greatest asset in building their empire wasn't letters of credit, or branch banking, or double-entry bookkeeping. It was this ethos of greed as a social good. It was their secret weapon.

What Cosimo did was absolutely smash to smithereens every rule that had held back the merchants who came before him. He *was* Aristotle's Magnificent Man. He was a commoner king, and once he had people within the church like Antoninus and the pope (actually, popes) backing him, the historic grudges held against not only merchants and usurers but all commoners were gone. Cosimo fused the virtues of the Magnificent Man with the vice of avarice and opened the floodgates for every other person who wasn't born a noble or a king to dream of becoming rich. All they had to do was embrace their greed, and they too could become magnificent. And it is here, I think, where you can for the first time see an ethos that would grow like wildfire and change Europe, and then the world. It is here where you can see the real birth of what would come to be called capitalism.

Whether Cosimo was devout or cynical isn't exactly clear. He publicly considered himself an "honest and good merchant."[20] He was obviously avaricious, but it's entirely possible he also absorbed and believed in this new positive view of avarice, and genuinely tried to live up to it. He seemed very truly inspired by the intellectual currents of the day. He cared about art and philosophy and literature as much as he did about banking and bookkeeping. He believed in these things and was so committed to them that today we still have a ton of priceless works of art, architecture, and literature that were directly financed by him. The San Marco convent, for instance, is now the Museo Nazionale di San Marco. But he was also controversial in his day, and not everybody was on board with this new way of building personal and public wealth. Under Cosimo's sub-rosa rule, Florence became "[U]n paradiso abitato da diavoli," according to one of his oldest, and later disillusioned, friends—a paradise inhabited by devils.[21] He also had many, many admirers. People liked what Cosimo brought to the city. The poet and scholar Giovanni Pontano was one of them, and in a work called *De magnificentia* he, well, waxed poetic about the new world that Cosimo de' Medici had single-handedly built: "Cosimo of Florence has renewed the ancient magnificence, both in building temples and villas and in founding libraries. And he has not only imitated, but also in my opinion he was the first to renew the custom of turning private money to public good and using it for the embellishment of his country."[22]

Cosimo didn't just invest in buildings. He invested in people. One day a bishop named Tommaso Parentucelli passed through Florence on a papal mission to France. Even though he was on official church business, the church in those days was in lousy financial shape, and the pope hadn't given Parentucelli any money for the trip. He was on his own. Parentucelli met da Bisticci at his bookshop in Florence and asked if he could talk to Cosimo about a loan. Cosimo did not give the bishop the loan. Instead Cosimo gave him a letter of credit entitling him to any amount he wanted to withdraw from any of the Medici Bank's agents. No limit. Parentucelli was told the generosity was only a trifle, a small gesture of the banker's goodwill. He withdrew two hundred ducats during his trip. When he returned to Florence, he met Cosimo personally at church, where he thanked him profusely—and borrowed another hundred ducats for the last leg of his trip, back south to Rome. Cosimo seemed to not care how much money he gave the bishop. "Cosimo had a beneficial eye, always friendly to men of merit, and knowing how to estimate their worth and to serve them," da Bisticci wrote.[23]

Parentucelli was even more of a commoner than Cosimo, but he was running around in the same circles as Cosimo and Bracciolini and operating under the same influences. He was part of the world that sought out and absorbed all the old knowledge, that revered books and education and writing, that read Aristotle and absorbed the concept of "magnificence" and the free-spending habits of Cosimo de' Medici. Cosimo's largesse, the ethos of beneficial greed, the revival of Rome's glory, it all made a great impression on the bishop. He carried these ideas with him in his career, and before he was done with that career he would completely reset Europe's path in the world.

5

THE BISHOP OF ROME

Tommaso Parentucelli was part of a circle of friends that included Poggio Bracciolini and Cosimo de' Medici, a group of men who imbibed the knowledge and wisdom of the ancients. Embracing that pre-Christian thinking introduced radical new ideas to sclerotic medieval Europe that would forever change the Continent. Parentucelli shot up through the ranks of the church, and to the surprise of everyone soon found himself in the big chair as Pope Nicholas V. But the big chair wasn't what it used to be. Rome wasn't what it used to be. The Eternal City was, frankly, a dump. Parentucelli devised an ambitious plan to restore it, and making that happen would involve spreading the radical new ethos of his friends to the very seat of Christendom.

The beauty of Rome lies in what is in ruin," Averardo de' Medici, Cosimo's cousin, wrote in a letter in 1443. "There are many splendid palaces, houses, tombs, and temples, and other edifices in infinite number, but all are in ruins." Every day, he said, residents burned porphyry and marble from the ruins for lime (used in new construction). The people were literally tearing the city apart. He summed up the men of Rome in a sentence: "They all look like cowherds." Most of them, he said, were "uncommonly dirty." He was told it was on account of all the cooking they did. While the Romans were agreeable, "one seldom sees them." As for Rome's social life, it didn't exist. "Amusements there are none." He signed the letter "*ex urbe delacerata*" (From the ruined city).[1]

For a thousand years Rome was the center of an empire that spread from Britain to Babylon, the largest and most important city in the world, a cradle of civilization. But the city itself was never a commercial or industrial center. It didn't even have its own port; that was on the coast in Ostia, by the mouth of the Tiber River. Rome's significance was always political, so when the empire collapsed, so did the influence. By the time of Bracciolini and Cosimo de' Medici, the Eternal City was a dusty burg where farm animals roamed as freely as people. The important Italian cities were Venice, Milan, Florence, and Naples. Even the popes had fled Rome, left and gone to Avignon in France. Nobody wanted to be in Rome. By the fifteenth century Rome's population had dwindled to only about thirty thousand. It was mainly a farming community, even inside the city walls. There were vineyards and orchards and vegetable gardens, and fields where cattle, goats, and sheep grazed. The fifteenth-century Romans *were* cowherds. The aqueducts, once a symbol of the empire's technological might, were almost completely shot; only one still worked.[2]

Even the Coliseum, which today is a revered and iconic symbol of the ancient city, was largely abandoned in the fifteenth century and the butt of jokes—and I mean that entirely literally, and on more than one level. In the 1440s a Florentine barber and comic poet named Domenico di Giovanni wrote a poem about Rome with these lines: "O, fresh/cool Rome, when the mantle is empty you would do well to make it into a compote and to give the *Culiseo* a suppository of pastoral staff, rather than of parsnip." I know, it doesn't seem very funny; I reckon it loses *a lot* in the translation across languages and centuries. To break it down: *the mantle* was a reference to the pope, who'd left the city. *Pastoral* was a synonym for penis. *Culiseo* was a play on the building's more Latin name of Coliseo, and a triple entendre. *Culo* was Latin for anus; *Culis* was Latin for asses. The "-eo" had a sexual connotation, too, meaning, well, to ejaculate. To the rest of Italy, the Coliseum was Rome's literal, round, ass.[3]

Rome's sagging fortunes mirrored those of the church as well. To quickly recap 1,000 years of Catholic and European history: In the 300s the Roman emperor Constantine makes Christianity the state religion, then moves the seat of government to Byzantium, renaming it Constantinople. Rome's influence wanes. It's sacked in 420. In the 800s, after Charlemagne's death, the bishops of Rome made a power play; relying on fraudulent documents made to look as if power had been given them centuries before, the so-called Forged Decretals, the bishops of Rome claimed to be the proper rulers over a global theocracy.[4] But both the papacy and the various monarchies had lost power over the years to various gangs of marauding vandals, and any unified European leadership further diminished. No ruler had any effective power. After several centuries, the Holy Roman Empire was revived and pulled together control over a vast swath of central Europe, but it was divided among dozens of small principalities. The Kingdom of the Franks likewise was more a patchwork quilt of competing feudalities than the nation of France we know today. Spain wasn't even Spain; it was called Castile. There was a kingdom called Aragon that just does not exist anymore. The English were the English. Italy was largely a plaything of all these other powers. The European map back then looked more like the

Westeros of *Game of Thrones* than the unified continent we know today.

In the early 1300s, French kings kind of just took over the pontificate and moved it to Avignon. For about a century, the seat of the Christian church in Europe resided in France, under the close alliance and supervision of the French king. This of course did not sit well with the English and the Germans. The Italians especially hated it, and the further loss of power and influence. You know who loved it? The church leaders. Life in Avignon was especially rich for the pope and the cardinals. In 1377, though, Gregory XI apparently got tired of being so pampered and decided to move the theocratic palace back to Rome. He died just a few months after arriving in the Eternal City, sparking a massive power struggle. The Romans wanted a Roman pope, and a mob beset the Vatican, threatening to tear the cardinals to pieces if they did not elect one. This was no idle threat. The terrified cardinals finally settled on an Italian, Urban VI, who promptly let his new power go to his head. He belittled the cardinals to such a degree that they tried to depose him, electing a different pope who would go back to Avignon. Now Europe had two chief priests, each claiming both ecclesiastical and temporal supremacy and, importantly, control over the vast property owned by the church and the money-generating network that was an integral part of it.

By 1410, this rift was so pronounced that myriad councils could not settle it. One in fact was so divided it elected a *third* pope. In 1418, all three—including Bracciolini's boss and Cosimo's client, John XXIII—were forced out, and a completely new pope, based in Rome, was elected. The bishop of Rome had been restored, but the centuries-long strife had depleted both the church's powers and Rome's influence. The papacy was a seriously degraded throne.

THE POPE NOBODY WANTED

Into this swirl came Tommaso Parentucelli. He was from such an insignificant family that it's not even clear what his last name was; some history books have it as Parentucelli, some as Sarzana.[5] In a papal bull from Felix V he was referred to as Thomas de Calandrinis, apparently his mother's maiden name.[6] In any case, he was born in 1389 in Sarzana, near the west coast in northern Italy. His father was a physician in either Pisa or Lucca, it's not clear. Da Bisticci says that Parentucelli's father was banished from his job by "civil strife," but explains no more. His father died from the plague when he was young, and he himself got so sick his mother assumed he would die, too.[7] When he didn't, both he and his mother took it as a sign from God (his mother had a dream about his recovery, da Bisticci says).

He left Sarzana for Bologna when he was about twelve to study grammar and Latin, logic, philosophy, and theology.[8] Two years later, he ran out of money. His mother had remarried, but not to a wealthy man; Parentucelli as a stepson got nothing.[9] Needing to work, he went to Florence, where he got a job as a tutor for the sons of one of the city's prominent citizens, Rinaldo degli Albizzi (yes, Cosimo's nemesis). A year later he tutored the children of another citizen, Palla di Nofri Strozzi, at the time one of the true power players of Italian politics. After those two years he had enough money to go back to Bologna and finish his studies. There he got yet another job, running the house of the local bishop, Niccolò Albergati. This series of seemingly menial jobs would have a huge impact on the impressionable youth, taking Parentucelli out of his life of obscurity and plunging him into the heart of the most dynamic movement in Europe. In Florence, he had his first contact with the social circle of Bracciolini, the Medici, da Bisticci and the others. In Bologna, he first was noticed by the church hierarchy. It almost sounds like a modern movie: a small-town nobody goes to the big city and finds himself in the room with the most powerful people in the country. And these connections would end up being lifelong ones. Parentucelli shared with Cosimo, Bracciolini, and da Bisticci a passion for books and learning and recovering the lost literature of ancient Greece and Rome.

Parentucelli became incredibly powerful in a stunningly short amount of time. In 1443, his employer Albergati died. He went and worked for another cardinal, who also died a few months later. He then went to work for Eugenius, who named him bishop of Bologna in 1444. On his return from a successful diplomatic trip to Germany in 1446, he was greeted at Rome's gates by church officials bearing a present from Eugenius: the red cardinal's hat. A few months later, Eugenius died. The election of the next pope was bitterly contested; there were factions within the College of Cardinals and they could not agree on any one candidate because every name pissed off some clutch of them. Powerful families like the Colonna and the Orisini, the Kingdom of Venice, the Duke of Milan, the King of France, and the King of Naples all had their own candidates in mind. But none of them could get enough of the others to agree. In fact, they couldn't find any candidate who didn't give one group an advantage that another group didn't want them to have. Finally, they zeroed in on the one person who carried virtually no political power with any group: Tommaso Parentucelli. Nobody was very happy about it, "but at least they had the satisfaction of considering that their opponents had gained as little as themselves," the historian Mandell Creighton wrote.[10] On March 18, 1447, he was coronated and took the name Nicholas V. The group that had formed around Bracciolini and Cosimo, which revered the ancient world and the magnificent man and promoted a more modern world that embraced avarice, finally had one of their own in a powerful position.

Nicholas was, by all accounts, an almost astoundingly good man for a position as decadent as the papacy, and though he served in the role for less than a decade, his was one of the most significant pontificates in the church's long history. He was physically slight with weak, abnormally small legs and an ashen face. His voice, however, was loud and harsh.[11] His manner was humble; he never looked to upstage others, and was kind to everybody in his presence. He chose diplomacy over force, claiming he wanted for his only weapon the cross,[12] and managed to talk his way into solving virtually every violent political squabble in Italy. He finally, through the execution of several treaties that all depended upon his considerable diplomatic skill, ended the church's century-long schism. Once again, there was only one pope, one chief priest leading all of Christendom. He worked out a new deal with the Holy Roman Empire that basically restored all of the church's old powers. He issued a papal bull in 1455 called the *Romanus Pontifex* that settled, for the moment, competing claims of Portugal and Castile over the lands their sailors were "discovering" in Africa (we'll come back to this). He even tried, albeit too late, to restore relations with Constantinople and reunite the long-disunited Roman Empire (we'll come back to this, too). The people almost uniformly loved him. (There was one pope-hating Roman named Stefano Porcari who consistently inveighed against popes in general and Nicholas in particular. At one point, he tried to have Nicholas assassinated. The plot was foiled, and Nicholas—kindly soul that he was—actually forgave Porcari. Rather than accept this act of love, Porcari tried again to kill Nicholas. The plot was again foiled, and this time the would-be assassin ended up hanging from a rope in front of Castel Sant'Angelo.) Nicholas had completely turned the church around.

In light of all his diplomatic successes and the church's newfound preeminence, Nicholas decided to celebrate with a massive jubilee in Rome. Technically, this was the same sort of "jubilee" as extolled in the Bible, the same jubilee that went back to Leviticus and was the Hebrew version of the Mesopotamian *amargi*. But the medieval jubilees were quite different: these jubilees didn't forgive *debts*, they forgave *sins*. And, quite importantly, they did it for a "donation" to the church. People were invited to come to the city, pray and confess, and receive absolution, for only a modest donation to the church's coffers. After decades of war, famine, pestilence, and death—literally, the four horsemen of the apocalypse—Europe's ragged survivors jumped at the chance to celebrate, to have their sins removed, and to have their everlasting souls promised to an eternity of peace in heaven. The jubilee began on Christmas Day 1449 and ran for the entire year of 1450. It was wildly popular. Rome, now a scrubby, rotting patch of ruins, had not seen such an influx of visitors in at least a century. Fully forty thousand people arrived every day from all over the Continent. Over the course of the year, millions came.[13] One German archbishop, one of the pope's most ardent antagonists, arrived with 140 knights and made peace. At least three future saints came. Princes from Italy, Austria, Poland, Slovenia, Germany, and elsewhere arrived. Scores of writers made the pilgrimage, and an entire jubilee literary scene emerged.

Importantly, the jubilee was a *massive* moneymaking enterprise for the church and for Rome. The city's moneychangers, apothecaries, artists, and innkeepers all made out well, but the church did even better. So much gold and silver found its way into the church's treasury that there was an actual, physical shortage of money elsewhere on the continent.[14] According to da Bisticci, Nicholas deposited one hundred thousand gold florins into the Medici Bank alone. This fortune allowed Nicholas to carry out his true, bold vision: nothing less than to restore Rome to its former physical glory, to make it a symbol and fitting capital for Christendom. Nicholas would take the ethos of beneficial greed and the concept of the magnificent man to heights not seen in Europe since the glory days of the empire.

REBUILDING THE ETERNAL CITY

In a deathbed talk with the cardinals in 1455, recorded by his biographer Giannozzo Manetti, Nicholas laid out his vision: "To create solid and stable convictions in the minds of the uncultured masses, there must be something that appeals to the eye; a popular faith, sustained only on doctrines, will never be anything but feeble and vacillating. But if the authority of the Holy See were visibly displayed in majestic buildings, imperishable memorials and witnesses seemingly planted by the hand of God Himself, belief would grow and strengthen like a tradition from one generation to another, and all the world would accept and revere it. Noble edifices combining taste and beauty with imposing proportions would immensely conduce to the exaltation of the chair of St. Peter."[15] Nicholas wanted Rome to be a physical, tangible expression of God's kingdom, and for that to be manifested, the city would have to blow away any other city in Europe. It needed to be magnificent.

Nicholas's plan encompassed just about every aspect of the city: improving its defenses, rebuilding its decrepit infrastructure, fixing and restoring dozens of churches, and of course creating that earthly manifestation of God's kingdom. The work was absolutely massive. He had crews repairing and replacing bridges and aqueducts. He had many of the ruins that littered the city removed, and then he relaid and repaved roads. And he rebuilt the heart of the Vatican itself: the Vatican Borgo, the Papal Palace, and St. Peter's (the basilica that is there today is the outcome of this project, though it is different from his original plan and Nicholas did not live to see it completed.) Nicholas's plans for what we today call Vatican City were audacious. In his own time, "Leonine City" was technically part of Rome but sat outside the city walls. His plan extended the city walls and brought the Vatican inside it. He had a plan to rebuild St. Peter's, with a huge open square in front of it, another large square in front of Castel Sant'Angelo, and three broad streets connecting them. In the center of the square in front of St. Peter's would be a massive obelisk.[16] That is more or less exactly what is there today.

One of the most solely utilitarian but critically important jobs was fixing the city aqueducts. It was a major need, and a major symbol of just how far the onetime capital of the empire had sunk. During the empire's heights, the city had fourteen aqueducts bringing fresh water to Romans. It was a major engineering feat for its time. When Nicholas was pope, only one of them was working; the city's residents were reliant on the Tiber for their water. In 1453, he commissioned Leon Battista Alberti to restore the Acqua Vergine, which ran from its endpoint at Trevi Fountain to outside the Porta del Popolo.[17] (The present-day fountain, a Baroque masterpiece, was built in the seventeenth century.)

All this activity had a profound economic effect on Rome. The dozens of projects created a massive demand for both skilled and unskilled workers, bringing them in from inside and outside Italy, along with, importantly, capital.[18] Nicholas didn't ignore intellectual pursuits, either. Like most of his circle, he was a voracious book hound. He brought

Greeks to Rome to help translate old Greek texts into Latin and the Latin texts into Italian (remember, to most Italians of that time, Latin was a lost language). So many came that they ended up forming a distinct literary group that stood in contrast to Bracciolini and the Florentines. Nicholas invested liberally in bringing in books and having them translated, handing out benefices—another word for church jobs—and hosting public lectures about the material. He financed the kind of book hunting that Bracciolini had been doing for decades—Bracciolini himself discovered several new works during this time.[19]

Pope Nicholas's efforts had a transformative effect on the papacy and Rome. He restored its position in European affairs, he got rid of competing popes, and he restored the church's moneymaking network. For a good example of that network, consider the city of Bologna, where Nicholas had spent so many years and which had been a key antagonist against Rome. Nicholas worked out a peace treaty that kept the city ostensibly independent of Rome, at least in name. A papal "legate," a representative of the pope, had a seat in the municipal council and magistrates of Bologna's government. The peace treaty gave the Bolognese control of their own militia and city revenues, and an agreement to protection from the pope's troops if needed. (Yeah, the pope had soldiers. Like, real soldiers.) The Holy See "only" received recognition of its suzerainty, meaning its supremacy, and the legate got a share of the patronage from public offices. The city paid a tribute to the pope on similar terms to other cities and states under the pope's influence.[20] Imagine that kind of setup in cities and towns across Europe. And consider this: the church was the biggest landowner in Europe. Its influence and power spanned the continent. And the man who restored Rome to its former level of, well, magnificence, was friends with and influenced by Cosimo de'

Medici and Poggio Bracciolini and that entire strain of Florentine thought that argued that greed was a social good. The Medici and the popes from this point on are preaching the same gospel. And it was around this time that these popes started getting tagged with a "new" title, one that had been bestowed back in the time of the empire on the emperors, one that you can see even today all over the city, and carved into the marble inside St. Peter's itself: the Pontifex Maximus.

Even though Nicholas closed the schism, restored the church, and started Rome back on its road to prominence, and even though he was universally considered to be a man of exceedingly high character, he didn't solve all the church's problems. Moreover, in restoring the church's revenue streams, he inadvertently opened the door to all the old ills. A well-known German monk and theologian, Jakob von Juterbogk, wrote a piece outlining the church's myriad abuses and implored Nicholas to fix them.[21] He argued for the pope to put himself and the church under the rule of a council, a sort of parliament for the church—this was a popular topic for reformers who felt that the pope and the Italians who were spreading this new gospel of greed had too much power. "No nation in Christendom offers such opposition to reform as Italy, and this from love of gain and worldly profit, and fear of losing its privileges," he wrote. In leveling this complaint, by specifically taking aim at the Italians' "love of gain and worldly profit," von Juterbogk was pointing directly at the ethos of beneficial greed. Nobody in Rome was listening.

I visited Rome once, about twenty years ago. It is a magnificent city, of course. The sense of history that hits you with every step is overpowering. I think every single age of Europe is represented somewhere along its winding streets, and you feel it intensely. I remember visiting the Vatican and walking into St. Peter's, and feeling this absolutely engulfing sense of awe standing inside it, taking in its size and grandeur. Of course, that is the point of the place. Nicholas's plan was to build the most stunning, staggering cathedral to Christ in the world, and his successors did just that. Everywhere you look in that temple there is something magnificent. In one corner, almost casually tucked away, is Michelangelo's *Pietà,* his statue of the dead Christ cradled in his mother Mary's arms. I swear to God it is the most beautiful thing any human being has ever created. Every step in St. Peter's is like that. You walk along and it's nothing but grand marble columns that seem to stretch forever, ornate tombs for different popes, and beautiful art everywhere; the place really is the very embodiment of the kind of magnificence I've been talking about. Michelangelo designed St. Peter's dome, and as you climb its narrow, curved stairs, you are in a way walking through the mind of one of the greatest artists who ever lived. The entire building is just wild.

But I remember, walking amid all that magnificence, that at some point a thought occurred to me: None of this really fits in with the things Yeshua thought and said (which, not for nothing, shows you that I've been thinking about some of the ideas in this book for a very, very long time). A simple carpenter who told the rich to sell all their belongings would be horrified, were he really to come back from the dead, to see this temple of excess built in his name. The church had actually gone past Aristotle's conception of magnificence. They weren't spending just the right amount for just the right works; they went way, way over the top. And they went way past anything their founder ever said. The church's newfound power in the era of Nicholas had virtually nothing to do with the man in whose name the religion had been created, and everything to do with the new ethos introduced by Bracciolini and Cosimo, and embraced by Nicholas. They were already pushing the idea of greed being good past any moral boundaries that could collar its excesses. They sparked a fire that would burn brightly for centuries. Nicholas died in 1455, and Cosimo in 1464, but their legacies carried great weight.

In a very small amount of time, from roughly 1430 to 1460, the influence of this group of Italian thinkers, bankers, preachers, and a pope laid the groundwork for a revolution. They created a new incentive structure for society, the ethos of beneficial greed, and embedded it in commerce and in the church. They gentrified greed. In the decades that followed, first Italy and then Europe would be transformed. The output from this new way of doing things was massive. Sculpture. Artwork. Convents. Monasteries. Churches. Rome itself was expanded, improved, and rebuilt. Entire cities were reborn. Artists who are today household names were nurtured in this new world. Donatello, but also Leonardo da Vinci, Botticelli, Michelangelo, Raphael, and others. Men like Cosimo and Nicholas and others of such stature in the generations that followed supported these artists, and their output was the material manifestation of this new ethos. Leonardo's *Last Supper* was painted on a wall of a convent in Milan. Raphael's *School of Athens* is on a wall in the Vatican. And of course hundreds of other works that would fill a massive catalog. These works are famous today, obviously, but most people don't understand the real reason for the changes in Europe that led to them. The ethos of beneficial greed was an important part of Europe's renewal, and it is still shaping our world because it launched countless imitators. With people like Cosimo and other non-noble bankers and merchants leading the way, it was clear to all that this ethos was adoptable by anyone. For more than a thousand years, the church had told peasants to embrace their poverty, to accept their lowly status, because the meek would inherit the Earth. But now they could see that the pursuit of wealth wasn't just for the nobility the way it had been in Aristotle's time. When seen through the lens of the ethos of beneficial greed, the lives and examples of Cosimo de' Medici and Nicholas V seem to represent a turning point. International trade with Europe had been mainly for luxury items only the wealthy could afford; for the serfs trade was local, and only for basic goods. But within decades of this era, trade absolutely exploded out of Europe. In the next chapter, I'll introduce you to a merchant, Benedetto Cotrugli, who enthusiastically embraced this new ethos, and showed others how to do so as well. At the same time, sailors were pushing the boundaries of the known world further and further, south and west. Yeah, you know what's coming. All the conditions were in place for Europe's commoners to embrace commerce, trade, and the pursuit of wealth. Nothing would be the same after that.

6

THE BALANCE SHEET

The ethos of beneficial greed was the spark that lit the fire that forced change in Europe. But the church was still around, God's law was still in effect, and the pursuit of wealth was still, overall, morally dubious. What merchants and bankers needed was a way to definitively show, to prove, that their activities were morally upstanding. They did, of course, find a way, which furthered the changes that started around Florence, and it may surprise you to learn that something that seems so boring today was at one time so radical that it helped to reshape the world.

In 1458, a bout of bubonic plague hit Naples. This wasn't unusual. The plague still showed up from time to time in different parts of Europe in smaller, localized outbreaks (it would continue for another couple of hundred years). In much the same way Covid has become "normalized," Europe normalized the plague. There was a standard plan for handling it. Lockdowns of the area. Quarantine of the infected. Individuals keeping apart as much as possible. Those who could afford to got out of the cities. Benedetto Cotrugli, a merchant from Ragusa (modern-day Dubrovnik in Croatia) who was in Naples when the plague hit, could afford to get out of the city, and that's what he did. He hid out in the countryside while the plague burned through the city. With a lot of time on his hands and not much to do, he decided to write a book.[1]

Between the example set by Cosimo de' Medici and other bankers and the embrace of the ethos of beneficial greed and the magnificent man by Nicholas, Antoninus, and others in the church, the status of the commoner merchant changed quickly. It was already evident before Cosimo died in 1464, and Cotrugli best exemplified the trend. Cotrugli, born around 1416, was part of the first generation to grow up in the era of Cosimo, Nicholas, Bracciolini, and that circle of educated men. They rubbed off on him. Cotrugli wanted to be a man of letters, too; he studied law and philosophy in school. Fate had other plans for him, however. His father died when he was about twenty and he was forced to take over the family business.

The Cotruglis were importers of wheat, cereals, salt, and saltpeter, mainly trading with merchants in Naples. The Republic of Ragusa was a key trade conduit with the East for the various Italian kingdoms, and the family business benefitted from this centrality. Cotrugli handled the actual trading side of the business, which took him to Barcelona, Venice, Florence, and, for the last eighteen years of his life, Naples. He traveled so often by sea in fact that he wrote a book on the subject, *De navigatione*. The Kingdom of Naples was a key partner with Ragusa, and Cotrugli eventually settled in the southern Italian city-state, becoming ambassador to Ragusa in the court of the king and the master of the Naples mint. He married and had children. After more than twenty years of building up this long and successful career, he sat down in that plague summer of 1458 and wrote down everything he'd learned from his decades in business in a manuscript titled *Il libro dell'arte di mercatura: The Book of the Art of the Trade.*

You've probably never heard of it. *The Art* existed only in manuscript form and none of the originals have survived. Cotrugli wrote it in Italian, not Latin, because he wanted it to be understood by common people. That was great then, but the language has changed so much that the original version of the book is barely decipherable today. And while Gutenberg had invented his printing press a few years earlier, *The Art* wasn't published in book form until nearly a century later. The version that was published was such a hatchet job that the true importance of the work was completely lost. *The Art* almost disappeared because it didn't seem to have anything important to say. Indeed, it essentially *did* disappear.

In the late 1500s, a Ragusan named Giovanni Giuseppi found a copy of *The Art*, which he passed on to a friend of his, Francesco Patrizi, a Neoplatonic philosopher and book nut who loved old Greek texts and bought and sold books out of crates. Patrizi also had a short-lived publishing house, which put out three works, all in 1573. One was a math book. Another was about the Roman military. And lastly came the book his friend had given him, Cotrugli's book. None of them sold very well, possibly because Patrizi wasn't very good at publishing. The one important thing that kept *The Art* from disappearing forever was that at one point Cotrugli mentions in passing that merchants should use double-entry bookkeeping. This gave *The Art* the minor distinction of being the first work in Europe to mention this method of accounting.

It wasn't until very recently that researchers came across copies of Cotrugli's manuscript that predated Patrizi's published version and realized that the publisher had badly butchered the original work; Patrizi wasn't only a bad publisher, he was also a terrible editor. The researchers took these copies and fused them into one master copy, and then translated that for a modern audience. The first English-language edition of *The Art* was published in 2017. What Patrizi published was a light work of business platitudes. The new translation makes it clear that Cotrugli had a much higher goal in mind.

THE MORAL MERCHANT

The Book of the Art of the Trade may have been the first true "how-to" business book ever written. Business was such a natural extension of the development of mankind, Cotrugli wrote, that nobody had ever bothered to write out the proper rules of businessmen. This led to "the confusion and abuse of proper procedures perpetrated daily by the merchants of our times," he said. And he made no bones about the fact that he was disgusted by merchants who abused these un-written rules, who made the entire profession look bad. "It pained me that this useful and necessary activity had fallen into the hands of such undisciplined and uncouth people." The business world, he said, had been "mangled and given over to those who know nothing, a forum for empty chatter where anything goes." It is a slim volume, and even though writers back then tended to drone on, Cotrugli didn't waste a lot of words. He had a point to make and he hit it. In that way, *The Art* is a surprisingly modern book.

Cotrugli's goal wasn't just to explain how merchants could make money. His goal was to explain how merchants could make money in a *moral* profession. His express purpose was to write a book that explained how a merchant could both pursue his own self-interest *and at the same time* be a morally upstanding citizen and do honor to God. Cotru-gli's book was a how-to guide to becoming the magnificent man in a Christian world and living within the religious rules of that world. It was an impassioned defense of commerce done correctly. He wanted to set the standard for the business class. His timing was great; opinions were already changing about commerce, banking, and money. Cotrugli poured everything he knew into his book, from the most mundane details of business life to the most philosophical ruminations on the role of the merchant in society, and how to meet those expectations. He gave a brief history of trade, explained foreign exchange, and provided a detailed explanation of double-entry bookkeeping. He dedicated an entire section to religion and its proper role in the merchant's life. He even explained how the merchant should pray.

Cotrugli was part of the first generation of businessmen to come of age in the time of Cosimo de' Medici, Bracciolini, and their ilk, when the reputation of commerce and money got rehabilitated, and it's clear that in a short amount of time they had a tremendous influence. Previously, nobody had been so bold as to write a book defending merchants and the business of making money. Indeed, in earlier eras that might have gotten one excommunicated, condemned to eternal damnation wandering one of Dante's circles of hell. *The Art of the Trade* shows how fast and how thoroughly the culture was changing. To be sure, commerce was still considered something that only commoners did. Cotrugli himself noted there were actual laws within the Justinian Code prohibiting the upper castes from taking part in commerce; the mere act of doing so would discredit them. Who exactly is that? "Kings, princes, barons, knights, gentlemen and any others of noble birth." By the time Cotrugli went into the family business, though, there was a model for being a totally upstanding, God-fearing merchant, one who had a full, profitable business for himself and while still doing right by the church and state.

Only it was mostly informal. Nobody had taken the time to set it in writing, to explain it, to codify it. This is what Cotrugli did, explaining for the first time what this new kind of merchant looked like. Cotrugli's book is like a Rosetta Stone of moral money. The vision he laid out is detailed and exacting. He held merchants to a higher standard than priests. He espoused a way of living that allowed a merchant to earn a good living, remain morally upright, contribute to society, and look forward to an eternity in the lofty embrace of heaven. The merchant should never lose sight of serving God at the expense of serving his business. "We must see to it that we recognize these earthly things for what they are and that the higher and eternal things are not unknown to us," he wrote. He is ruthless on the topic of merchants who didn't espouse Christian morals in their business dealings. In his experience, the profession seemed run through with sinners. "Merchants are far from devout, addicted as they are to earthly and corrupt things so that it is hard for them to live without sinning constantly," he wrote.[2]

Cotrugli's book as translated into English is extremely readable and has much to say to the modern businessman. He's a lively writer and clearly cares deeply about his subject. His passion comes through on every page, his exhortations to his fellow merchants to do better, to be better. It doesn't feel like a bone-dry old book talking to a different world. On the contrary, he feels very relevant. Cotrugli is ruthless in his condemnation of bad, unscrupulous merchants. It's not hard to imagine Cotrugli looking at our world with some satisfaction. After all, we as a society view the merchant class the same way he did. But he'd also probably have the same mix of passion and condemnation, because today we still have our unscrupulous businesses. It is absolutely fascinating and telling that the world's first how-to business book spent as much time on religion as it does on accounting.

"Merchants must practice among themselves a sort of religion," he wrote, and offered a laundry list of things the holy merchant should avoid. They should stay away from dice games or card games or other kinds of gambling.[3] If he does win some money gambling, he should return it. The merchant should avoid gluttony. Food is only for nourishment, and wine should be minimized. Indeed, he goes on at length about getting drunk and how it reflects on the merchant. "This habit is more abhorrent in a merchant than other men." And it's harder to operate your business with a hangover. The merchant should avoid quarrels, his own or others', avoid "nefarious and evil men," and limit his number of "empty-headed or indigent friends." He is forbidden from practicing alchemy and should avoid jousting (really, that's in there), which Cotrugli considers "frivolous." He is against any extravagance. He exhorts merchants to avoid any kind of showy clothing. Everything should be simple and plain. No bright colors. "Dark color is a sign of a serious and reliable man."[4]

To Cotrugli, religion and commerce were completely intertwined. In order to do the latter well, a merchant had to embrace the former. He spends as much time talking about religion as anything else, and he in fact seems far more emphatic on the matter than Bracciolini or de' Medici or even, in a way, Nicholas. To Cotrugli, saving one's soul in the afterlife is as important a goal as turning a profit. More important, in fact. He advised merchants to follow Jesus's precepts, to observe mass daily, which "encourages holy works and the will to perform them."[5] He offered another laundry list— thirteen conditions—for the proper practice of praying. "We add our prayers spoken aloud to pay tribute to God for our debt of all we have received from him," he wrote.

He was adamant about the fact that merchants have a social responsibility and should give back to the community.

And not just token gestures. He quotes Matthew 25, the parable of the sheep that I mentioned in chapter 1. To not provide alms, he said, was a mortal sin, and he mentioned seven deeds of compassion that are incumbent upon the merchant: "to feed the hungry, to quench the thirsty, to dress the naked, to house the pilgrim, to visit the sick, to bail the prisoner, to bury the dead." He was virtually quoting Matthew directly, and if you think about it, that is a tall, tall order. But Cotrugli wasn't done. How much should the merchant give? Anything that isn't necessary for the support of the people who depend on him. "Although this surplus, strictly in terms of property, belongs to its owner, in terms of its use it belongs to the needy." (Remember this statement. It'll pop up again.)

It's hard to say how popular the book was when Cotrugli first wrote it. He was a successful businessman with contacts in several regions, so probably people were aware of it; there is evidence that Luca Pacioli—who we'll get to in a minute and who did write a hugely popular book on accounting—was aware of Cotrugli's works.[6] But Cotrugli's work itself didn't have much staying power. The book was largely forgotten across the centuries, and if not for Cotrugli's first-in-Europe mention of double-entry bookkeeping, it probably would have been forgotten entirely. In the version published by Patrizi, there was one line about accounting, and it said merchants should use double-entry. It was the modern researchers who resurrected the book who made a critical discovery: Cotrugli didn't make just a passing reference to double-entry. He wrote an entire chapter about it. Patrizi was such a bad editor, he just cut out things he didn't understand. And he didn't understand double-entry accounting at all. So what, you ask? The importance of a work that seeks to meld religion and morality with double-entry bookkeeping is more relevant to our relationship with money today than you might suspect.

THE "BALANCE" SHEET

The system of double-entry bookkeeping described by Cotrugli in 1458 is essentially the same one we use today: In double-entry, every transaction is recorded twice, once as a debit, once as a credit. At the same time as you are taking in something (the credit), you are putting out something (the debit). At the end of whatever period, a day, a week, a month, a year, you add up all the entries in both columns. If they match, then you have successfully recorded all your transactions. If they don't, you made a mistake, and finding it is just a matter of going back over every corresponding credit and debit until you find the place where they don't agree anymore. Before this, European businesses used a single-entry accounting system. In that system, finding the error was harder. Double-entry was a decided boon in efficiency and record-keeping. And most people seem to think that alone is why it became so popular. But one curious thing in Cotrugli's book is his passionate insistence that double-entry was somehow aligned with morality. As we'll see, accounting and morality were related through double-entry bookkeeping in a way that had a profound impact on the business world.

Double-entry bookkeeping was developed by an Islamic mathematician named al-Khwarizmi. An Italian mathematician and merchant's son named Leonardo Pisano came across the system while traveling in the twelfth century. Pisano, better known today as Fibonacci, introduced Hindu-Arabic math to Europe through his writings. The oldest existing record of its use in Europe is the ledgers of a business in Genoa called

Messari, dated to 1340. But it's clear from Messari's ledgers themselves that the system was already fully fleshed out. The Medici used it as well, of course. Double-entry's popularity exploded late in the fifteenth century. In 1494, two years after Christopher Columbus landed in the Americas, a Franciscan friar named Luca Pacioli published a masterwork, *Summa di arithmetica, geometria, proportioni et proportionalita,* a textbook that explained all of the known mathematics of the day. Like Cotrugli, he published it in Italian rather than Latin to make it more accessible to the public. It was, at the time, the most comprehensive book on the topic, mixing the practical with the technical, and was in part a self-help manual for an emerging business class. The book was incredibly popular, so popular it quickly sold out. The publisher printed another run. That sold out. What they soon figured out was that there was one section in particular that people loved: the section on double-entry bookkeeping. There was so much demand for it, in fact, that the publisher carved it out and sold it as a separate book, *Particularis de computis et scripturis.*

Particularis itself is mostly a straightforward explainer, something that any reader today could understand. There is a chapter describing how the merchant can use different kinds of books, like a day book and a journal, and then reconcile those to a master ledger. (One benefit of this method, Pacioli pointed out, is that if any one of the books gets destroyed, the merchant can recreate it with the other two.) One chapter defines inventory, another merchandise, with explanations on how to keep track of them. There is a chapter explaining how to record cash, how to set and maintain the debit and credit columns, and how to divide the page for small and large accounts. In the accounting world, Pacioli's work was long considered the definitive beginning of double-entry bookkeeping as a business practice; go Google him and you'll see he's called the "Father of Accounting," even though Cotrugli's work came decades earlier.

A couple of things in Pacioli's work were a bit peculiar, though. For one thing, Pacioli insisted that every page of the merchant's ledger needed to have this printed on the top: "In the name of God." Second, he suggested that maintaining these books was about more than counting money. "Without double entry, businessmen would not sleep easily at night," he wrote. The merchant has myriad responsibilities to his business and family and is often on the move. Having clean books is a way to maintain vigilance and keep one's mind clear for the bigger things in the world. "In the divine offices of the Holy Church, they sing that God promised a crown to the watchful," he wrote.[7] It's possible he was just talking about the comfort that comes with knowing one's records are in order. But given his chosen profession, it's likely he was also talking about something else.

Cotrugli was even more explicit about the use of double-entry. Cotrugli very forcefully made the point that *only* merchants who use double-entry bookkeeping were credible. Those who used single-entry were "the basest and most iniquitous." It seems odd that something as anodyne as accounting would produce that reaction. Like Cotrugli, Pacioli seemed to suggest there was some moral component to keeping clean books. Another Florentine, Leon Battista Alberti, made it even more explicit. He talked about keeping business records under a lock and key in a study, "almost as if they were sacred or religious objects," he wrote. For Cotrugli and Pacioli, and I'd imagine the people who bought and read their books and followed their systems, the care taken in maintaining "the books" was on a par with daily mass and prayer. This starts to explain why Cotrugli was so emphatic about using double-entry. Cotrugli's insistence on the virtues of double-entry makes sense once it is put in its entire context: what drove double-entry bookkeeping's popularity in the fifteenth and sixteenth centuries wasn't just its effect on business efficiency.

It was a way for merchants to prove their piety.

In the macabre world of Europe after the Black Death, when war was unending, famine was common, and bouts of the plague kept springing up across the continent, people were in a constant state of panic about death and their sins, and that they would die with a sin deficit that would condemn them to an eternity in hell. People *believed* in hell and were morbidly afraid of ending up there, especially bankers and merchants who plied trades that were already viewed dimly by their local priests and bishops. Quite unexpectedly, this new form of bookkeeping became a way for them to quantify the value they were providing to society. Bookkeeping became in effect an extremely detailed form of confession.

The European mind in the medieval age and after the Black Death was positively obsessed with confession.[8] The condition was called by modern scholars "moral scrupulosity," an always present anxiety that even the smallest, most minor transgression or sin could lead one to a life of eternal damnation. True believers start to see sins and failings in every single waking moment, in every action, even when there is none (apparently the condition still exists). It drove a compulsion among the laity to fixate on recording and arbitraging away every single possible sin. Parishioners kept detailed ledgers of their supposed sins, and went to confession weekly or even daily. They wanted to keep their "books" up to date and clean.

Merchants and bankers weren't immune to this moral anxiety. Indeed, given the church's rules against usury, they were even more conflicted than the average person. While many of the bankers' methods were designed to find the loopholes in canon law, it wasn't *just* the law they were trying to steer clear of. They desperately wanted to prove what they themselves wanted to believe, which was that their livelihoods were not inherently sinful. They did not want to die with those sins on their souls, such that when they reached the gates of heaven and God took out *his* book— the ultimate ledger—he would not find them in the deficit column. Indeed, it was not unusual for merchants to put into their wills a stipulation that all their usurious profits should be returned to the people from whom they had been taken.[9] As early as the 1300s, bankers started convincing themselves that their business was not, in fact, sinful, and they were not engaged in usury and therefore were not sinners. But they could never be quite sure. What they lacked was a way to craft a narrative around their business that showed, in black and white, that they were not just greedy usurers. That they were not just taking from society and giving nothing back.

In the book of Revelation, the narrator talks about seeing a "great white throne" and a God sitting on it, "from whose face the earth and the heaven fled away." All the world's dead, even those already sent to hell, come before him. In front of God are a number of open books, one of which is the book of life. "And the dead were judged out of those things which were written in the books, according to their works." This is the ultimate, final judgment of men. "Whosoever was not found written in the book of life was cast into the lake of fire."[10] The book of Revelation is notoriously inscrutable, but this passage seems very clear: when you die, you will be brought before God, who has every single thing you've ever done recorded in a *ledger*. You stand there, one among the countless dead, as God adds up the good and the bad of your life, and renders a final tally.

If your *final balance* is a positive, it's off to the fluffy white clouds. If your final balance is a negative? The lake of fire. This was a powerful narrative in the medieval mind. For the merchant or banker whose very livelihood was considered something that was automatically a demerit in God's book of life, this kind of thing was constantly on their mind, it was like a double helping of moral scrupulosity. Think about Cosimo de' Medici confessing his moral anguish to his pope (and being told to fund a monastery.)

In the 1200s, a French writer named Lorens d'Orleans wrote a work called *The Book of Vices and Virtues* that illustrates how sins and accounting were a mixed metaphor in the medieval mind. In this popular account, a wicked steward is using confession to give an accounting of himself to God and to God's bailiff. In this confession, the confessor is required to "yield account of his receipts and of his dispenses." The confessor is implored to do a thorough accounting, because "even if thou fail at thy account, God will not fail at His when he commeth."[11] D'Orleans was the tutor of the children of France's Philip III, as well as the king's confessor. The book is a moral instruction guide for the king and his royal progeny, but for our purposes what's interesting is the use of accounting terms and the reference to that final accounting with God and the book of life.

Today accounting ledgers are mainly about math and spreadsheets, but in medieval times they were far more narratively driven. The single-entry ledgers comprised not just numbers but long, explanatory sentences;[12] guild statutes expressly forbade the use of Arabic numbers and columns (the less-familiar numbers were considered more susceptible to deception).[13] With double-entry, what the medieval businessman finally had was a way of telling that narrative that offered a final accounting, like the one in the book of life, that proved the value he provided to society, since for every thing the merchant *took in,* every credit, he *gave something back,* every debit. The banker wasn't just an avaricious predator, using the unnatural practice of usury to take from society more than he received. No, no, the ledgers showed, conclusively, in numbers, that he was also giving back, that he was in fact providing a useful service to society! Double-entry bookkeeping was the solution they didn't even know they needed. In that final accounting, that final reckoning, the medieval merchant or banker could point to his ledgers and show, using math, that he gave back as much to society as he took, that his life and soul were in both temporal and ecclesiastical harmony. Hell, it was right there in the name: *the balance sheet.*

Does Cotrugli's curious passion for the topic make more sense now? Accounting was a form of confession, a pouring out of every little thing the businessman had done, and double-entry allowed the medieval merchant and the medieval banker to flip the script. Amazingly, it worked, and this I'd argue is the real secret to the Medicis' success, and the real reason why an entire generation of merchants like Cotrugli were no longer content to just make their money and try and keep out of the church's eye. They had long felt like they weren't sinners, like they belonged. Now they had a way to prove it.

This new acceptance of merchants produced an absolutely visceral effect on Europe. After the empire moved to Constantinople, Europe spent about a thousand years looking inward. Trade routes that had brought riches between the East and West disappeared. Europe became feudal, tied to its lords and the land. Slowly, that started to change. The Venetian merchant Marco Polo went east in the back half of the thirteenth century and spent nearly two decades working for the Chinese emperor Kublai Khan.[14] The tales he brought back eventually fired up the imagination of Europeans. The change reached critical mass in the fourteenth century, with Bracciolini, Medici, and Nicholas leading the way. They weren't afraid to live a life that embraced greed, that posited it as a good thing. By the time Cotrugli was an adult, being a seafaring merchant seemed pretty respectable. Suddenly there were scores of sailors trying to find better, faster routes to the East, new ways to expand trade and find profitable things to trade. The two leading countries in this charge were Castile and Portugal, and in 1494 they did something audacious that would affect the entire world for centuries.

Agreeing to a division proposed by Pope Alexander I, the two countries basically split the entire world outside of Europe.[15] Everything east of a certain meridian in the Atlantic Ocean belonged to Portugal, everything west of it belonged to Castile. Imagine the stones it took for some European rulers and a pope to slice up the entire world and expect that to stick. It's the most incredible evidence of just how far the European mind had traveled in a short time. And it shows how much the Catholic mind had absorbed the ethos of beneficial greed. Money and God, separated ecclesiastically for millennia, were back together again.

7

THE MEDICI POPE

The church effectively used greed to rebuild its power, but this created new problems, for greed leads to rapacity and corruption. This new era of a greed-fueled church reached an unprecedented level of excess, and it was led by the Medici, who went from being bankers to the popes to being the popes themselves. Eventually, some of the faithful became fed up with the corruption brought on by avarice and rebelled against Rome. These protesters sparked a schism more profound than any that had come before. It tore Europe in two, Catholic and Protestant. Surprisingly, though, both resulting camps found a place for avarice within their philosophical hierarchies, which only served to further the ethos of beneficial greed.

Nicholas held the pontificate for less than a decade, but he created the template for the office for the next hundred years, putting the church back on a path to predominance in European affairs. Across the careers of a string of popes after him—Callistus III, Pius II, Paul II, Sixtus IV, Innocent VIII, Alexander VI, Pius III, Julius II, and Leo X—the church became quite possibly more wealthy and more powerful than ever. The bold gambit from the 800s, built off the lie of the Forged Decretals, was finally being realized. The bishop of Rome was one of the most powerful people on the Continent, the church was truly a player in political affairs. And money continued to pour in. The memory of the jubilee of 1450, and the insane wealth it generated, remained strong. For all its wealth, though, the centerpiece of Nicholas's vision remained unrealized: the construction of a new St. Peter's Basilica to replace the crumbling, nearly millennium-old house of worship then in place. Nicholas wanted to build the biggest, most excessive, most overwhelming temple the world had ever seen, a physical symbol of the church's importance. Sixty years after Nicholas's death, only the bones for a new St. Peter's stood, next to the rotting carcass of the old one. What the church needed to make this vision real was money, and in its zeal to raise money it embraced greed on an industrial scale.

For Leo X, becoming Pontifex Maximus wasn't just something that happened to him. He was elected pope on March 9, 1513, but had been headed for the job his entire life. He was granted "the tonsure"—a practice where they shave the top of your head as a sign of religious devotion—when he was only seven. He was made cardinal of Santa Maria in Dominica when he was thirteen, and joined the College of Cardinals when he was twenty-four. He was named papal legate to Bologna and Romagna in 1511, a diplomatic post that also could, naturally, be quite lucrative. All of this had been orchestrated by his father, and who *he* was also matters for our discussion.

Leo's birth name was . . . Giovanni di Lorenzo *de' Medici*. His great-grandfather was Cosimo. The generations of the family after Cosimo expanded the Medici empire and became fantastically wealthy, the unquestioned rulers of Florence. They had essentially become royalty. Leo's father,

Lorenzo the Magnificent, ruled Florence and had specific plans for his three sons. He planned Leo's entire church career, buying him his positions from the time he was a child. "To be united with the Church is advantageous to Florence and you must be the bond of union between the two—and the welfare of our house depends on that of the city," Lorenzo wrote to his son.[1] Lorenzo paid lip service to the idea that his son would dutifully serve God, but it was clear that devotion and fidelity to the love of Christ were a concern to Lorenzo only insofar as they'd help advance Leo's career, and they seemed to have never been a concern to Leo himself. A church career was about money and power for himself and his family, and Leo relished both. "How very profitable this fable of Christ has been to us through the ages," he once remarked to a colleague.[2]

Leo was educated and admired the arts. Indeed, he spent lavishly supporting some of Europe's greatest artists, like Raphael and Michelangelo. Some of the treasures hanging in museums around the world are there because of Leo's patronage. Like many in his family, Leo suffered from ill health. He had longstanding, painful ulcers. He needed to be attended by his personal physician just to make it to the conclave that elected him. Indeed, one of the reasons the cardinals elected him pope at such a young age was because they reasoned he wouldn't live long. Raphael captured him in one iconic painting. Wearing deep crimson robes, he's got a round face, permanent beard stubble, and eyes fixated on something in the distance. I don't know if Raphael was trying to make him look holy or temporal, but he looks wholly temporal. Even in this image, it seems like Leo's mind is machinating about money and schemes.

Leo's pontificate was absolutely notorious for profligate spending. Indeed, Leo was an eager practitioner of the ethos of beneficial greed. He courted revenue aggressively, and spent it just as aggressively. The goals of Leo's pontificate mashed up the needs of the church and the needs of his family. He backed wars, planned Crusades, schemed to get his family back into power in different city-states, and used the church to raise money to help his family schemes. He backed a war against the French that ultimately put his nephew Lorenzo in control of the state of Urbino, but which also led to an assassination attempt against him. The plotters were foiled; most were imprisoned. One was executed. The war was also costly, draining the papal treasury. Leo's pontificate was one moneymaking scheme after another.

INDULGENCES

Leo made it clear from the very outset that his was going to be an in-your-face papacy. His coronation ceremony was a complete spectacle.[3] He was crowned in a tent outside the crumbling old St. Peter's, a gem-encrusted, triple-layer tiara put on his head that was so heavy it actually caused him physical pain. A procession then followed through the streets of Rome. The route had been lined with statues and columns carved specifically for the parade by a variety of suppliants from all over Italy, each one more ornate and expensive than the last. The Florentines built a massive arch with myriad symbols carved into it representing the Medici family and its various members. Different houses of Rome's elite had banners and tapestries along the parade route. Mounted spearmen led the parade, followed by the cardinals and more banners carried high. Leo's younger brother Guilio had his own place of honor in the parade. The next day he would be named archbishop of Florence, a stepping stone on his own trip to the papacy. There was a procession of white mules from the Vatican stables and stable hands all decked out. Then scores of Roman barons, followed by the

Florentine elite, bankers and merchants who held the physical keys to untold riches. Then the clergy, deacons and subdeacons, followed by hundreds of lower-ranking members of the Papal Curia, lawyers and clerks, the bureaucracy of the church. Then the members of the College of Cardinals, on white-draped horses. Then the conservators of Rome, the city's political leaders. Lastly came Leo, surrounded by the pope's traditional armed troops, the Swiss Guard, in their green, white, and yellow uniforms. He was riding a massive, white Arab stallion. Attendants held a silk canopy over his head. Behind him two officers carried bags of gold and silver coins, throwing handfuls of them into the adoring crowds. Rome had come a long way from the days when Florentine barbers would make bawdy jokes about it.

What Leo's actions show is how the ethos of beneficial greed had already begun to morph. The original idea of it—make a lot of money and spend it lavishly for the betterment of society—he did. His money went to artists, writers, translators, architects, engineers, and multitudes of others. But he had already started jumping the lines past the idea of *beneficial* greed and into plain old greed. He juiced the church infrastructure for all it was worth. His immediate predecessor, Julius II, left him the moneymaking church apparatus and a treasury comprising about 800,000 ducats. He blew through 100,000 on his coronation alone, a vast sum for those times. He spent another 150,000 up front to finance his war against Urbino, and ultimately spent about 800,000 on it. And remember, that war was basically for no other reason than to set up his nephew in a position of power, in order to further the power of the entire Medici family.

Besides the treasury left to him by Julius, Venetian bankers estimated that Leo was making about 400,000 ducats a year for himself, both through the extensive network of church revenue—benefices, fees, indulgences, and the

sale of jobs—as well as money from his family businesses.[4]
He had preachers roaming the countryside selling "indulgences," basically absolution for sins, as a way to fuel his
profligate spending. The most notorious was a German
named Johann Tetzel. Tetzel was an eloquent speaker and
a brilliant marketer; he claimed his indulgences could save
not only the souls of the people buying them but also the
souls of their dead relatives. He even came up with a jingle:
*So wie das Geld im Kasten klingt; die Seele aus dem Fegfeuer
springt.* "As soon as the gold in the casket rings, the rescued
soul to heaven springs."[5] Tetzel made his bosses a lot of
money.

If you're thinking that all of this would have been abhorrent to a lot of people, you're right. It was. And they tried
to do something about it. A group of cardinals tried to poison him (the plan's originator, Alfonso Petrucci, originally
wanted to stab the pope publicly, Brutus-on-Caesar style,
but didn't have the gumption for it). The pope got wind
of the plan, called the conspirators to his chambers, and
had them arrested. Petrucci was tossed into Castel Sant'-
Angelo and tortured until he gave up everybody. Leo holed
up in Sant'Angelo and had his soldiers patrolling the streets,
ready to put down any inkling of a rebellion. Petrucci was
publicly hanged, along with his servants. The other rebel-
lious cardinals were fined and sent packing. And even this
threat Leo turned into a moneymaker. A few weeks later,
Leo named thirty-one new cardinals, each of whom paid
cash for his post. All in all, Leo turned a profit of about
500,000 ducats from the attempt on his life. The assassination attempt wasn't the only challenge to Leo's rule, or even
the most material. Another was brewing up in Germany.

There was a significant overlap between the church and
the nobility. Church positions were bought by nobles for
their children, who then had both their own landholdings

and church landholdings, and taxed their subjects heavily from both. They were extremely deficient in their knowledge of the Word and concern for their flocks.[6] Bishops were more concerned about the fights and quarrels that involved their families than their church duties, leaving those to underlings. "The episcopal revenues are spent on this world's possessions, sordid cares, stormy wars, and world dominion," the bishop Berthold Purstinger declared in his anonymously published criticism of the church, *Onus ecclesiae*. People like Leo, people in power, may have been blind to the effect this had on the population, but average people were incensed. The entire edifice of the church was rotten, they knew it, and hated being under its thumb. They needed a spark to actively rebel.

Tetzel was the spark. Now, like I said, Tetzel had his critics, and his methods outraged many, especially in Wittenberg. There was a reason, after all, they'd banned the practice there. On October 31, an obscure priest and theologian at Wittenberg University was fed up with the corruption within the church, which he saw most plainly illustrated and represented by the work of Tetzel and the whole practice of selling indulgences. He went to the university's chapel, where staff often pinned messages and notices on the main doors, held a piece of paper up against the doors, and nailed it there. On the piece of paper was a series of ninety-five assertions and condemnations of church practices, mostly focused on the selling of indulgences. The priest's name was Martin Luther.

"He who sees a needy man and passes him by, yet gives his money for indulgences, does not buy papal indulgences but God's wrath," Luther wrote.[7] Luther condemned the practice of selling indulgences wholeheartedly, he ripped people who thought indulgences were a way to get around being truly contrite for their sins, a clever loophole. He also *very* carefully tried to absolve the pope. He was a critic, but he was still a Catholic. "If the pope knew the exactions of the indulgence preachers, he would rather that the basilica of St. Peter were burned to ashes than built up with the skin, flesh and bones of his sheep." In this, he was extending Leo an indulgence the Medici pope certainly had not earned. The "indulgence preachers," meanwhile, Luther demeaned as hawkers of fake goods, an empty salvation, demagogues, blasphemers, enemies of God. The purported bargain they offered was "madness," he said. "The true treasure of the church is the most holy gospel of the glory and grace of God."

Luther never mentioned Tetzel by name in what came to be known as the 95 Theses, and Tetzel for his part defended his actions. In January 1518 Tetzel published a formal response prepared by a professor of theology. Luther replied a few days later with a sermon. Tetzel replied again, zeroing in on what he surmised to be Luther's true motive: a broad attack on the entire church, its practices and beliefs, and the pope. In this, he was almost certainly dead-on right: Luther was justifiably aghast at the church's rampant, unchecked greed. Of course, Luther wasn't the first to bemoan church corruption; indeed, Bracciolini himself had attacked the church's hypocrisy a century before, and he wasn't the first either, for that matter. The myriad councils and schisms and antipopes over the years were basically about the same thing. The church for the better part of a thousand years had engaged in a hypocrisy of professing the philosophy of Yeshua but embracing the greed that killed him. After Bracciolini and Nicholas's time, the church didn't just indulge in the hypocrisy anymore; it fully exemplified it. This was too much for Luther and many other Europeans. They were fed up, finally broken, done. Luther rebelled, and half of Europe came with him. It was the biggest split in the religion's history.

At first, Leo gave the debate between Luther and Tetzel little notice. Maybe Tetzel had gone a little too far. So what? But Luther's arguments were quickly evolving, and as they evolved, and as his movement grew, the threat to the church became more pronounced. Luther's arguments wound around and around his central, unavoidable point: to him, the Bible was the ultimate authority, not the pope. Early on he tried to tiptoe around that belief, but in short order he shifted from just criticizing the abuses of indulgences to proposing an entirely new belief system. To Luther, the true communion between God and the people was between *only* God and the people, directly; the church had nothing to do with it. He believed this so much that he said the church's ultimate threat, excommunication, was empty, hollow, it could not affect the soul.[8] Leo put it to the test: On January 3, 1521, he excommunicated Luther.

MONEY AS A SIGN OF GOD'S FAVOR

I can't tell you with 100 percent certainty that Leo's excommunication had its intended spiritual effect; I reckon it's something you and I will all discover for ourselves after we each in turn shuffle off the mortal coil. I can tell you with complete certainty that it did not have its intended temporal effect. If anything, it only increased the reformers' zeal. In retrospect, it was probably too late for Leo to stem this tide. The church's behavior over the course of centuries had embedded deep resentments among the people. Luther's rebellion against the church quickly became a spreading reform movement. Individuals adopted his precepts on Christianity, then individual parishes turned to him, then individual regions. Within a few decades, what we now call Protestantism had spread through most of Germany and the Icelandic states, into England and Austria-Hungary.

It was a violent split. In 1524, a band of German peasants rebelled against the church. The so-called "German Peasants' War" lasted a year; about a hundred thousand Germans died in it. In France, there were widespread, violent attacks on reformers. In 1529, to give just one example, a lawyer named Louis de Berquin was burned at the stake for his refusal to recant his beliefs, one of countless to die so hideously. The English Civil War was fought largely along Protestant-Catholic religious lines. Amid this widespread violence, many just fled. One theologian left France for the relative safety of Switzerland, where he whipped up a furious pace of writing. His work had almost as big an impact on Christianity as Luther's. But what interests us is that this man's impact on the ethos of beneficial greed may have been greater than even that of Bracciolini or Cosimo de' Medici. He really changed the game, for good. His name was Jehan Cauvin. The world knows him as John Calvin.

Not long after he fled France, Calvin wrote and published his most important work, the *Institutes of the Christian Religion*. The early editions were aimed at vindicating the martyrs; later revisions were directed at attacking perceived Catholic faults.[9] The work is considered the first fully fleshed out explanation of Protestantism, and in it Calvin explained his two most important concepts: providence and predestination. In a nutshell, Calvin's position was this: that God is all-powerful and has control of people from birth to death (and, of course, into their afterlife). He asserts this in vivid language (Calvin was an excellent writer, one of the reasons he was so influential):

> If any one falls into the hands of robbers, or meets with wild beasts, if by a sudden storm he is shipwrecked on the ocean; if he is killed by the fall of a house or a tree; if another, wandering through deserts, finds relief for his

penury, or, after having been tossed about by the waves, reaches the port, and escapes, as it were, but a hair's-breadth from death—carnal reason will ascribe all these occurrences, both prosperous and adverse, to fortune. But whoever has been taught from the mouth of Christ, that the hairs of his head are all numbered, will seek further for a cause, and conclude that all events are governed by the secret counsel of God.[10]

The idea that things happen by chance, that random fate plays *any* part in our lives, is "erroneous," Calvin asserted. Every single action, every day's work, every meal, every interaction, every battle and celebration, every breath we take, every morning we wake and go about our day, the very moment of our death, has been directed and controlled by God. Even the precise number of hairs on our heads. Your reading this book and these lines at this very moment. All of it. Every last bit. "The providence of God, as it is taught in Scripture, is opposed to fortune and fortuitous accidents," Calvin said. "Not a sparrow of the least value falls to the ground without the will of the Father." He admits that while many things may *seem* random, that's only because our dull minds can't fathom the master plan of the creator. And indeed, he continues, we shouldn't try to fathom that plan, since it is so clearly beyond our abilities. Our only job should be to do what we *perceive* God wants us to do, because if we perceive it, God intended for us to perceive it, and to act upon it. Thus, no matter what we do, we are doing it because God wanted us to do it. There can be no mistaken actions, no unplanned happenings. Even bad things, evil things, things that lead a person to hell, all those were planned by God as well. "God only requires us conformity to his precepts," Calvin wrote.

In Calvin's mind, there is virtually no man or woman

alive who is truly deserving of salvation. "There was never an action performed by a pious man, which, if examined by the scrutinizing eye of Divine justice, would not deserve condemnation."[11] The savages with no knowledge of God, the hypocrites, and even the righteous are somewhere in their hearts "tarnished by some carnal impurity." Therefore, *nothing* that people on earth do is worthy of the Lord's favor on its own. Anything that any person has comes solely from God's grace. Good deeds, he says, are "pleasing to God, and not unprofitable to the authors of them." But the reward is not being granted because it's been earned. No deeds are worthy. No, the reward is "not because they merit them, but because the Divine goodness has freely appointed them this reward."[12] If this sounds unduly harsh, well, it was. Calvin also believed in a concept called "double predestination." Not only did God plan out everybody's lives, he created some to be saved, and others to be damned. All those people who weren't Christians, who didn't know God? No matter how good they might seem, they didn't deserve any merit; in fact, they were deserving of punishment, because they contaminated "the pure gifts of God with the pollution of their hearts."[13] And you know what? Well, that was intentional, and they deserved whatever fiery fate was waiting for them on the other side because, as Calvin already stated, God controls everything, down to the life of the least sparrow.

Calvin never worked out a detailed theory of economics but did offer broad brushstrokes. He saw mankind as originally living in a perfectly equitable state, all the people of the world sharing its bounty, since of course it was all a gift from God. Jesus's commandment to treat your neighbors as yourself—and Calvin was quite clear here in saying that "neighbor" should be read as all mankind—loomed large to him. It was the basis of everything, really. We should all be working together and cooperating to build a better society for the benefit and glory of God. Any inequality in society was a corruption of that original state of grace, and thus a sin. But it was also kind of just the way it was, so Calvin seemed content to let it go with calling it a bad name. Trying to get wealth by means of taking it from one's neighbor was a sin, and it seems almost certain he was talking with an eye toward usury here, since the language he used mimics the language used as far back as Aristotle. However, any money earned honestly was totally fine. "We should accept the gain that comes to us as coming from God's hand."[14] Calvin also was big on charity, feeling that it was part of the Christian's calling, that it should be voluntary, and that it should be lavish to the point of excessive. This went doubly so for the rich. "Those, then, that have riches, whether they have been left by inheritance, or procured by industry and efforts, [should] consider that their abundance was not intended to be laid out in temperance or excess, but in relieving the necessities of the brethren."[15]

To Calvin, charity wasn't just a way to be nice, or to absolve one's guilty conscience. To him, charity toward one's neighbors was a characteristic of God's divine law.[16] He wasn't just talking about donating money; he was talking about an entire way of looking at your fellow man. Calvin saw the principal division of that law as breaking it into two parts, one focused on the duties of religion and the other focused on the duties of charity. This split was even more foundational and primary than the Ten Commandments. These two are intertwined, piety and charity, and both rely on people's fear of God and His righteousness.[17] They are primary to worshipping God. Calvin goes on about this for page after page after page, describing it with a level of detail that taxes the modern, often distracted mind (or, at least, my mind). But to Calvin, the point of God's law is clear: we are commanded to love one another, and that means treating each other with charity, in the broadest definition of that word. To do otherwise is to violate God's law.

Calvin's impact on attitudes toward money and business and usury can't be overstated. He was hugely influential, and that influence extends even to today because it informs most of our attitudes about money. The attitudes first expressed by Bracciolini and put into practice by Cosimo de' Medici morph through Calvin into a way of operating that isn't just acceptable but part of God's moral framework. That last should not be discounted. While Calvin formally brings money into religion, it is extremely important to note that he brings it into a moral system. "Charity" reappears endlessly in his work. He is adamant about his view that people are *supposed* to be charitable toward one another, that it is in fact God's *law* that they be so. Calvin says the rich are rich because God wants them to be rich, but he also exhorts them to give away their riches because God wants that, too. It is a tragically nuanced point, and the most consequential development in this story of money I'm telling is that somewhere between Calvin and today, that understanding got lost. Calvin, like Cotrugli, Bracciolini, Yeshua, and Aristotle before him, was trying to draw a picture of a just society, an equitable world of men. He also was practical and acknowledged that such a world didn't actually exist. What I'm not sure he could have envisioned, though, was just how his own theology could and would be twisted to create something almost wholly opposed to the ideal world he saw as the ultimate goal of mankind.

THE CALL TO WEALTH

The generation that sparked all this rancor eventually died. Poor Tetzel, wracked by the controversy, passed on in 1519. Leo followed in 1521 (the cynical cardinals were right about his short life). Luther died in 1546, and Calvin made it to 1564. Make no mistake, the Catholic Church centered around Rome was still incredibly powerful; they could by the pope's decree do just about anything. Questioning the church or its doctrine was an offense for which you could lose your life. An inquisition was a powerful tool they could bring to bear against virtually any citizen of Europe. In 1633, Galileo was threatened with torture and death unless he recanted his assertion that Copernicus had been right in saying the Earth revolved around the Sun (Copernicus had had the good sense not to publish that argument until he was almost dead). Galileo recanted. Others were burned at the stake for heresy. People were raised in a dogma, they believed in that dogma, and the church itself was part of the dogma that was used to indoctrinate people into their beliefs. This imbued the church with the power to tax, to rule, and to murder in the name of the Faith. It was an illustration of how deeply ingrained Christianity was in Europe.

Despite the church's overwhelming power, the arguments that Luther and Calvin made continually found new believers and followers. Because Luther and Calvin stressed the direct connection between people and God, the religions that grew around them in the seventeenth and eighteenth centuries evolved without the kind of central authority the Catholics had; there's no pope of Protestantism. That gave rise to a number of smaller sects, like the Puritans in England. This was a time of rapid economic and social change, leading up to the Industrial Revolution in England, when the modern world we live in today was coming into being. Calvinist priests and theologians did not shy away from that world. They dove right into the issues of the day. Protestant priests and ministers began to apply their religion and the concepts underlying it—the idea that all of this was predicated on some ethereal afterlife—to the society in which they lived. And none had a bigger influence than a reverend who was extremely popular in his day, Richard Baxter.

Baxter was born in 1615 in England and by his twenties was already making a name for himself as a theologian. He became both famous and influential and controversial. He was a leader of the "Nonconformist" movement—the same movement that produced the Pilgrims—and he served as an army chaplain on the Parliamentarian side during the first English Civil War. He was a rebel against both the monarchy and the church, eventually driven out by both. I'm not going to focus on all that, though. What most interests me about Baxter is how his work foreshadowed the work of Adam Smith more than a century later. Baxter links labor and morality, and details the various aspects of work in a way that presaged Smith's famous division of labor. What Smith would later present as a secular, almost scientific endeavor began before he was even born, and it was distinctly religious.

Most of Baxter's work is familiar to us as classically Puritan: the passionate drive for work to the exclusion of virtually any and all idleness, the constant denial of any little luxury, the demand that work must be hard and continual as the only means to salvation, the absolute disgust with anything considered unnecessary, frivolous, or, God forbid, enjoyable. The repeated emphasis that absolutely any little thing designed to satisfy oneself rather than God was a sin. Baxter goes on for page after page after page on this point. There was a purpose to this: it was commanded by God, it was the way to bring about His glory, it was the only path to redemption. Every person, no matter how rich or poor, must put in ceaseless toil. For the Lutheran, this was God's plan. For the Puritan, it wasn't planned, it was something else. This was a subtle but significant theological difference.[18]

To Baxter and other Puritan writers, labor was a *calling* from God himself. Every job, no matter how menial, was there specifically to help further the ends of increasing God's bounty. Some men earned their keep through their minds, some through their bodies. Some were very rich and others very poor; but every single person had a calling, a thing they were good at that came from God, and they were commanded to put that calling into use.[19] "It is action that God is most served and honoured by; not so much by our being able to do good, but by our doing it." Every person, from the workers in the tobacco fields to the plantation owner, was performing one part of a whole. Indeed, Baxter specifies that the rich need to work, too, no matter how rich they really are. And Baxter makes it very clear that the goal of all this labor is not to store up riches for oneself, but to do so for the good of society as a whole, and the dictates of God.

"The public welfare, or the good of many, is to be valued above our own," Baxter wrote. "Every man therefore is bound to do all the good he can to others, especially for the church and the commonwealth. And this is not done by idleness, but by labour! As the bees labour to replenish their hive, so man being a sociable creature, must labour for the good of the society which he belongs to, in which his own is contained as a part."[20]

And the end result of this effort—you know, the profit of a business measured in money—was the ultimate tally of how well or poorly somebody was serving God. The Puritans weren't against *making* money. They were wholeheartedly in favor of it! In the Puritan mind, every single opportunity for profit had to be seized upon. The Puritan was in fact *commanded* to make money. To pass up a chance to pile up profits was a rejection of God's providence. Work must be a constant, never-ending endeavor. Instead, the Puritans were

totally against *enjoying* money, like those blasphemous Roman Catholics. Baxter was so dedicated to the idea that
work and what it produced not just for the individual but
for the common good was critical in advancing God's plan
that he felt it shouldn't be ignored even if you wanted to be
a monk and spend all your time in meditation. "God hath
commanded you some way or other to labour for your daily
bread and not to live as drones of the sweat of others only,"
he wrote.[21]

I haven't read the complete works of every fifteenth- and
sixteenth-century Protestant preacher, but the proverbial
thought leaders like Calvin and Baxter were very clear on
one point: that working for money for the sake of just the
money itself was a sin. It went against God's wishes and
it hurt rather than helped mankind. "It is a perverting of
God's creatures to an end and use clean contrary to that
which they were made and given for: and an abusing God
by his own gifts, by which he should be served and honoured," Baxter wrote, and wrote, and wrote.[22] He goes on
for pages about the proverbial wages of sin while elsewhere
explaining how money can be a sign of piety. You can see all
these preachers trying to thread the needle like this, looking for just how far one can go in terms of pursuing wealth
and still be a good Christian. It is the same needle Aristotle
tried to thread nearly two thousand years earlier. And it is
still something we are working on today; the problem is our
concept of money has changed radically, the moral undertones of money that are evident in Aristotle, Bracciolini,
Calvin, and Baxter are gone today. I think most people today understand in theory the things Baxter and others were
saying about how money can be perverted and malignant,
but do you see that in practice? I don't.

To Baxter, the value of a calling was primarily expressed
in moral terms, in that the work resulted in some tangi-

ble goods that helped advance the common good, which in turn was useful in advancing God's providence. But, importantly, there was another way to measure the usefulness of such a calling: in monetary terms.[23] To Baxter and other Puritan writers, money was a key way of measuring the success of one's calling, and thus the piety of the parishioner. Philipp Jakob Spener, a German theologian, reasoned that the importation of tobacco, for instance, was okay. "The cultivation of tobacco brings money into the country and is thus useful, hence not sinful."[24] John Wesley, the English theologian and founder of the Methodists, struggled with this paradox as well, that as people became wealthier, they tended to become more material and less religious. His solution was just to sort of throw his hands up and hope that people can both get rich and get religion. "We must exhort all Christians to gain all they can, and to save all they can; that is, in effect, to grow rich."[25]

For the Puritans, therefore, the pursuit of wealth was part of God's calling, and the pursuit and accumulation of wealth itself was virtuous. It was the use of that wealth for any personal pleasure that was sinful. The practical result of this is something with which we are all familiar: the Protestant Work Ethic. The German economist Max Weber explained it like this:

> For, in conformity with the Old Testament and in analogy to the ethical valuation of good works, asceticism looked upon the pursuit of wealth as an end in itself as highly reprehensible; but the attainment of it as a fruit of labor in a calling was a sign of God's blessing. And even more important: the religious valuation of restless, continuous, systematic work in a worldly calling, as the highest means to asceticism, and at the same time the surest and most evident proof of rebirth and genuine faith, must have been

the most powerful conceivable lever for the expansion of that attitude toward life which we have here called the spirit of capitalism.[26]

Weber noted the very plain reality that wealth eventually corrupts even the purest, most pious soul. "These Puritanical ideals tended to give way under excessive pressure from the temptations of wealth," he wrote.[27] Which is something that's been noted among thinkers and philosophers going all the way back to Aristotle. *However*, while these august thinkers, sitting off somewhere in a quiet place where they can contemplate the nature of man, can point out this very obvious reality and wag their fingers about how it defiles their pure religion, the truth is that the people who professed piety but have been tempted by wealth *saw no contradiction* in their actions. Baxter, Calvin, Luther, and all the other Protestant leaders set up a hierarchy where wealth was acceptable, and maybe in their purer minds there is a fine but firm distinction between wealth achieved under God's plan and wealth gotten by less noble means. To most people, there is no such distinction. The ethos of beneficial greed becomes simply the ethos of greed. Getting rich becomes a sign of God's blessing both to the Protestant and to the Catholic.

The work of Calvin, Baxter, and other theologians had a huge effect. It drew closer the realms of economics and religion. The upshot was that ordinary, secular labor was put on a par with the work of priests and churchmen.[28] Both were doing the job of building God's kingdom. This resulted in an embrace of money and labor among the Protestants; something that had happened earlier with the Catholics. The Protestants so elevated ordinary labor that it gave rise to a new, extreme, work ethic. Around 1620 a group of Puritans arranged for funding to start a colony in the Americas that they called Plymouth. They wanted to be free of the

Church of England and to build a society based on their Calvinist, pro-work, pro-money worldview.

Look, I don't want to overstate my point about the ethos of beneficial greed. The ethos upon which the United States was founded—that all men are created equal—is one of the most world-changing ideas that's ever existed. You can argue how well the United States has lived up to this founding principle, and who exactly was then and is today included in the word *men*, but the principle itself spearheaded what would eventually become a global movement toward self-rule that changed the face of human society (even if today that principle is under attack in many places). But what I believe has been *understated* is that when those religious refugees came over to the Americas, when those conquistadors hacked their way through the Americas, when all those teeming masses of Christian Europeans sailed across the Atlantic, they all brought with them a less lofty but no less potent principle: that the accumulation of wealth was a material sign of God's blessing, and that therefore working to accumulate wealth was a pious endeavor. Eventually that morphed into a logic where any money made is good, no matter the endeavor and no matter the means. And the less lofty principle came to the Americas' shores *first*, before the colonials embraced the more lofty principles. The effects of the ethos of beneficial greed could be seen as soon as the first European landed, and it is still with us today. Exploring how that less lofty principle became the cornerstone of a new world order is the focus of Part II.

PART II

Greed, for lack of a better word, is good.

—Oliver Stone and Stanley Weiser, *Wall Street,* 1987

8

THE AGE OF AVARICE

Now that the Europeans had absorbed the ethos of beneficial greed and accepted the pursuit of wealth as a God-given command, they set about searching for ways to get rich. The fall of Constantinople closed the old routes to the East, so they were forced to look westward and southward, across the oceans. Soon enough, of course, they stumbled across the Americas, a vast land teeming with resources. The Europeans set about invading and taking every piece of land in this new world, and commandeering every natural resource they could get their hands on. It was all part of their era of colonialism and world domination. Spurred on by their new ethics, they considered themselves ordained to do it all. And to make it all viciously efficient and monstrously profitable, they scaled up the most immoral, oppressive system of slavery the world has ever seen.

Behind the example set by Cosimo de' Medici, Europe's merchant class was for the first time finding itself in the position of being legitimized and respectable. They could practice their profession out in the open, in the knowledge that they were part of God's plan. But the old trade routes to the East were slowly being closed. In 1453 the city of Constantinople fell to the Ottomans. The last vestige of the Roman Empire was gone, and the ancient trade routes— the ones I referenced in chapter 2—that had been used so profitably were cut off.[1] The timing is so ironic as to be almost unbelievable. Nicholas V was still in power, a man raised in the same circle as Cosimo de' Medici and subscribing to the same philosophy. The ethos of beneficial greed was washing over Europe. Now was a time to make money! And the Ottomans made that harder. Greed is a powerful force, however. The Europeans didn't just crawl back into their shell, as they had after the sack of Rome in 420. This time they improvised. If the Ottomans wouldn't let them go through the Near East to get to the Far East, they'd have to find a way *around* the Ottomans. That meant sea routes.

There is today a shorthand explanation among historians for the motivations of this era: gold, God, and glory (the order sometimes is God, gold, and glory), and it perfectly sums up how religion and money had interlaced themselves around each other in the European mindset, and how that combination unleashed the greatest explosion of rampant, unrestrained greed the world has ever seen. The worst nineteenth-century robber baron or twenty-first-century tech bro doesn't hold a candle to the wanton destruction wrought by the first wave of European colonizers in the fifteenth and sixteenth centuries. We don't need to spend too much time on this—the field has been examined exhaustively, there are countless excellent books on the topic that will give you far more insight than I can here—but I do just want to point out how this entire age takes on a different shading when you understand the backstory of the embrace of greed by both Catholics and Protestants. The church in Rome had always been eager for money and power, but after the pontificate of Nicholas it was remade, its reach extended, its infrastructure shored up. It became as efficiently profit-driven as any modern corporation. And it showed, in tangible form, that it both would take in money and spend it lavishly. The takeaway was clear: money was to be gotten, at any and all costs.

As the attitudes fostered by the ethos of beneficial greed expanded, Europe's appetite for wealth expanded as well. After all, if everything in the world is under the purview of a Christian god, and everything you do is done to gain favor with that god (or even predetermined by God Himself), and accruing wealth is a manifestation of your efforts, then it stands to reason that there isn't anything you *can't* do with any resources anywhere in the world. It's a twisted reasoning to be sure, but it's exactly the reasoning that had spread across Europe like wildfire.

OH, DIABOLICAL GREED

The Portuguese had a considerable head start on naval navigation. By the first decades of the fifteenth century, Portuguese sailors were already exploring the sea to their west and south. They found the Madeira Islands and the Azores, and landed in present-day Senegal and the Cape of Good Hope. Vasco da Gama took it a step further, going around Africa's southern tip and sailing all the way to India. The Ottoman conquest of Constantinople made these voyages even more important. By the early 1490s, Portugal and Castile, given their geographies and access to the Atlantic, were in a fierce competition for land and resources. Today we think of the sailors from this era as great explorers, and they certainly were explorers, but their motivations were often very simple. They wanted to make money. And they believed they were ordained by God to do so. Christopher

Columbus dreamed of creating a trading empire in Asia.[2] Columbus had been trying for years to persuade either Portugal or Castile to finance his proposed westward exploration. Queen Isabella of Castile finally took him up on it.

In 1492 Columbus landed in what is today the Bahamas (we think, nobody is totally sure), and the stories he told must have made the Europeans' mouths water. His diary from that first trip to the Americas is littered with references to gold. He presses practically every native he encounters on the topic. There are myriad times he makes notes of a gold trinket or bauble being carried by one of the islanders. They wore bracelets of gold on their arms and legs and golden earrings, nose rings, and necklaces. He repeatedly references a king who supposedly had control over a gold mine. On the twenty-first of October he wrote, "I intended to search the island until I had speech with the king, and seen whether he had the gold of which I had heard." He didn't find any great gold mine, but he did realize the commercial value of the natural resources on the islands he found, and how easily the islanders could be overwhelmed by the better-armed Castilians. "With fifty men they can all be subjugated," he wrote on October 14.

His discovery—at first erroneously assumed to be Asia—brought the competition between Castile and Portugal to a head. Pope Alexander V issued a series of papal bulls that sought to settle the dispute, which mentioned Columbus and his discovery by name. The declaration drew a straight line from the north pole to the south, sliced its way around the already known Azores and Cape Verde islands, and "gave" the Americas to Castile and Africa and Asia to Portugal. This was the Inter Caetera ("among the rest"), and it built on top of Nicholas's 1455 bull that settled the claims between Portugal and Castile.

At this point, the face of Europe had already been radically changed by the ethos of beneficial greed. The Catholics carved up the known world, with Castile, Portugal, and France in a fierce race to dominate their spheres (the Italians were too busy trying to keep other powers out of their peninsula to really get into the colonizing game). The Protestants weren't waiting around, though. The English and Dutch sent their fleets across the sea as well. The Spanish and Portuguese dominated in what is today South America, while the English and Dutch dominated what is today North America. The French held some sway for a while, too. The northern colonies, dominated by the Dutch and English, were mainly Protestant-based endeavors, and they brought with them Luther and Calvin's focus on the individual. Thus, their colonies were self-consciously built on a smaller scale, favoring the middle-class small businessman. The southern colonies, dominated by the Spanish and Portuguese, were more Catholic-based and, like the church back in Rome, far more industrial in their scale.

Now, as influential as the pope was, nobody really observed the territorial claims ensconced in the Inter Caetera. Still, the document was incredibly significant; it was taken by the colonizers as essentially a license to treat the world as European property. The bull demanded that the Castilians and Portuguese should be in the business of making sure that "barbarous nations be overthrown and brought to the faith itself," and Pope Alexander commended both King Ferdinand of Portugal and Queen Isabella of Castile for being dedicated to that cause. According to Alexander, the natives of the lands Columbus discovered were *already* somehow magically open to becoming Christians. "These very peoples living in the said islands and countries believe in one God, the Creator in heaven, and seem sufficiently disposed to embrace the Catholic faith." Alexander commanded the Castilians and Portuguese to convert everybody they met. In return, they were given, by the authority of the pope as God's representative on earth, perpetual ownership and control of any land they "discovered." It was theirs for themselves and their heirs, forever. This had such a lasting effect that more than five hundred years later—only a couple of years ago, actually—there were still real efforts to try and get the church to revoke the Inter Caetera and render its "rights" null.[3]

The expedition of Hernando de Soto through Florida and the Southeastern United States is a good example of the Europeans' regard for the new lands and people they'd come across in their mad quest for wealth. De Soto had already done serious damage in present-day Guatemala and the Yucatan Peninsula. He was governor of Cuba and tasked with checking out the reports that there was gold in Florida. He took an expedition of hundreds of men, mounted on horseback, with enough supplies to last them for four years. The party made quite an impression on the locals, and de Soto and his men pressed their advantage. Everywhere they went, they demanded things. Not just pearls, and emeralds, and other valuables, but people. De Soto and his men demanded both men and women from the natives: men to carry all the treasure they were collecting, and women to satisfy the lusts of the soldiers. These were, for all intents, slaves, and the expedition almost continually needed new slaves because they were being worked to death. There was only one reason for all this, according to the diary of Rodrigo Rangel, de Soto's private secretary on the trip:[4]

> As to where they were going, neither the Governor (de Soto) nor they knew, except that his intent was to find some land so rich that it might sate his greed, and to find out about the great secrets that the Governor said that he had heard about those places, according to many reports that

had been given to him. And that as regards disturbing the land and not settling it, nothing else could be done until they came upon a site that would satisfy them. Oh, lost people; oh, diabolical greed; oh, bad conscience; oh, unfortunate soldiers; how you did not understand in how much danger you walked, and how wasted your lives and without tranquility your souls!

De Soto never did find a site that satisfied him. After three years of wandering through what is today the Southeastern United States, he died, leaving behind about half of his men. They were low on supplies, most of their horses had died, and presumably they discovered that you can't eat gold. Not that they'd found much anyhow. They gave up the search and headed back, eventually ending up in Mexico City. Nobody knows for sure where de Soto died, where he was buried, or even if he was buried.

It's easy today to look at Columbus, de Soto, Coronado, and the rest and say they were evil. Certainly in retrospect the things they did look evil. They were directly responsible for generations of deaths, for wiping out entire civilizations, and indirectly responsible for bringing with them the viruses that killed the rest. It was absolutely a genocide. However, it is important not to forget that these men were operating within the laws and morals of their time. Just as we today live in a world dominated by an ethos of greed, the world they were living in was dominated by it, and it was new to them. The Europeans convinced themselves that the quest for gold and wealth was on a par with the quest for God, and did absolutely horrible things because of it. The men who left Europe and took these new lands were lauded, they were regarded as heroes, doing God's work. One wonders what the "heroes" of today will look like in five hundred years.

THE DEITY OF INCREASED PRODUCTION

As bad as the explorations and invasions and annihilations themselves were, they were supplanted by an even worse development. The plantation system the Europeans imported into the Americas in the sixteenth and seventeenth centuries was something they created many centuries earlier in the Mediterranean basin.[5] When the Europeans sent armies into the Middle East during the Crusades, they discovered and developed a taste for sugar, as well as other crops to which they'd never been exposed. Once they had more or less successfully invaded a region, they would set up enterprises focused on growing, cultivating, and exporting crops like sugarcane, rice, coconuts, lemons, and limes. The massive farms built for this task operated under a mash-up of the feudal system and what we'd today recognize as capitalist foundations, and used laborers from wherever they could be found. Largely, this meant enslaved locals, and these businesses were a major driver of the slave trade that existed around the Mediterranean. Christian and Muslim captives from wars, crews of ships captured at sea, Tatars from the Black Sea, Mongols, Russians, and Ukrainians; the ethnicity, religion, or nationality didn't matter.

After the fall of Constantinople, the Portuguese began establishing trade routes along the African coast, and this is when the first African slaves started showing up in the marketplace. Then Columbus sailed across the Atlantic. While the Portuguese were more content to open up trade routes and establish commercial ports on their way into the Atlantic and across Africa, the Spanish were from the start hellbent on conquest.[6] Columbus intimated as much in his 1492 diary with that comment about fifty armed men. Columbus was followed by Hernán Cortés and Francisco

Pizarro, who proved the Genoan's point by quickly overrunning the Aztec and the Incan empires.

Plantations started appearing across the Caribbean and in Central and South America soon after Columbus's first voyage. The first English plantation was established at Jamestown in 1607 in what is today Virginia. The Americas were abundant in natural resources that the Europeans quickly commercialized, and one can only imagine what the natives thought of all this. The Europeans used native populations as forced labor. There were pockets of resistance, but the superior arms and technology of the Europeans, as well as the absolutely unremitting avarice that fueled them to use any means necessary to increase production and profits, were simply too much for the natives to contend with. The Americas were taken over by the conquerors.

The conquerors brought with them something even worse than their muskets. The local population wasn't just exposed to new people, new conquerors, and new religions. They were exposed to new bacteria and viruses they had never experienced and for which they had no natural immunity. While the waves of Europeans who came across the Atlantic were definitely responsible for the carnage they wreaked, from 1492 right through to the last of the "Indian Wars" in 1896, when US troops slaughtered countless unarmed natives, violence wasn't the cause of the most native deaths. It was the diseases they brought with them that killed far more people. The population of the entire Americas was estimated at roughly 50 million in 1500. A century later, it was only about 8 million. The populations of Mexico and Central America fell from around 8–15 million in 1520 to only about 1.5 million a century later. The population of the Andes fell from around 9 million to 1 million.[7] That kind of devastation is magnitudes worse than even the

Black Death (albeit the latter did its damage in a shorter period of time). The entire population of two continents, people varied and rich in culture, language, empire, life itself, was virtually eradicated by disease.

Meanwhile, the Europeans were making so much money off their new trade that it quickly became an absolute national imperative in Spain (formerly Castile), Portugal, England, France, and the Netherlands to drive this business, spurred on by the now-fanatical desire for gold and for converting the world to Christianity. In their zeal for gold, God, and glory, they'd were quickly "becoming used to the idea of sacrificing human life to the deity of increased production," as the historian Eric Williams put it.[8] And this is where the ethos of beneficial greed really starts to shift. It swaps one adjective for another. It became an ethos of *unmitigated* greed. In the savagery of the European conquerors it is clear that they had reached a point where they considered any profit a justified profit, and any action in the service of that profit was righteous. Greed could do no wrong.

Columbus, Cortés, and multitudes of others who followed set up plantations for sugar, tobacco, and other crops. Gold mining was a constant endeavor. All of these businesses required a ton of labor. The Spanish didn't reinvent the wheel in the New World; they didn't come up with new ways to grow things. They just grafted their own system of control on top of agriculture that had been developed by the locals. The Aztecs and Incas had cultivated myriad crops like maize and potatoes, and the Spanish, sometimes with support from local leaders, kind of just took it all over.[9] They made money by growing and exporting crops, and they made fortunes by searching for and mining gold. The Spanish even made money just by selling the *licenses* to sell slaves in territories they controlled.

They converted all this new wealth into power, building up armadas and armies.

The slave trade was critical for these profit-making ventures. During the first few decades of colonization, the native population was put to work, mostly cultivating food and panning for gold.[10] The death rates were so catastrophic that the colonizers were constantly in need of new laborers. More people died on the plantations than were born, at least in the early centuries. That meant a continual influx of new bodies was needed to keep these enterprises going. The biggest challenge was finding enough people to do all the labor. In the old plantation model imported from the Mediterranean, nobody cared where the slaves came from. The colonizers in the New World felt the same way, at first. So when the native population was devastated by disease and overwork, the Europeans turned not to Africa but to Europe.[11]

Indentured servants, convicts, poor whites; all were sent across the sea. It not only solved a problem, it fit with the prevailing Protestant ethos that held that work was good for the soul. It was a bustling trade; two-thirds of the immigrants to Pennsylvania in the eighteenth century were white servants.[12] These immigrants endured the harsh conditions of the ocean crossing, long voyages with ill-preserved food on overcrowded vessels that resulted in scourges and epidemics.[13] Just getting to the New World was its own ordeal. But they endured it mainly because of the promise of a better life, an escape from the hardscrabble reality of subsistence farming or endless war. After a period of some years, these servants had the promise of "earning out" their contracts. Given the vast tracts of land "available" to them, many were able to just wander off the plantation and start their own life on their own farm. This solution worked for the plantation owners, to a degree. It provided bodies, yes, but they had to be continually resupplied, and such a stream of bodies from Europe actually meant depopulation back home, which created its own set of economic problems.

Enter a new kind of slavery. In the Americas, the native population had been devastated, and the European emigrants weren't economically feasible, given how often they had to be replaced. The deity of increased production forced a new solution on the colonists: Africans. It was a devastatingly efficient equation. Native slaves were all dying from a combination of disease and weakness from disease. White European servants either earned out their indenture or simply vanished. But the Africans, forcibly taken off their own land, didn't have the expectation of eventual suffrage of the poor white Europeans nor did they have the disease-driven weakness of the native Americans (decades of contact had essentially immunized them). In 1510, the first 250 African slaves were brought from Lisbon to the Americas.[14] Yes, slavery had existed in the Old World going back to Mesopotamian times, and probably even earlier. But slavery in the Americas took on a complexity and brutality it had never had before. We all know that. What is less well understood is what drove that brutality in the first place.

"A MAKE-SHIFT FOR HIRING"

The driving force behind the especially inhuman brand of slavery that developed in the Americas, the British colonizer Edward Gibbon Wakefield wrote in 1830, wasn't racist.[15] It wasn't necessarily that the Europeans felt superior to the Africans they kidnapped (though they of course did). Critics of slavery, he wrote, attributed the rise of American slavery to "the wickedness of the human heart." This had become widespread common wisdom among abolitionists, he said, blaming "the infernal spirit of the slave-master." But the plantation owners don't engage in slavery because they love the cruelty of it, Wakefield said. They don't love the oppression. These slavers engage in slavery, he argued, because of the circumstances that "forced" them to engage in it. In a word, it was about money.

"They are not moral, but economic circumstances," he wrote. "They relate not to vice and virtue, but to production." The problem, Wakefield said, is that the plantation owners couldn't find bodies for the plantation. They had no choice, he argued, but to turn to slavery. In the history of the world, he said, labor had been supplied only by one of those two means. "Slavery is evidently a make-shift for hiring; a proceeding to which recourse is had, only when hiring is impossible or difficult."

Now, let's get one thing out of the way straight up: this is an *incredibly* self-serving justification for the violent bondage of generations of people who were treated like animals. Slavery, especially as practiced in the Americas, was not just indefensible but outrageously indefensible. Wakefield was a colonizer, but not especially a slaver; indeed, he was most famous for a colonization plan called the Wakefield Scheme that sought to create a self-sustaining economy for these new colonies. It involved criteria for selecting only certain people for emigration, concentrating settlers in a given area, and selling land at fixed rates that would create a revenue stream for the owners that would allow them to pay the settlers and workers decent wages. But as evidenced by his ham-handed justification for slavery, he didn't see it in moral terms at all. To him, it was pure economics.

Of course, the slave trade was *enormously* profitable, and thus enormously important to the European economies. Ships left Europe with goods bound for Africa, sold the goods in Africa and loaded back up with human beings bound for the Americas, sold the humans into bondage, loaded back up with commodities, and sailed back to Europe. Without slavery, it didn't work. The English economist Malachy Postlethwayt described the slave leg of the trade as "the mainspring of the machine that sets every wheel in motion."[16] If making money was right, and slavery allowed them to make money, then the slaving had to be right, too. Still, they needed to rationalize the absolutely inhumane treatment of the Africans they sold into slavery, and their descendants. That or just give up all the money.

As time went on, the justifications piled one on top of the other. It started early. The Africans' immunity to European viruses, compared to the natives of the Americas who died at incredible rates, led the Europeans to believe that Africans were *born* to be slaves. The justifications would grow more convoluted and extreme. They would often rely on a twisted reinterpretation of the Bible (or even a straightforward interpretation; remember, slavery was a common feature of the ancient world). Myriad preachers defended slavery; indeed, most of the formal defenses were authored by clergymen. And of course they would be written into law in the Southern US states. In 1806, Virginia's supreme court ruled that Blackness in and of itself created the presumption of slavery. Every slave state (except for Delaware) simply wrote it into their laws. Being born Black meant legally that you were a slave, forever.[17]

By the nineteenth century, the racism that suffused slavery in the US was so deep-seated that fully half the country was ready to go to war to defend it. In 1861, just before the Civil War started, the vice president of the Confederate States, Alexander Stephens, argued that slavery was "truth," and it was the kind of truth that would be appreciated in time, the same way the truths that Galileo and Adam Smith uncovered weren't initially appreciated, either.[18] Seriously, he name-checked Galileo. The cornerstone of the CSA, the great truth that animated it and made it work, the entire singular belief around which this new nation was being founded and built upon was this, Stephens said: "the negro is not equal to the white man." Really, that was it. That belief had become so foundational that the Southern states believed it to be fundamental truth, and refused to be moved off it. You all know this, of course, though the Cornerstone Address is so emphatic on the point I just have to quote it some more: "Slavery, subordination to the superior race, is [the negro's] natural and moral condition. [The version of this speech I referenced noted that at this point, Stephens was met with applause.] This, our new government, is the first, in the history of the world, based upon this great physical, philosophical, and moral truth." People who didn't believe this, he said, were suffering from "an aberration of the mind, from a defect in reasoning."

At least he acknowledged not everybody believed him. Now, that is some profound hatred, and it has haunted this country ever since. I bring it up to make this point: *Before* slavery became a moral quandary, it was an economic one. Wakefield was right about that. The colonizers rifled through natives and Europeans before turning to Africans, and it was only after they found a population they could abuse and dominate that they started dreaming up all the racist justifications for their immoral economic system. With the idea now baked into American society that making money was serving God, the idea that enslaving and exploiting an entire slice of humanity in order to make money also became accepted. It became part of the culture. But it was such a perversion that the only way to justify it was to mentally reduce Africans to subhumans. You see this clearly in Stephens's speech.

The idea that the racism of slavery, and the centuries-long subjugation of Africans and African Americans, came as a result of the economics of the plantation system in the New World is an argument the historian Eric Williams made in his 1944 book *Capitalism and Slavery*. "Slavery in the Caribbean has been too narrowly identified with the Negro," Williams wrote. "A racial twist has thereby been given to what is basically an economic phenomenon. Slavery was not born of racism: rather, racism was the consequence of slavery. Unfree labor in the New World was brown, white, black and yellow; Catholic, Protestant and pagan."

Williams is a fascinating figure in his own right; born in Trinidad in 1911, he had creole heritage, received his doctorate at Oxford, and led Trinidad and Tobago from being a British colony to an independent republic in 1976. The nation's first prime minister, he is known as the "father of the nation." He was also a historian, and *Capitalism and Slavery* is his boldest, best work. I highly recommend getting a copy and reading it apart from anything I write here. *Capitalism and Slavery* was Williams's doctoral thesis, originally titled "The Economic Aspects of the Abolition of the Slave Trade and West Indian Slavery."

In *Capitalism and Slavery*, Williams digs through the records and discovers a buried history. His basic thesis is simple and straightforward: that slavery in the Americas began as an economic necessity. The racism that eventually became its all-pervading feature only came later, as a justification for employing such an obviously immoral system. Williams wasn't focused on the institution of slavery itself; his book doesn't get into all the horrible details of the day-to-day life of a slave. He is focused on his point about slavery and economics. And what he also surprisingly argues is that economics also played a role in the *decline* of slavery, at least in the West Indies. He tried unsuccessfully for years to publish it. Both the subject matter and the fact that he was a Black man worked against him. And the book's central thesis didn't play well with his contemporaries who wanted to believe that abolishing slavery had been a moral crusade. Williams's work actually *undermined* their imagined moral superiority. They just didn't want to hear what Williams had to say. It's one of the reasons Williams had trouble finding a publisher. But what he's saying, besides being right, is important for the purposes of our discussion. Williams's focus on the economics of slavery and the fact that it was an economic decision *before* it was a racial one makes perfect sense when you plug it into the context of everything we've been talking about here. Money and religion merged, money was believed to be a sign of God's favor, getting it was a goal of the church, and anything that advanced that goal was acceptable. And the evolution of slavery into a specifically racist system actually shows exactly how entrenched and deep-seated the money-religion belief had become.

Stephens's Cornerstone Address is a famous example of how deeply rooted racism had become in the South, but for sheer audacity he doesn't come close to Thomas Reade Rootes Cobb. A Georgia lawyer, Cobb in 1858 wrote the most elaborate, extensive defense of slavery that has probably ever been written, *An Inquiry into the Law of Negro Slavery in the United States of America.*[19] Cobb's stated goal in his preface was to do something that had previously never been done: write an "elementary treatise" that would define slavery within the law. He wasn't writing this necessarily for the South; they were all slavers to begin with. No, Cobb was writing this for the *North;* his goal was to try to convince Northerners that slavery was just and right.

"Cobb did not merely collaborate with a system of evil," wrote University of Tulsa College of Law professor Paul Finkelman in 1999, "he worked hard to recast the very notion of evil to remove slavery from within its definition."

It was a biased work, obviously—Cobb himself admitted as much—but it was also an exhaustive work. The book is huge, more than three hundred pages. He cited hundreds of cases in contemporary law, and more in ancient law, and related virtually every instance of slavery he could find in the entirety of recorded human story. Slavery, he said, has been "more universal than marriage, and more permanent than liberty." Cobb acknowledged up front that slavery in general—the idea that one person's life should be lived shackled and chained—is considered contrary to nature. That all people are in general presumed to be free at birth. So, what did Cobb do to overcome this obstacle? He set out to prove it wrong, of course. Slavery, he argued, has been so common in history, so endemic in civilization, that it must be part of the law of nature. Slavery is a natural state much like freedom is a natural state.

You can hear echoes of Cobb's arguments in Stephens's speech, and hopefully this shows just how elaborate the racism was—how much thought the slavers put into it. Cobb's book is, of course, completely *bonkers*; just chapter after chapter of convoluted arguments that are obvious garbage. There is something incredibly offensive on virtually every single page. I flipped through it randomly and found the following: He asserted that God himself made Africans indolent and slothful (page 38). Africans are "inferior mentally to the Caucasian" (page 34). Africans have such a "weakness of intellect" that they are fortunate to live under a "wise director" (page 35). "Reason and policy" demand that the "superior race" control the "inferior" (page 106). Since masters can't watch their slaves every minute, and since slaves left alone will invariably gather together where "mischief and evil" are the result, states must create quasi-police squads to watch them (page 107). It is church law and custom that fugitive slaves must be returned to their masters (page 115). Children born to mothers enslaved must also be slaves, because it's a universal law going back to Leviticus (page 69). Because slaves have a "want of liberty" they can't be witnesses against freemen (page 226). A slave has no right to private property (page 235). On and on and on, for hundreds of pages. And this was a man who was called the James Madison of the South.

I brought Cobb into this to make two points. First, to show how far the human mind can take a notion and run with it. I don't think there has ever been a starker example of the extremes to which the love of money can push people. In their absolute lust for profits, Europeans took over three entire continents, enslaved their indigenous populations, worked them to death, and kept their offspring in chains for generations. They endeavored to do all this as efficiently and comprehensively as possible. And then they had the audacity to argue that this was the *natural* state of mankind, indeed that it was somehow God's will. Because it had to be, right? After all, it was profitable, and God's will was for profits to be made.

The second point is that these kinds of assertions did have a profound effect on some people, especially and particularly in the slaveholding American South. Cobb and his fellow travelers argued that Africans were not people and thus should not therefore be given the same protections under law as white people, claiming the Bible and God himself as supporting evidence. It took a bloody civil war to put an end to slavery, but that war didn't change the thought patterns that had hardened over the centuries. And we are *still* dealing with the fallout from that. After the war, "chattel slavery was abolished, but a program to transform slaves into citizens was omitted," as Martin Luther King Jr. wrote in 1966.[20] "The omission inexorably caught up with them, and their enemies, only partially defeated, gained the breathing spell to reassemble and renew their power. The [postwar] era of hope ended with the return of Negroes to a more sophisticated form of slavery."

To Dr. King, economic equality was every bit as important as social equality. It was something he pushed hard for in his final years, and it was something that many of his previous allies resisted, as he noted in that same essay (much like Williams's work, linking racism and economics was something that made even purportedly progressive whites antsy). It would be easy to raise the minimum wage and pull millions out of poverty, Dr. King said, but a "formidable wall" stood between idea and execution. The reason was very simple. It was the same reason that had created American-style slavery in the first place, centuries earlier. "Someone has been profiting from the low wages of Negroes," he wrote.

Cobb's work didn't do anything to change the hearts and minds of Northern abolitionists, but it clearly had a lasting effect on Southern segregationists. In the pages of his terrible book, in all those offensive things he said—things he argued were objective and even scientific—you can see the modern prejudice they'd produce. The pervasive racism that has been a feature of the United States since before its founding is not some amorphous force of nature that cannot be tackled. It very clearly was built on top of an economic foundation that itself was built on top of an ethos of unmitigated greed.

9

TALK TO THE (INVISIBLE) HAND

The more malignant effects of Europe's new commerce-based society became clear in the eighteenth century. Native Americans were being wiped out, and African Americans were enslaved. The gap between the rich and the poor of Europe was expansive. Financial crises proliferated amid nation-level speculative schemes. It was enough to get some people, like the philosopher Jean-Jacques Rousseau, to question if any of it was morally defensible. Rousseau's attack on the new economics was damning and demanded a response. The response came from a colleague of Rousseau's and a man who would become the father of modern economics . . . Adam Smith.

While the danger of Europe's embrace of a commercial-driven religion with avarice at its heart was obvious to the Africans and Native Americans whose people and nations were wiped out by it, it was less obvious to the Europeans themselves, or rather, conveniently ignored by the Europeans themselves. Initially, it seemed, all they recognized was the fantastic wealth entering the Continent. Spain, Portugal, France, England, and the Netherlands were transformed as their plunder was sent back home. Navies were constructed, capitals acquired grandeur. Commercial ventures flourished. The outrageously decadent royal court in France that eventually sparked a revolution was an outgrowth of this embrace of the ethos of unmitigated greed, and no one person illustrated it better than a man named John Law. Soon enough, his schemes came to typify the very real downsides of this new brand of commercialism.

Law was a Scotsman who killed a man in a duel in London, escaped the gallows, stole another man's wife in Paris, gambled compulsively, hobnobbed with Europe's elite, and had a compulsive attraction to money. Along his travels, he picked up enough of the new ideas about money and commerce floating around the continent to become a dangerous person.[1] He wormed his way into the court of the young Louis XV in France and convinced the French to orient their economy around these new ideas. Law founded a bank called Compagnie des Indes in 1716 and somehow wrestled his way into exclusive rights to develop the massive lands around the Mississippi River claimed by France. It didn't matter that he didn't have the actual wherewithal to develop all that land. Within three years he had completely monopolized French trading in North America. The allure of riches in the Americas caught the fancy of the investing public, and shares in the bank skyrocketed, rising from five hundred to eighteen thousand livres[2] (that 3,500 percent increase would blow away the gains of virtually any stock you can think of today). Law brought the Crown into the scheme, and his bank essentially became the central bank of France. Its stock became currency. Law dreamed up a plan to issue more stock and use the proceeds to pay off France's public debt, which had soared under the corruption and mismanagement of King Louis XIV.[3] Demand for French debt went through the roof as well, the French issued more currency, which was used to buy more shares, and soon enough the whole scheme had flooded markets in France, England, and across Europe. People got so fantastically rich off Law's scheme that the French had to come up with a new word to describe them: millionaire.[4]

By the eighteenth century, the ethos of beneficial greed combined with the benediction of both the Catholic and Protestant churches had created a free-for-all. European merchants, missionaries, soldiers of fortune, and political outcasts had stretched virtually around the world. God, gold, and glory were the driving forces behind it all. But this was a perversion of the ethos initially described by Bracciolini, put into practice so effectively by Cosimo de' Medici, and amplified by Cotrugli. In those first and second generations, the *beneficial* part of beneficial greed was paramount. Cosimo seemed to at least be somewhat worried about his eternal soul and whether his deeds were good or bad for society at large. Cotrugli's entire point was to craft a daily living plan that created a symmetry between morality and business. Later generations lost this appreciation for the moral implications of this system. It became an all-consuming drive for profits fueled by the Calvinist argument that God controlled everything, and therefore anything any person did, especially to accrue profits, must be good. Every man for himself was what the Christian god *wanted,* according to this line of thought. Who were mere mortals to argue with God?

At the same time that Law was making the French fantastically rich (on paper), the British had a similar scheme going. They were becoming financially sophisticated. Assets were traded informally by investors and merchants in coffeehouses; in 1698 a man named John Castaing started tracking the prices of commodities, currencies, and stocks, an endeavor that would eventually turn into the London

Stock Exchange.[5] Parliament had created a joint-stock company, the South Sea Company, and granted it a monopoly in trade, including the incredibly lucrative slave trade. The expected payouts sparked a wave of investment and speculation. Its shares became so valuable that Parliament sold the national debt to the company, expecting that the government could pay off the debt just through sales of the company's stock. In reality, neither the South Sea Company nor the Compagnie des Indes were remotely profitable enough to meet the wild expectations of their investors. In 1720, the stocks of both companies crashed. Both nations were thrown into turmoil. Law fled France, and another appointment with the gallows. The French government had no choice but to take over his bank and company and raise taxes to pay off the debts. Britain passed laws banning joint-stock companies. But thousands of people had already been wiped out.

The twin bursting of the South Sea Bubble and the Mississippi Bubble felt very familiar in the Netherlands. The Dutch had already invented the stock market and gone through their own financial madness. The Netherlands had gained their independence and become quite prosperous from trade and from employing the new economics—indeed, Amsterdam is where Law picked up the basics of his economic theories. The Dutch East India Company held the world's first initial public offering of stock in 1602,[6] and in 1611 the world's first stock exchange opened in Amsterdam. After some lackluster years, the Dutch East India Company became ruthless in its exploitation of islands and regions in Asia, and of course was wildly successful by the 1630s. The Dutch were on their way to becoming a world power. Tulips had been introduced to Europe via Turkey and over the decades were an increasingly popular flower—and for the well-to-do Dutchman, the tulip was the ultimate status symbol. In 1633, the trade went stratospheric, peaked, and then crashed.[7] So when the crash of 1720 was washing over Britain and France, the Dutch recognized the cycle. An anonymous tract started circulating in the Netherlands, *Het groote tafereel der dwaasheid.* In English, that means "The Great Mirror of Folly." It was marketed as a "warning for posterity," and satirized the entire Mississippi affair with poems, playing cards, caricatures, and even prospectuses. It traced the entire ordeal, from its start with Law through its height and crash.

The Great Mirror of Folly showed that people had already caught on to how stupid—and dangerous—greed could be. It was enormously popular. A number of editions were put out by a group of Dutch publishers, so there are myriad copies; almost no two are exactly alike. The Great Mirror was a sharp satire, but it was just part of the rising backlash against the new ethos of unmitigated greed. Another popular work, kind of like the *Succession* of its day, was a satire and farce by the French playwright Molière called *L'Avare (The Miser).* It's about a man named Harpagon, a usurer who makes his money off lending at excessive interest. He cares more about his money than his children, and won't even buy his servants new clothes. The play struck a nerve among Europeans. There were versions of it adapted in Germany, England, and Italy. It was turned into an opera. *The Miser* portrayed and parodied the attitude on a personal level that was driving these insane, damaging, financial crises. It was becoming clear to some at least that the full-throttled embrace of greed, which three hundred years prior had been held up by Bracciolini as a great beneficial driving force for society, was also sparking hugely damaging problems for people, both Europeans themselves and even the "savages" overseas.

THE IMMOVABLE BASIS

The question became, what was the logical endpoint of this kind of world? If you took an ethos of every man for himself to its extreme, what kind of society would you have? The answer, at least for some, was that you would have no society at all. The French philosopher Montesquieu addressed the question in his work *Persian Letters* (1721), a series of fictional letters between two friends. In one of the letters, the writer tells the story of a now-extinct tribe, the Troglodytes. They had once had laws, but decided to abandon them, to live under conditions where each man looked out for himself and only himself. "Why should I kill myself working for people I don't care a thing about?" is the argument they make. The bonds of brotherhood that held nations together were torn apart by these Troglodytes.

Montesquieu took Bracciolini's ethos to its logical end, a society in which nobody has any responsibility for anybody else. It is, of course, a disaster. Everybody works for themselves, and only themselves. Farmers grow crops to feed only themselves and their family. One year, the highlands have crop failures, and everybody starves. The next year, the lowlands are flooded and the crops fail. They starve. One man abducts his neighbor's wife. As the neighbors are quarreling over the wife, they bring their case to a man who had once been respected back when the Troglodytes had laws. They want him to make a ruling. He tells them to go scratch. "What does it matter to me whether the woman is yours, or yours? I have my field to cultivate." One man works up a very healthy, bountiful farm. Two other men kill him and take it, and agree among themselves to maintain it for the both of them. Six months later, one man kills the other. And on and on, until they're all dead. It is not a subtle story.

Even if you didn't go to such extremes, it was obvious just from daily observation that the kind of society produced by this ethos of greed was one of vast imbalances. Some people were fabulously wealthy and powerful, others were destitute. Was *that* what God intended? Was that the correct way for society to be structured? By the eighteenth century, it was obvious that a certain kind of society had emerged in Europe and its colonies, but was it a good society? Had mistakes been made along the way that warped society? These backlashes would culminate in a work that may have been the greatest intellectual challenge the new commercialism ever faced: the *Discourse on Inequality* (1755) by Jean-Jacques Rousseau.

Rousseau was a major European philosopher, and his work had a profound impact on political and economic debates that we are still having today. He was a Protestant and a Calvinist and an integral part of the movement that would end up redefining, in sometimes messy ways, how people govern themselves. Rousseau was interested in designing, and helping to build, the ideal state, one where the interests of the leaders were perfectly aligned with the citizens, where people knew each other and had no reason to either cheat their neighbor or suspect they were being cheated, where people were free to pursue their own particular nirvana at their own leisure. He was, in essence, an idealist looking for utopia when all around him he saw nothing but greed and selfish proto-fascists using the state and religion for their own benefit at the exact expense of their people. It was a world powered by new ideas and technologies, and it was leading to one where too many people were being left behind. The many were being sacrificed for the good of the few. This was unacceptable to Rousseau.

Like many in his time, Rousseau's intellectual curiosity was sparked by the interaction between the "savages" of the

Americas and the purportedly enlightened men of Europe, and he would flip those adjectives so thoroughly that the Europeans were put on the defensive. Rousseau dedicated his *Discourse* to the city of Geneva, which he apparently held up as a model state, and even in his dedication he is attacking the avaricious. "I notice, with a pleasure mixed with surprise and veneration, how much they detest the frightful maxims of those accursed and barbarous men, of whom history furnishes us with more than one example; who, in order to support the pretended rights of God, that is to say their own interests, have been so much the less greedy of human blood, as they were more hopeful their own particular would always be respected."

Rousseau sought to distinguish what was natural and inherent in mankind and what wasn't—what was a later addition, a result of developing civilizations. And the question he was looking at was: How did the latter end up producing the kind of ingrained inequality that seemed to be taken for granted rather than seen for what it was: something artificial, something taped onto our natures? Something *un*natural. Discovering mankind's natural rights, he felt, was the key to creating a just society. It's impossible to read Rousseau (at least, if you're an American) and not think about the Declaration of Independence. In its insistence that people have unalienable rights, you can hear an echo of the exact things Rousseau was seeking. The American experiment in self-governance as a whole stemmed from the ideas Rousseau was probing. To Rousseau, "natural law" was essentially a result of two strands of thought within people, a sort of first principles, if you will: one in which people were "deeply" interested in their own welfare and preservation, and the other in which there was a "natural repugnance" in seeing others "suffer pain or death." Everything we have built up in civilizations throughout the ages has been built up on top of those two emotions, he said. "If we look at human society with a calm and disinterested eye, it seems, at first, to show us only the violence of the powerful and the oppression of the weak," he wrote. "It is only by taking a closer look, and removing the dust and sand that surround the edifice, that we perceive the immovable basis on which it is raised."

Rousseau accepted the basic Protestant tenet that every person's station in life was a result of a determination from God himself. But he asserted that looking at nature, probing for a sort of natural state of mankind (though he denied it ever actually existed) is how one can find the cause of inequality. Rousseau engaged in a somewhat fanciful recitation of how mankind developed, from a point when we humans were no different than any other animal, following along as we got clever and used our smarts to overcome challenges, learned how to use fire and make tools, to control other animals, and finally, to recognize that there were others like us, that we were a distinct group of beings. From there came civilization.

As soon as money came into being, he said, equality among men disappeared. Whether rich or poor, once there was a separate *thing* that existed that could measure possessions—shekels, drachmas, florins, francs, dollars—people wanted it to such a degree they put themselves before their fellow man. "As the most powerful or the most miserable considered their might or misery as a kind of right to the possessions of others, equivalent, in their opinion, to that of property, the destruction of equality was attended by the most terrible disorders." The "natural man" that Rousseau held as an ideal was destroyed. Rousseau therefore flips the script on the idea of "progress" from natural man to modern man. In his view, the narrative ran opposite. Natural man was the ideal, modern man was the despot. All the economic systems represented by the division of labor had the effect of making one group subservient to another. This flew in the face of the burgeoning capitalism and colonialism that was making Europe rich, but the very reality of what had come of Europe's embrace of money as a sign of the gods' favor was the biggest proof of Rousseau's criticisms. The English, Spanish, Dutch, French, and Portuguese had become fantastically wealthy at the expense of multitudes of human beings across three continents who were murdered, killed by disease, and enslaved. What all this eventually leads to, Rousseau concluded, is utter misery; a world of people fighting each other for whatever scraps they could get, unable to live on their own and dependent upon others for their livelihoods and survival, a world where a small cadre of the rich controlled most of the wealth and exercised that control through expansive and corrupted political systems and ultimately despotism. Rousseau made a powerful argument against the New Europe, and he wasn't making it in a vacuum. The pain being caused across multiple continents was impossible to miss. All you had to do was look into the great mirror of folly.

Rousseau's essay was a powerful damnation of the entire commercial apparatus that had developed from the early 1400s through the mid-1700s and it had long-lasting effects. Rousseau put the entire system on defense. Truth be told, it's hard to imagine that anything could have waylaid the commercial interests that were taking over the Americas; there was too much money and momentum. But Rousseau mounted as strong an attack as anyone ever had before him. What the bankers and merchants needed was their own intellectual defense, their own philosopher. They got one in Adam Smith.

THE WEALTH OF NATIONS

"The greatest improvement in the productive powers of labour, and the greater part of the skill, dexterity, and judgment with which it is any where directed, or applied, seem to have been the effects of the division of labour." Not exactly one of the most scintillating opening lines ever written, but it is how one of the most influential books in the history of the world begins.

In 1776, while British colonials in Philadelphia were starting their famous revolution, the Scottish philosopher Adam Smith published his masterwork, *The Wealth of Nations*. To most people, what we today call economics began with Smith and his book. The division of labor, the magic of the market, the proverbial "invisible hand," all these things are known primarily because of *The Wealth of Nations*. It's one of a small handful of books that almost literally changed the world. I say almost because what Smith does here is not so much create something as record something. Smith was just the first to lay it all out in minute detail. And while that's what most of us think *The Wealth of Nations* is actually about, that isn't really the point of the book. It's a dry read, to be sure, and it comes across as a dry exposition of economics—a really, really long and dry exposition of economics. But what Smith was actually doing was defending a system that had come under withering attack.

Rousseau and Smith ended up on opposite sides of an intellectual divide, but they were not really enemies. They were contemporaries and even to a degree colleagues. Smith helped edit some of Rousseau's work, and Smith put some of Rousseau's ideas into his own work. Unlike later economists, Smith is acutely aware of, and concerned with, the morality of economics. His earlier, and second-most famous, work is *The Theory of Moral Sentiments*, and as a professor at the University of Glasgow, he studied moral philosophy as one of his fields. The period of time when he taught that subject he considered the "most useful" of his career, indeed his life.[8] As part of these teachings and inquiries, he investigated state power, the law, and wealth. Though he came to different conclusions than Rousseau, the two were attacking the same questions.

Rousseau was a utopian. Smith was a pragmatist. Smith dismissed the idea espoused by Rousseau that the kinds of undeveloped societies found in the Americas were in any way superior to what was found in Europe. In the "savage nations of hunters and fishers," he wrote in the introduction to *The Wealth of Nations,* everybody worked but these nations also regularly were forced to abandon their weak or old or even young, anybody who couldn't contribute to the whole. In "civilized and thriving nations," by contrast, some people never work but still enjoy the fruits of the productive society. "A workman, even of the lowest and poorest order, if he is frugal and industrious, may enjoy a greater share of the necessities and conveniences of life than is possible for any savage to acquire." You can hear echoes of that statement even today.

While Rousseau's *Inequality* is just an essay, if a long one, Smith's *The Wealth of Nations* is an opus. It's a massive, exhaustively detailed exploration of every aspect of the emerging commercial world. Nobody at the time used the term *economics,* at least not in the way we do today. To the ancient Greeks, who came up with the word, economics was just the process of managing one's household. Cotrugli's *Art of the Trade* staked out some of the same ground Smith did, inasmuch as he was trying to lay out a formal explanation of business, but its focus was on the individual merchant, and even more specifically on how the merchant could both make money and be moral. Smith's aim was far grander. It was on one level a compendium of the entirety of global commerce, the most comprehensive that had ever been written. But it was more than just a dry recitation of facts and theories.

The importance of Smith and his *Wealth of Nations* cannot be overstated. For the first time in the history of Europe and the Near East, Smith constructed and offered up a vision of society that was not dependent on either a deity-like king or an actual deity, a god to worship, around which was built a temple and around which an entire society was structured. Remember, what we today think of as commerce was once considered so lowbrow that nobles were not even allowed to take part in it. Smith took this lowbrow activity, painted it in a new light via an exhaustive, methodical, systematic analysis, and elevated it, placing it right alongside the kings and gods themselves. In fact, in Smith's eyes the three weren't level at all. He clearly considered commerce as a system for widespread prosperity to be superior to anything offered up by a king or seemingly offered up by a god. He pretty much pulled it off, too. The same year that he published *The Wealth of Nations*, colonists in North America rebelled against the British crown, and the power of kings, which had begun an almost imperceptible diminution a century before, fell into a drastic and irreversible decline. The power of the Christian God would not suffer as drastic a decline, but it's hard to argue against the plain reality that European and American societies became focused more around economics than religion. God's influence would no longer extend far beyond the walls of the church. Economics would find its way into every single nook and cranny of daily life. This was what Smith longed for, a society based upon the reason and intelligence of people, around scientific principles that could be applied equally and evenly everywhere.

Today *The Wealth of Nations* is considered one of the

great books of the Western world: it was ranked thirty-ninth in a 1952 edition I used published by the *Encyclopedia Britannica*, which included a great-books list on the inside cover.[9] (For the record, several other authors I've cited also made the list: Aristotle came in at eight and nine, Lucretius was at twelve, Tacitus fifteen, Montesquieu and Rousseau tied at thirty-eight.) Smith was the first person to describe economics in purely technical, scientific terms. Even his one main reference to the religious underpinnings of money and commerce was couched in such an obscure way that most people miss it. I'll get to this, because it's critical, but the top-level takeaway here is that Smith didn't transform commerce or finance itself. The systems he explained had existed for centuries before he came along. What he did was reframe them in a way that made them seem objective and scientific, that took them out of the realm of faith and religion. This resonated tremendously in Europe, which had been fighting religious wars for centuries. It resonated in America, too, where people saw themselves as fleeing the religiously addled old country and forging some new, nebulous path. Smith gave them a nonreligious roadmap, a way to create society anew without a god arbitraging every human action. God was still there, of course, but now he was off to the side. The temple was replaced as the focal point of society. That is the true significance of *The Wealth of Nations*.

THE GREAT ANTIDOTE

As previously noted, the first sentence of the book is about the division of labor, and the entire book is an exposition on that first sentence. Unlike Rousseau, who spent ten pages waxing poetic about the city of Geneva, Smith gets right to business (pun intended). You know the concept even if you've never taken an economics class or read an edition of *The Wall Street Journal*. Picture a modern factory, say one making cars. Every worker is responsible for only one specific job in the process of putting together a car. The idea is that an enterprise is more productive when it employs different people doing different parts of a single job. Imagine one person trying to build a car on their own. Even if you could find somebody who knew how to put together every part and component, how many could they conceivably build in, say, a year? The division of labor is the foundation of modern commerce.

Smith introduces the division of labor with the example of a pin factory. In this factory there are multiple workers each responsible for one single part of the pin. One guy measures the wires for the pins and separates them, another straightens the wire, another cuts it; another grinds the top of it, two or three workers make the head of it and attach it to the wire. There might be twenty people in a warehouse, all working on very specific aspects of these pins. By operating this way, they can make upwards of forty-eight thousand pins in a day, Smith estimated (I have no idea if this is an accurate estimate or not, but if it is, well, boy howdy, those are some valuable workers). If there was no division of labor, if by contrast each worker was building one pin from start to finish, he doubted if any of them could make twenty in a day. It might even be that they couldn't make more than one, he said. "The division of labour, however, so far as it can be introduced, occasions, in every art, a proportionate increase in the productive powers of labour," he wrote. The entire rest of the book is dedicated to explaining how this division of labor creates this productivity miracle, how it affects societies where it is employed, the minutiae of commercial society, how companies and commerce operated (at that time), and how it slots into history.

He goes back to ancient Rome, through its collapse, and shows how commerce in local towns laid the foundation for Europe's rebirth. (If you're going to read Smith, take note of which edition you get. The work is gargantuan, and there are myriad editions around, many of them abridged. I have one slim edition that notes it comprises just "selections." I have another that makes no mention that it leaves anything out but does. For this book, I worked off an edition that comprised the entire text.)

In Smith, you can hear the full-throated denunciation of taxes that today is a major plank of many politicians. Taxes in ancient France were so oppressive, he said, that it was in the farmer's interest "to appear to have as little as possible, and consequently to employ as little as possible in its cultivation, and none in its improvement." Growing more and being more prosperous would only result in more taxes, is the argument; therefore, the tax itself is an inhibition to productive commerce. These taxes, he seems to be saying, were a major reason why Europe spent a thousand years in darkness. Now that's an anti-tax stand.

In Smith's telling, religion was corruptible, and government was corruptible. Even business was corruptible. But business, he thought, was *less* corruptible. In general, he rails against the interests of myriad parties who were more concerned about their own wealth, and indulged their own avarice, than the welfare of the state: monarchs, lords, and landowners who bent the laws and customs as far as they could to enrich themselves. This left most regular folk as virtual slaves to the local power, impoverished and without any realistic means of improving their lot, and without any motivation to even try. Thus, Europe sat dormant for a thousand years. "A person who can acquire no property, can have no other interest but to eat as much, and to labour as little as possible. Whatever work he does beyond what is sufficient to purchase his own maintenance can be squeezed out of him by violence only, and not by any interest of his own." As you imagine, Smith took a very dim view of the value of slave labor. He said it is due to the "pride of man" and a desire to dominate those he sees as inferior. But then Smith somehow ties himself in knots to justify it in the British colonies.

Religion is another potential roadblock to creating a better society in Smith's eyes—at least, *organized* religion is a roadblock. He writes a dissertation about how the Catholic Church operated, especially during the medieval years; essentially he covers in more detail much of the ground we've gone over in this book, and he draws even more damning conclusions. The organized clergy operated as a power quite apart from the sovereign. Not only apart, but beyond the control of the sovereign and able to wield enough of their own power to bring down a sovereign. They were not only equal in terms of power, they were equal in terms of wealth and ability to tax the people. And not only were they a political power unto themselves, able to tax the people and accrue their own massive wealth, they had a power the sovereign couldn't even hope to replicate: the power of faith. "This authority depends upon the supposed certainty and importance of the whole doctrine which they inculcate, and upon the supposed necessity of adopting every part of it with the most implicit faith, in order to avoid eternal misery."[10] So strong is this power that the sovereign could not even counter it with a standing army, Smith says. Since he traditionally has no role in propagating faith, he can't fight them on that front. He is essentially defenseless against the clergy. "Their great interest is to maintain their authority with the people." He has absolutely no qualms about where the church stands in his hierarchy of *things that help people*: "The constitution of the Church of Rome may be considered as the most formidable combination that ever was formed against the authority and security of civil government."

Smith sets the church up as this unassailable institution. No king or prince, no amount of science or reason can stand up to it. What can counter it? He has an answer, and it won't surprise you. It's the rise of commerce itself, which over time weakened the bonds between the general mass of people and the clergy. As the power of Europe's barons and monarchs was rising in the fourteenth and fifteenth centuries, eras we just spent considerable time examining, the power of the church was waning. The church was, he said, "by the natural course of things, first weakened, and afterwards in part destroyed." Then he makes a bold prediction: The church "is now likely, in the course of a few centuries more, perhaps, to crumble into ruins altogether."

Smith talks a lot about religion and "superstition." He noted that most education was handled by religious institutions and was more focused on teaching the faith than any objective subjects. And while back then that seemed like a pretty good thing, Smith comes out against it. He uses the words "superstition" and "enthusiasm" a lot, basically saying that the mass of people are not educated, and thus are susceptible to all manner of what we today might call misinformation. It is a fundamental impediment to the kind of world Smith thinks best. He sees two remedies for this.

The first is education. He argues that the study of science and philosophy should be universal—an entreaty that would be realized in the next century with public education. "Science is the great antidote to the poison of enthusiasm and superstition," he wrote, "and where all the superior ranks of people were secured from it, the inferior ranks could not be much exposed to it." The second is, perhaps surprisingly, "public diversions." As in, entertainment: painting, poetry, music, and dancing, which would overwhelm "that melancholy and gloomy humour which is almost always the nurse of popular superstition and enthusiasm."

It's pretty funny that Adam Smith, who seems one of those stone-faced, very serious Dead White Men, would be a fan of entertainment, which is why I mentioned it, but the first point is the one I really want to focus on. To Smith, science was an antidote to the superstition of religion, and religion was a blockade against the kind of society he thought offered people their best chance at a good life. And *that* is why he wrote *The Wealth of Nations*, this gargantuan book that laid out, in painstaking detail, every aspect of commerce. Smith was trying to elevate it to a science. Where to Calvin and Baxter commerce was still just a part of their God-centered society, Smith wanted to pull it away from that. In the centuries since *The Wealth of Nations* first appeared, a lot of others have taken up his quest. The book was incredibly influential, and did more on its own than any other work or any other captain of industry ever did to cement modern capitalism as the dominant organizing principle of the Western world.

Smith was *this close* to pulling it off. Then he went and threw a religious curveball into his opus.

THE INVISIBLE HAND

Unlike modern economics in which people are largely assumed to be "rational actors," Smith clearly saw the importance of human emotion. This shows up all over *The Wealth of Nations*. At one point, he notes that "the avarice and injustice of princes and sovereign states" was responsible throughout history for the habitual debasing of money. The word "greed" never appears in introductory economics textbooks like Paul Samuelson's, but Smith uses the word

avarice several times. The greed of the nobility and landowners, he says at one point, is responsible for creating
conditions that made people unwilling to work any harder
than they needed to, because anything they made beyond what was needed for subsistence was just sucked up
through taxes. At one point, when discussing corn prices,
he notes that prices are basically a balance between dealers
and merchants looking to sell at the highest prices the market will bear, and consumers looking to buy at the lowest
price they can force. Merchants who get greedy and try to
jack up prices beyond what the market will bear not only
risk upsetting this balance but will find themselves stuck
with bushels of unsold corn that they'll later have to sell
at unprofitable prices. But greed wasn't Smith's main pre-
occupation, though he did explore the incentive structure
behind commerce, and his most important conclusion is
buried so deep inside a different topic you might miss it.

In the second chapter of the fourth book, Smith focused
on regulations that block overseas trade. High tariffs in
Great Britain on foreign imports of cattle, salt, corn, wool,
and silk secured a monopoly for those industries in the
nation, he wrote (linen manufacturers apparently did not
enjoy such a monopoly for some reason but were "making
great strides toward it," he reported). This is obviously a
benefit to the owners of those businesses, but it's not clear
that it's a benefit to society, Smith said. These regulations
do not increase commerce on their own, they just divert
it, and it's not clear the diversion is a good thing. Then he
explains exactly why.

A nation's industry cannot employ more workers than it
has capital to pay, which means that every person within
that country is trying to find the job that will pay him (or
her in modern times, of course) the biggest slice of that

overall pie. People aren't necessarily concerned about the state of society when they're out there looking for a job or someplace to invest their capital. "It is his own advantage, indeed, and not that of society, which he has in view." Individuals were more interested in investing their capital in domestic industry, he said, because there was a greater chance of profit; the more of them that did that, the better the profits for the overall industry. And every good capitalist is looking to find the best return on his investment. And this, Smith argued, had a totally unintended effect:

> By preferring the support of domestic to that of foreign industry, he intends only his own security; and by directing that industry in such a manner as its produce may be of the greatest value, he intends only his own gain and he is in this, as in many other cases, led by an invisible hand to promote an end which was no part of his intention. Nor is it always the worse for the society that it was no part of it. By pursuing his own interest he frequently promotes that of the society more effectually than when he really intends to promote it. I have never known much good done by those who affected to trade for the public good. It is an affectation, indeed, not very common among merchants, and very few words need be employed in dissuading them from it.

You've likely at least heard the phrase "the invisible hand." This idea that Smith sketched out here—that every individual looking out for their own needs and profit collectively creates a more prosperous society—is one of the most, if not the single most, used defenses of personal greed. You hear echoes of it every single time a member of a board of directors defends putting the pursuit of shareholder profits above all other considerations. You hear echoes of it every single time a CEO or some corporate executive defends firing a warehouse's worth of employees in order to cut costs and boost profits. You hear echoes of it every single time some corporate raider takes over a company, loads it up with debt, and takes a huge payout for himself. In all these cases and more, the defense is the invisible-hand defense: yes, what I'm doing may appear to be really selfish and even destructive, but this is what I'm supposed to do. I'm supposed to look out for myself. When we all do that, society wins. Smith wasn't looking to mount a defense of no-holds barred mercantilism with his invisible-hand metaphor. He didn't dwell on it. The above reference is the only time he mentions the invisible hand in *The Wealth of Nations*. Yet in the centuries since, that is exactly what it's become. There is absolutely no corporate or capitalist action that can't be defended with an appeal to the Invisible Hand.

But if all you know of the invisible-hand metaphor is Smith's lone reference to it in *The Wealth of Nations,* you do not understand it at all. Because it isn't a concept he came up with in that work; he developed it in an earlier work, and in *that* work he made clear exactly what he was talking about: the "invisible" hand belonged to God.

In *The Theory of Moral Sentiments,* Smith makes this clear.[11] It comes in the middle of a long discussion about avarice and the pursuit of wealth. Smith traces a hypothetical man's life from youth to old age. He traces the youngster's desire for more wealth than he has, for a home larger than his father's small shack. He spends his life working laboriously at some trade, spending countless hours becoming so good at one thing that he is better than any competitor, and he uses this skill to amass the purported good things. Then old age hits. He gets sick. He's on his deathbed. There, in his "last dregs of life," he discovers this truth: "that wealth and greatness are mere trinkets of frivolous utility." He realizes, in that aged tranquility, that the peace of mind he sought his entire life was there all along. He was deceived by the lure of material things. He was tricked by a "splenetic philosophy." (No, I'm not going to tell you what it means; I had to look it up, you can, too.) But this is actually okay, Smith said, because "it is this deception which rouses and keeps in continual motion the industry of mankind." Yes, we are all tricked into pursuing baubles that have no real value, but that mad pursuit has been the driving force behind everything, every inch of progress mankind has made since our most distant ancestors built the first hut. And, yes, in this endless pursuit of material wealth some do seem to make out better than others, Smith admitted. However . . . well, let me just quote the whole thing here, it's pretty important you get it from the man himself.

The produce of the soil maintains at all times nearly that number of inhabitants which it is capable of maintaining. The rich only select from the heap what is most precious and agreeable. They consume little more than the poor, and in spite of their natural selfishness and rapacity, though they mean only their own conveniency, though the sole end which they propose from the labours of all the thousands whom they employ, be the gratification of their own vain and insatiable desires, they divide with the poor the produce of all their improvements. They are led by an invisible hand to make nearly the same distribution of the necessaries of life, which would have been made, had the earth been divided into equal portions among all its inhabitants; and thus, without intending it, without knowing it, advance the interest of the society, and afford means to the multiplications of the species. When Providence divided the earth among a few lordly masters, it neither forgot nor abandoned those who seemed to have been left out in the

partition. These last too enjoy their share of all that it produces. In what constitutes the real happiness of human
life, they are in no respect inferior to those who would
seem much above them.

Now, there's a lot to think about there, and I'm going to
leave that for you to do on your own. I want to focus you on
one word: Providence, with a capital P. When Smith wrote
this, he was talking about god. Or, rather, God. The Christian God. Providence was God, and God was directing all
people's actions, even the selfish, rapacious, really rotten
ones. The "invisible hand" mentioned so obliquely in *The
Wealth of Nations* is really Smith arguing the exact same
thing that Calvin and Baxter both did: that people who pursued wealth were doing so because it was God's will. Smith,
of course, goes even further than that. People who were
poor were poor because *that* was also God's will. Smith, like
Calvin and Baxter before him, essentially absolves anybody
of any action they undertake, because the real cause of all
of this *isn't* people and the things they do, it's God.

And *this* becomes the supreme defense for the mind-
less pursuit of money and wealth, this is what gives people complete moral justification for giving into their greed
and selfishness, this is what allows them to enslave other
human beings and not think twice about it. And that's not
even the worst part! With Smith, businessmen were provided with a completely new, nonreligious justification for
their activities that had submerged underneath it the exact
same justification as religion: that money and wealth were
a sign of the "the gods'" favor. All that changed was where
the favor was coming from.

What to Calvin and Baxter were matters of morality and
religion, to Smith they were not. He recasts everything in
purely secular terms. No more did the businessman have to

calculate the wages of sin. Cosimo de' Medici had to confess his moral quandaries to the pope himself and repair monasteries. Cotrugli had to kitbash double-entry bookkeeping into a moral ledger to justify making money. Smith erases those concerns. Making money, being a merchant, commerce, it is all just rational actors making rational decisions. There is no need to justify it in anybody else's terms or to anybody else's satisfaction. Smith freed commerce from the bonds of the Christian religion and its moral code and that code's effect on how people operated in civilized society. In doing so, however, Smith erected a *new* code and a new morality and ultimately a new religion centered around money and commerce that absolved people of their greed with a wave of an invisible hand.

10

A MORE PERFECT UNION

The British colonies throw off the crown but struggle with issues of economics and government, while Smith's masterwork sparks a revolution. Other thinkers and philosophers follow in his footsteps, proposing myriad theories and concepts and "laws" of nature focused on money, and in a few decades the field we know today as economics emerges. It was wildly popular, and gave the newly independent United States a guiding principle. Get rich, in any way possible. The new nation is driven by speculators and industrialists, it is volatile and prone to crisis, but in an astoundingly short amount of time it produces some of the greatest private fortunes the world has ever seen.

On January 25, 1787, Daniel Shays marched through a snow-covered field outside Springfield, Massachusetts, and he wasn't alone.[1] Shays led a fearsome group of about fifteen hundred somewhat ragged but armed men. For months these "Regulators" had been tramping across the state, wreaking havoc with the government, shutting down courthouses, and preventing the judiciary from operating. Most of them, like Shays, were local farmers and veterans of the recent war for independence. In that war, they had been fighting for freedom from the British crown. This time, they were fighting for a different kind of freedom: freedom from debt.

Shays joined the colonials' cause in 1775. He fought at Bunker Hill, became a captain, and was in a number of battles across Massachusetts, New York, and New Jersey. He left the army in 1780 and settled back in his home in Pelham, Massachusetts, to begin a new life as a farmer. The colonial government never paid him for his service, and in that circumstance his was a typical story. The new federal government was totally unreliable. Many soldiers from the war got paid in land grants, or got worthless IOUs, but they didn't get paid in actual currency. Many, therefore, were left in debt. After the revolution, the former British colonies were loosely united under a framework called the Articles of Confederation, which gave very limited power to the central government. Effectively, the states were on their own, and the postwar landscape was unsettled and volatile. The citizens of the new country were in many ways in a worse situation than before the war. Economically, the new nation was a mess. The government's credit was terrible. Its debt traded for a fraction of face value. Most circulating currency was worthless. Foreign merchants wouldn't accept it. That made it hard for American merchants to compete. British merchants, ironically enough, still dominated trade and commerce. Merchants in Boston got squeezed by their customers in Europe, and in turn the merchants tried to squeeze their suppliers, the local farmers. Those merchants, though, basically ran the Massachusetts government, and pushed tax levies to force the debtors to pay up. Most of the debt was held by a small cohort of Boston speculators.[2] The outlines of this conflict are not, therefore, much different than any of the conflicts

I've mentioned going all the way back to the ancient world. It's always creditors vs. debtors.

Shays had been hauled into a court on debt arrears and learned that there were multitudes just like him. Men were still trying to get paid by the government for their war service and couldn't afford to pay their creditors, or their taxes for that matter. Many lost their farms. Some landed in jail. Finally, in the summer of 1786, scores of them were fed up enough that they banded together and did the only thing they could think of: they marched on the courthouses and shut down debt-collection proceedings. They effectively tore up their contractual debts by preventing the mechanism for enforcing those contracts from being able to operate. Beginning in August, this semi-organized army marched through the Massachusetts countryside, descending on courthouses, and shutting them down. They dubbed themselves the Regulators, and they marched across the state for months, from Great Barrington in the west to Northampton, Worchester, Concord, and Taunton in the east. It was essentially a modern-day version of Yeshua's assault on the temple in Jerusalem. A colonial debt jubilee.

The Regulators were able to keep this up at least partially because many citizens sympathized with their cause. Even the governor was reluctant to call out the militia to stop them. Local officials had tried to organize their own militias but they had trouble finding enough willing men, especially armed men, to mount an effective deterrent. Regular people, the kind of men who'd end up in such a militia, didn't want to be seen confronting their own kind. The memory of the war was still fresh. If they fought the injustice of the British, they were unwilling to turn around and become the injustice. And, of course, the new federal government didn't have the resources to put together its own army to meet the rebels. On that snowy pitch in

Springfield, though, it ended. The Regulators finally met an organized and armed local militia. The rebels were told to retreat but did not. The militia had one cannon available to it. They fired it twice. Three Regulators were killed, and that was that. The rebels dispersed.

Despite the loss on the battlefield, the rebellion was relatively successful for the people involved; Shays for one was granted a pardon rather than hanged, and he managed to hold on to his farm (though he didn't really prosper and died poor). Its lasting impact, though, wasn't in what it achieved for the participants. "Shays's Rebellion," as it came to be known, was a clarion call for the young nation. The specter of mobs and anarchy terrified the new nation's creditor class, the merchants and speculators and landed gentry who'd pushed for the revolution in the first place. The Articles of Confederation didn't provide the government with the means to protect their interests and their wealth. Shays's Rebellion threatened everything they wanted to build, and they needed a defense against it. That defense would turn out to be the Constitution.

The American Revolution and the adoption of the Constitution and the founding of the United States is one of the most significant developments in the history of the world. That at least is the myth, and more or less how the history of the country was taught to me in grammar school. For all I know, it's still taught that way. And it's not entirely wrong. For sure, the nation was founded on one of the most radical, liberal, progressive ideas ever put forth, an idea that is radical even today: that all men are created equal. That idea's implementation had a profound effect on all humanity. The problem is, that isn't *entirely* what the nation was founded on.

The fledgling United States had myriad economic problems. It started with veteran farmers like Shays who were owed back pay. In fact, almost nobody who was owed money by the government was getting paid. The federal government had no legal ability to tax, and so it had no money. There wasn't any federal judiciary, either. Creditors were finding that local officials were often more sympathetic to debtors; many states—excluding Massachusetts—passed various forms of debt relief, and courts often sided with the debtors as well. But the same states had little impact on commerce. State laws carried no weight beyond their own borders, and sometimes not even within them. The entire state of affairs was bad for the creditor class: the government debt they held was worthless, their commercial enterprises were being undercut by more well-financed Europeans, and they had trouble collecting private debts.

In 1913 a Columbia University professor named Charles Beard published *An Economic Interpretation of the Constitution of the United States,* and it completely upended the national lore of a nation founded on the idea of human equality. It was wildly controversial at the time, and would probably be just as controversial if it were published today.

Beard took a detailed look at the economic conditions of the colonies and broke the various factions up by their moneyed interests rather than the more traditional approach of splitting the new country between north and south, or between the thirteen individual colonies. He identified three main cohorts: the "manorial lords," meaning basically well-off businessmen who weren't farmers; the large, slaveholding plantation owners in the south; and the small farmers who lived mostly inland and were spread from New Hampshire to Georgia.[3] There was a fourth cohort, he noted as well: people who had absolutely no voice in the new government. These were the slaves, indentured servants, men who didn't hold property and therefore couldn't vote, and women.[4]

The first two factions comprised a collection of "merchants, money lenders, security holders, manufacturers, shippers, capitalists, and financiers," and they were the ones who got the new Constitution passed. Who was against it? "Non-slaveholding farmers and debtors." (Incidentally, the same groups opposed to each other in Shays's Rebellion.) It's entirely possible the slaves were against it as well, or women, or anybody else who didn't have a vote in the new nation. But nobody asked them. Looking at it this way, he said, undercut the argument that the Constitution was a document designed to protect the entire citizenry. Moreover, he said, those who pushed for it and adopted it were not guided by ideals about justice or the welfare of "all." Rather, "the direct, impelling motive in both cases was the economic advantages which the beneficiaries expected would accrue to themselves first, from their action."

I've been thinking about this a lot since I first read it. What strikes me is that the founding fathers had a problem. Just about every nation can trace its history back to some distant past. The English, the French, the Germans, the Italians. The Egyptians, the Greeks, the Turkish, the Tunisians, the Ethiopians, the Ottomans, the Arabs, the Chinese. The Incas, the Mayans, the Aztecs. For almost all of those nations, their founding myths went all the way back to the mists of time. The history I've been recounting here—the temple, the gods, the cities—is the basis of most of these civilizations, and we to some degree or another still identify with those things. They all have a deep culture any leader can call upon to rally the citizenry. For as long as anybody could remember in Europe, monarchy and religion had been intimately connected. One derived its power from the other, and all were united underneath it. The new United States, however, wasn't just sundering its ties to monarchy, it was also cutting its official, legal ties to religion. But the founders wrestled with this; after all, you need to give people something to believe in. There is an acute human longing for meaning in our lives. We want to belong to something, to come from something, and to be working toward something. We need a godhead, a starting point from which to move forward. What would it be, if not the Christian religion?

There was still a strain of deism among at least some of the revolutionaries. Thomas Jefferson, the man who wrote the Declaration of Independence and would be the new nation's third president, was so disillusioned with Christianity as practiced that he took a copy of the Bible, literally cut out all the references in the New Testament to any element of the "miraculous" or the divinity of Jesus, and pasted what was left into a completely terrestrial tale of a man with a lot of good ideas that he called *The Life and Morals of Jesus of Nazareth* (yes, not unlike what I did in chapter 2). Thomas Paine, the pamphleteer whose stirring *Common Sense* in 1776 rallied the colonials to the cause of revolution, went a step further than Jefferson. In 1794 he published the first part of a work called *The Age of Reason* that was a complete dismantling of the Christian religion. "The suspicion that the theory of what is called the Christian Church is fabulous is becoming very extensive in all countries," he wrote. By "fabulous," he makes clear, he means rubbish. He absolutely savages both the Old and New Testaments as works of myth filled with inaccuracies that could not possibly be true and which therefore were in no way to be relied upon or believed. He does, like Jefferson, suggest that Jesus was a man who espoused a moral philosophy that was worth studying. But the church that grew up around that man and his philosophy, Paine said, was a complete bastardization. Paine pulled absolutely no punches. He railed against the church and its practices of indulgences and the idea that it could grant people absolution. He argued that the entire church was based on a false reading of Jesus's death, the idea that one person could sacrifice themselves to absolve the sins of others, and that the church's entire authority arose from this. In Paine's eyes, the entire church was nothing more than a money-making scheme. "The doctrine of redemption is founded on a mere pecuniary idea corresponding to that of a debt which another person might pay; and as this pecuniary idea corresponds again with the system of second redemption, obtained through the means of money given to the Church for pardons, the probability is that the same persons fabricated both the one and the other of those theories."

Paine wanted to demolish the church, but he understood, as did the other leading colonials, that there had to be some kind of moral structure to the nation. He suggested replacing organized religion with an amorphous deism guided by logic and reason, which isn't really a bad idea, though it obviously didn't take. The new nation was not about to make science its religion. In fact, the backlash to Paine's work was overwhelming; there was an absolute explosion of writers who penned scorching rebuttals.[5] As voluminous and passionate as these rebuttals were, though, they inadvertently illustrated the waning power of the church. In previous centuries, people could be burned at the stake for questioning church dogma, but Paine's antagonists could do nothing but flail against him in writing (and flail with vigor; some of the rebuttals were longer than Paine's original work). When Paine said he suspected people were doubting the veracity of the Bible, he wasn't kidding. Even though the church forced Galileo to recant, even though they murdered people in the name of the faith, the march of progress was inexorable, and every new discovery cast further doubt on the millennia-old tales of gods and supernatural beings.

To be sure, religion still played a big role among the people in the new nation, but it had no official role; there wasn't a Church of America like there was a Church of England. And in reading Beard's work, it hit me: what was the nation's godhead? It *wasn't* equality; most of the new nation's citizens were distinctly second-class. It *wasn't* God, either, despite what some still argue. The First Amendment makes this perfectly clear. It wasn't royalty or dynasty. What was left?

The godhead of the United States was money.

This may sound, well, it may sound crazy. But it wasn't crazy to Beard, and he argued it wasn't crazy to the people who created our laws, either. James Madison, who played such a pivotal role in the new government that he is called the "father of the Constitution," plainly stated it, Beard said. He quotes Madison's own words in the Federalist Papers, the series of essays published in newspapers that were written to build support for the Constitution. In the tenth essay, published in New York in November 1787, Madison addressed the "violence" of factions within the country vying for power (he didn't mention Shays by name but he was pretty clearly subtweeting him). Madison's explanation of how factions form in the first place makes Beard's point quite clear:

> Those who hold and those who are without property have ever formed distinct interests in society. Those who are creditors, and those who are debtors, fall under a like discrimination. A landed interest, a manufacturing interest, a mercantile interest, a moneyed interest, with many lesser interests, grow up of necessity in civilized nations, and divide them into different classes, actuated by different sentiments and views. The regulation of these various and

interfering interests forms the principal task of modern leg-
islation, and involves the spirit of party and faction in the
necessary and ordinary operations of the government.

Money, in a word, is what separates people, and protect-
ing moneyed interests is the first order of government. That
is essentially what Madison argued. In a 1935 edition of
his book, Beard noted his theory was bitterly opposed, and
more than one person called him a Marxist. But Karl Marx,
he said, was just picking up on an argument that had been
ongoing for millennia. Think about the story of the Spartan
kings Agis and Leonidas. Factions split by money interests.
This has been going on for a long, long time indeed.

What you see in the adoption of the US Constitution
and the formation of the new nation is the culmination of
that process. In the city-states of ancient Mesopotamia the
king, the gods, whatever qualified as "truth," and money
were all tightly lashed together. There was virtually no sep-
aration. Over the course of centuries and millennia, money
created its own path. The temple and the palace grew further and further apart. Money was rejected, and then rehabilitated through Bracciolini and Medici. The merchant
class, the moneyed commoner, started to rise and became
a powerful faction of its own. In colonial America, for the
first time, those factions outright rejected the crown. They
denied religion a central role as an organizing principle. But
there still had to be some *thing* for the people to believe in.
What was left? It had to be money.

THE ORIGIN OF SPECIOUS

The Europeans didn't cede the love of money to the Americans, though; after Adam Smith there was an absolute explosion of thought on the questions of economics. Throughout

the nineteenth century, a slew of thinkers added on to what Smith created, and most of the market myths that dominate our world today emerged from these various thinkers and writers. They took any concept they could think of and basically just mathified it and dressed it up as scientific. Sometimes they even took a purely scientific concept—like Charles Darwin's theories on evolution—and adapted it into something that further justified having money sit at the top of the new pyramid. Most of it was written and intended for the ruling classes and intellectuals, but the movements filtered into the general public as well. Through it all, the idea that we should let people be greedy came out unscathed. Not only unscathed, but dressed in new robes that reset the theory and drove it even further.

To Smith, melting the concept of the invisible hand into the mechanics of the market meant that anybody operating within that framework could not be wrong. Or rather not be very wrong. A merchant could try and jack up prices on his merchandise, but the magic of the market would soon enough make him pay for the mistake, ideally in the guise of customers demanding lower prices and a competitor coming from somewhere to meet that demand. The market itself could never be wrong. Smith actually put together one of the most incredible feats of all time: he created something that worked equally well on both a completely rational level and a totally magical level. (I'm not exaggerating; "let the invisible hand work its magic" is a totally normal thing to say on Wall Street.) It's kind of amazing, really. Like Bracciolini before him, Smith was both pushing the conversation forward and reflecting the larger trends around him. From before Aristotle all the way through to Smith, economics was about morality. After Smith, economics was about math. It is a change in focus that gets absolutely zero attention in modern economics, but if you're looking for it, it's impossible to miss.

A particularly sticky idea came from a clique of French thinkers. These "physiocrats" worked out an economic system that was largely based around farming. Farming was the only productive labor, they held, and was the real source of all national wealth. Everything flowed out from the crops grown on a farm, and on a certain level, of course that makes sense: without food, everybody starves to death. From this idea they created their core ideology, which was that the individual was the main economic unit, and thus an economy should be built around individuals—and everything, in fact, should be largely subservient to the individual, especially government (and for that matter, religious authorities). They called this idea *laissez-faire*, French for "let them do."

Laissez-faire was, at least as originally conceived, a relatively positive and progressive idea, even if the centuries to come would reveal its flaws. But some of these ideas were just dark to begin with. One of the best examples of how these new ideas could result in almost dystopian policies came from the English economist Thomas Robert Malthus. Born in 1766, he came of age just after Smith published *The Wealth of Nations*. As a student, Malthus excelled in Latin, Greek, and mathematics but wasn't just an egghead; he was ordained in the Church of England at twenty-three and worked as a member of the clergy. In his thirties, he published a work called *An Essay on the Principle of Population* that was so influential its impact can be felt even today and its author's name became an eponym: Malthusian.

The conclusions Malthus reached in the essay are so grim that the entire phrase "Malthusian" carries with it a connotation of dystopia. This is what he argued, in a nutshell: that the increase in the human population was exponential—2, 4, 8, 16, 32, and so on—but the production of food was linear—2, 3, 4, 5, 6. The result of this math, he stated quite surely, was that a society could *never* grow enough food to feed all its people, and that a portion of the population is destined to starve or live in a constant state of desperate need. "The power of population is so superior to the power of the earth to produce subsistence for man, that premature death must in some shape or other visit the human race," he wrote.[6]

The math, Malthus contended, was inescapable. There are too many people, there will not be enough food, people will die as a result. No European nation, so far as he knew, had ever avoided this conclusion. "In every state in Europe, since we have first had accounts of it, millions and millions of human existences have been repressed from this simple cause."[7] It is in his opinion a law of nature. Because of this utter imbalance, people fall to vice and misery. Not only is there no escape from this, he argued, but there can never, ever, be a fully just and equal society—utopia is a fantasy. "It appears, therefore, to be decisive against the possible existence of a society, all the members of which should live in ease, happiness and comparative leisure; and feel no anxiety about providing the means of subsistence for themselves and families."[8] The ramifications go beyond theoretical utopias.

The very existence of this relationship between procreation and food, Malthus said, meant that the limited amount of food available was a natural check on population growth, so that humanity would not just grow exponentially forever. If the rate got too far out of whack, mankind would be served up with famines, and death. Lots of death. Precisely because it is impossible to feed everybody, the government should limit what it gives the poor, and to otherwise make them fend for themselves. Malthus really does not equivocate about this since he believes it stems from a law of nature, that it may as well be a proclamation coming from God Himself. Beyond a certain threshold, helping the poor is simply bad for society: "If, from the numbers of the dependent poor, the discredit of receiving relief is so diminished as to be practically disregarded, so that many marry with the almost certain prospect of becoming paupers, and the proportion of their numbers to the whole population is, in consequence, continually increasing, it is certain, that the partial good attained must be much more than counterbalanced by the general deterioration in the condition of the great mass of the society."[9]

More than two hundred years' worth of denunciations of the poor and of any and all kinds of welfare can be traced directly to Malthus and his math on population and agriculture. And that's not even the worst of it. Countless population-control and eugenics efforts have their roots in Malthus, too. All of it based on purportedly objective math, supposedly derived from science and Truth. This was the new economics. Every conclusion was presented as a result of logic and math, and if it didn't work at first, they'd just keep trying to make it work. Malthus spent decades rewriting his essay—it eventually became the length of a book—trying to smooth its rough edges, make the math work, and even walk back its most dire implications.

David Ricardo was another early and influential economist. Coming from a family of Sephardic Jews who emigrated from Portugal to England, he fell in love with a Christian and converted to Unitarianism. He made a career for himself in banking, served in Parliament, and eventually started writing essays on economics. Ricardo railed against excessive money printing—England didn't have any official central bank responsible for money printing, and there was a notorious run of forged bank notes at the outset of the nineteenth century during the French war against England. He argued for the establishment of a central bank to control the money supply, something that eventually came to pass after his death, in the form of the Bank of England. He also found fault with one of the precepts in *The Wealth of Nations,* Smith's theory on labor and wages: how they controlled value and what a merchant or farmer therefore needed to or could reasonably charge.

Then there was French businessman and journal editor Jean Baptiste Say, who was a fanboy of Adam Smith and one of his most strident proponents. Say, born late in the eighteenth century, was raised to be a man of commerce and undertook several different commercial ventures. He also worked as an editor, and wrote a number of publications that spread the gospel of Smith. What Say argued was that because obviously there could not be anything for consumers to buy until it was produced, therefore production had to come before sales. "Inherent in supply is the wherewithal for its own consumption." This has been boiled down to the more simple and direct: "supply creates demand," and even if that isn't *exactly* what Say said, that's how most people have interpreted it. It has since become a cornerstone idea in the markets.

This is what the time after Adam Smith was all about; all these different people, whom we today call economists, drawing all these different conclusions from their observations, and dressing them up in ways that seemed scientific. Many of them knew each other. Malthus brought a clutch of them together and formed the first economics society. In 1821, they gathered at a friend's house for the first meeting of the Political Economy Club (more than two hundred years later, the club still meets monthly). They had an obvious zeal for this new world they were creating, and the profession has tried to follow the scientific method: propose a hypothesis, test it, keep testing it until it either stands up or falls down. A lot of times, the hypotheses didn't stand up to reality. A lot of people still inherently believe in "Say's Law" even though supply doesn't always create its own demand. Anybody who remembers the Edsel, New Coke, or the Zune could tell you that. The ability to grow enough food to feed people is not inherently overwhelmed by population growth, either. Malthus was often just wrong, but many of his ideas became ingrained market myths. There's a good reason economics is called the "dismal science." The real problem isn't whether or not economics is a scientific endeavor. The real problem was that economists didn't actually understand what they were studying, and this is something that has gotten only worse in modern times. Economics is not the study of markets and math and quadratic formulas. Economics is the study of people and their irrational impulses, including of course greed and all the moral implications of money that so concerned Adam Smith. But in the nineteenth century, there was one woman who understood all this and became famous for explaining it to the public. At one point, her work outsold Charles Dickens's. She was a light of London's literary scene. Examining her work shows a path economics could have taken, and should have taken, and maybe would have taken, if not for the irresistible lure of the Almightier.

DEMERARA

While Malthus, Ricardo, Say, and others were busily coining their clever little laws, they were writing with other intellectuals and elites in mind. They weren't really trying to convince the common folk about their ideas. That role fell to somebody most of you have probably never heard of but who arguably did more than any of these legendary economists to popularize the field: Harriet Martineau.

Martineau was born in 1802, one of eight children in a well-off family. Her father owned a textile mill and was a Unitarian deacon. She was educated and had a voracious curiosity and artistic bent. By the time she was fifteen, she was well acquainted with Malthus's writings and already considered herself a political economist.[10] She was also practically deaf and used a large trumpet in order to hear people. She got engaged when she was twenty-one, but her fiancé died, and she never again took that plunge. She began writing freelance pieces and novels. When she was twenty-seven, her father's business collapsed, and Martineau threw herself into her writing in order to earn money to support the family. As any writer can tell you, this is hard to do, even today. To do it then, especially as a female in male-dominated England, took special gumption. But Martineau had plenty to spare. She was a ferocious writer and soon became very successful. She wrote about women's issues and was a staunch critic of the meager state of women's education. She would in time become a strident abolitionist and defender of the working poor.

In the early 1830s she was commissioned to write a series that aimed to take the work of Smith, Malthus, and other economists and "translate" it for a general audience. This became a nine-volume epic called *Illustrations of Political Economy*, in which she wrote fictional stories that explained various economic topics. At the time, the entire field of economics was so new that most people were entirely unaware of it. Even among the various fields of academic study it wasn't highly regarded (if it was regarded at all), as she explained in the introduction of the first volume. Most people found it to be "obscure and the study of it fruitless."

"Very few," she wrote, "inquire into the principles which

regulate the production and distribution of the necessaries and comforts of life in society." Economics, she said, "we would fain see more popular than at present," and so she endeavored to make it understandable. The books in the field, great as they were, were of no use to most people. She called *The Wealth of Nations* "a book whose excellence is marvellous when all the circumstances are considered, but which is not fitted nor designed to teach the science to the great mass of the people."

Martineau's publisher printed up fifteen hundred copies of the first volume, a low number indicating he didn't have high expectations for it. But the combination of subject matter, reader curiosity, and Martineau's lively, clear writing style proved to be a big hit. The first volume quickly sold out, another edition was ordered, and that sold well, too. Over the next two years, Martineau wrote eight more volumes, each as popular as the last. *Illustrations of Political Economy* outsold Charles Dickens and catapulted Martineau into the London literary and intellectual elite. She'd have all the work she wanted for the rest of her life. She could take care of her family on her own.

The fact that Martineau and Dickens were England's bestselling writers of the era is very interesting, because the exploration of how the new economics was affecting society was a major theme in both their works. Dickens's tales are dripping with condemnation and stuffed with social critiques of the dark side of the Industrial Revolution. *David Copperfield* is the story (largely autobiographical) of a young man trying to navigate the harsh Victorian society. In *Great Expectations*, Pip is a young, poor orphan who comes into the orbit of the rich but half-mad Miss Havisham. And, of course, *A Christmas Carol* gives us Ebenezer Scrooge, perhaps the most iconic portrayal of the miserly, mean, nearly soulless money-lover ever written (even though he gets redeemed in the end). Dickens thumbed his nose at a system that left large swaths of the population in poverty, and the reading public absolutely loved him for it.

Martineau addressed economic and social issues through her work as well, but in a much more direct way. One of her best-known stories is *Demerara,* which was based on her travels in America and included in the second volume of *Illustrations of Political Economy.*[11] It shows the workings of a sugar plantation in the British West Indies. Alfred is the son of the plantation's owner, and the story is seen through his eyes. Having returned after being educated in England, he attempts to improve the plantation's operations, but finds it utterly impossible. The reason, he realizes, is this: slavery. He finds it both morally and economically awful. "The very sight of slavery is corrupting, to say nothing of the very evil of holding property under the system," he says. He concludes that slavery must be abolished if there is to be any real progress. Martineau was channeling her own reactions to the slavery she saw in the New World. Indeed, she argued that the way to understand society and economics was to look at the total effects of its machinery on society.[12] What was the status of those who held the least power? Did every person have access to the same freedoms and potential? Did society provide them with enough resources? To Martineau, the answers to those questions explained how inequality existed and how much a society was progressing. This actually was her key and lasting contribution to the intellectual tradition. Studying society in its totality as she advocated would soon become its own discipline. French philosopher Auguste Comte gave the field a name: sociology.

Like Adam Smith's, Martineau's economics existed fully within a moral universe. She was a strident abolitionist and vocal about women's rights. You can hear in her writings the same kind of consideration Aristotle gave to economics. If it helps people in their daily lives, then it's a positive. If it's just out there being used for the sake of being used, if it's just money making money, then it's immoral and should be opposed. Both Smith and Martineau injected economics with a much-needed moral center, but it just got lost somewhere in the nineteenth century. It's difficult to pinpoint the exact moment where that happened, but I'm pretty sure it had something to do with Charles Darwin.

Martineau was very close with Erasmus Darwin, the older brother of Charles Darwin. It's not exactly clear what their relationship was. The Darwin boys came from a wealthy family; neither needed to work. Charles pursued—and eventually perfected—the evolutionary ideas pioneered by his grandfather, and Erasmus was a London literary gadfly, content to bring together smart people for dinner parties and salons. He was highly enamored with Martineau, who kept him constantly busy with her many projects and interests. "Our only protection from so admirable a sister-in-law is in her working him too hard," Charles quipped to his sister in a letter.[13] It was through his brother that Charles came to read Martineau's work, which led him to learn of Malthus's dim views on human population growth. This ended up being the spark that put all the pieces of his evolutionary theories together in Darwin's mind. While reading Malthus, Darwin said, he had an epiphany. "It at once struck me that under these circumstances favorable variations would tend to be preserved, and unfavorable ones to be destroyed. The result of this would be the formation of new species. Here, then, I had at last got a theory by which to work." There apparently has been a fierce debate among Darwinists about exactly how much influence Malthus's work actually had, even though Darwin himself cited it.[14] Some take the man at his word, that Malthus's work opened up Darwin's mind to things he had not before appreciated or understood.

Others downplay Malthus's impact. The degree to which they credit Malthus probably depends more on their opinion of Malthus than of Darwin.

Either way, the ideas Darwin was working on were far more controversial than anything Malthus wrote. While religion was beginning to lose its position as the central focus of society, it was still an era where God was universally considered the creator of heaven and earth; to suggest otherwise was to risk professional ruin, attacks from the church, maybe even the anger of a mob (yes, many people are still religious today, but you can disavow God and not face ruin). Darwin spent nearly twenty years working on *On the Origin of Species* before publishing it in 1859. It brought the clash between science and religion to a head; it was the culture war of its day. Hell, some of us are *still* debating it. Regardless, soon after the book's publication, "Darwinism" became a legitimate thing, and much like Malthus's theory, people started trying to extrapolate the ramifications of Darwin's ideas. And the slice of the world that had already absorbed the ideas of Calvinism in regards to money and had accepted Smith's invisible hand as some kind of secular-slash-divine, supernatural-but-not-really guiding force jumped all over Darwin's ideas. To that crowd, it was one more confirmation that the pursuit of wealth was the totally correct way to go.

Darwin's theory was quickly adopted by conservative economists and thinkers, especially in the United States. He explained that various species evolved through a process that selected some to go on and others to be left behind. Those who went on were the victors of a process he called natural selection; they were *supposed* to win. It was a Law of Nature. You can imagine how this concept would appeal to somebody like John D. Rockefeller or J. P. Morgan, or somebody tussling around every day on the New

York Stock Exchange like Cornelius Vanderbilt. It was a secular version of the same kind of argument Calvin had made. In Calvinism, God selected the winners. In Darwinism, evolution selected the winners. But in both cases, the winners were still *selected*. You can see how somebody at the top of society's anthill could take an idea like this and just run with it. It gave them a self-serving reason to be ruthless, an excuse to indulge their greed.

SOCIAL DARWINISM

And indulge it they did. After the revolution, the former colonies and newly united states found themselves in control of a vast land bursting with natural resources and opportunities. But they needed the kind of financial infrastructure that existed in London, Paris, and Amsterdam to take full advantage of it. As anybody who's seen *Hamilton* knows, Alexander Hamilton was a key player in erecting that infrastructure. He came up with a system that allowed the fledgling nation to issue debt and collect revenue and set up the first national bank. All of that provided "liquidity"—a fancy way of saying capital or money—for the capitalists and merchants doing business in the new nation's cities and farms and waterways. In 1792, a group of New York brokers who used to meet under a buttonwood tree on Wall Street signed an agreement that bound them to trade with each other at set rates; that agreement was the founding document of the New York Stock Exchange (which still has a buttonwood tree outside the building). What the nation did not have was a strong central currency. Hamilton's bank was bitterly opposed by some, and in the end it issued debt and coins but not paper currency (its critics feared paper money would be debasing). What this allowed was for private interests, including banks and many of the new companies operating far out in the wilderness, to issue their own paper money.[15] This flooded the country with "liquidity," but it also was an inherently unstable and volatile setup. There wasn't any kind of Securities and Exchange Commission, which wasn't formed until 1934, or regulatory agency to monitor the markets. So this is what you had: limitless resources to consume, a philosophy that encouraged greed, the financial infrastructure to make it all work, and virtually no way to collar man's worst impulses. It really was the Wild West.

The kinds of financial ruin seen earlier in the Mississippi Bubble became common in the new nation. The history of the nineteenth century in the United States is littered with financial crises and scandals. "Panics" were a completely regular occurrence. In the US, there were panics in 1819, 1837, 1857, 1873, 1884, 1890, 1893, and 1896. Wall Street was as unruly as crypto markets are today. Speculators and manipulators ruled the Street. For example, in the 1850s the "King of Wall Street" was a New Yorker named Leonard Jerome.[16] Jerome was like a character out of a novel. His grandmother was related to George Washington; his grandson was Winston Churchill. He was one of the Street's great speculators, making and losing several fortunes. He was often involved in the stock schemes of Cornelius Vanderbilt—who was to the market back then what Elon Musk is to it today. During the 1863 draft riots, Jerome reportedly defended the *New York Times* office with a Gatling gun. Jerome had good reason to defend a newspaper office; he used them to help his stock manipulations. Keep in mind, we're talking about a time before the Dow Jones Industrial Average and other stock indexes, before *The Wall Street Journal*, and before the SEC. Wall Street was an opaque market where manipulators could operate unhindered. Jerome was one of them.

Jerome, who'd once been a newspaperman himself, had

a brokerage firm in New York and wrote a business column for *The New York Herald*. He used the column to attack a railroad, Michigan Southern, that he'd bet against. Betting against that particular railroad, it was assumed, was folly. "The shares of no [rail]road stood firmer," the writer James Medbery said in his 1870 book about the market called *Men and Mysteries of Wall Street*. But Jerome didn't care. He insisted that the market was in a bubble. He talked about imminent crashes. He said most stocks were rotten. This kind of talk mattered back then: there wasn't any central bank to bail out the Street like today, there weren't any objective news sources, and crashes and panics were common. Soon, public opinion began to turn on Michigan Southern. "Holders began to sell their stock. The panic spread," Medbery wrote. Jerome kept up his doomsday talk and kept betting against specific stocks. Before long, he'd wiped out Michigan Southern and made a fortune, all based on complete fabrications and lies. Far from being punished, he was richly rewarded for it, and the lying only bolstered his reputation. Even today, there are still two streets in the city named after him: Jerome Avenue in the Bronx and Jerome Avenue in Brooklyn.

Of course, it's never been just powerful insiders that fueled Wall Street's greed. Medbery talked about the "flush days" between 1863 and 1867, when people from every city, town, and hamlet were plugged into the stock market. Tell me if this mania sounds familiar, and keep in mind that the dollar figures mentioned would probably be in the millions today:

> Women pawned their jewels for margins. Clergymen staked their salaries. One man sent his horse to his broker, and realized in the end $300,000 from this small beginning. Brokers cleared from $300 to $3,000 a week in commissions alone.

But, as we've witnessed in contemporary times, it always turns ugly. Medbery continued:

> An author in two months lost the profits of three books. A bank clerk, in one of that chain of towns between Albany and the city, on the Hudson railway, made $30,000, in successive strokes. Then he offered himself to a fair young girl, and put the whole of his gains into the Street, promising his affianced the rarest of bridal gifts. Three days after he received a dispatch with the warning word, "ten per cent more margin."

It didn't end well for the young suitor. He lost his entire fortune and went back upstate a broken man. Medbery didn't tell us what happened with his bride. "There are hundreds upon hundreds of such human wrecks scattered through towns and cities," he wrote, "dazed or crazed by the swift shock of ruin."

Why is this kind of greed tolerated if it's so destructive? Medbery had an answer for that. The greed of the stock operator was ultimately okay, he said, because the value the stock market provided to society was greater than the pain of the booms and busts on the exchanges. "Liquidity," which I brought up a moment ago, was like a super ingredient for society, he said. Liquidity "has bought crowns. It has sustained governments. It is a perennial flower of auriferous bloom, whereby all there is splendid or solid or beautiful in Europe is made possible." The kind of liquid capital that the Street can provide powers the world, Medbery said. "The large economies consequent upon the symmetric working of the bourses and stock-marts of Europe compensate a hundredfold for all excesses of speculation." It worked in the Old Country, he intimated, and it would work in America, too.

Men and Mysteries of Wall Street is a curious book. I first came across a copy of it randomly years ago in the news-room of *The Wall Street Journal*. It interested me in that it went into great depth to describe the market, going so far as to describe physically the building in which the New York Stock Exchange operated. At first, I thought it was interesting because back then most people probably had never seen the NYSE building, where today I bet just about everybody has. But when I got toward the end, and Medbery was making his big argument about why the offenses of Wall Street's speculators should be forgiven, I realized that it wasn't a tour guide. It was an apology. Medbery was detailing Wall Street culture in an attempt to get people to accept it, to forgive the speculators for all the damage they had caused. It was around this same time that a new phrase was being coined: Social Darwinism. The idea was basically just taking Darwin's theory of evolution and "applying" it to the business world. The idea was simple: whoever succeeded in business, no matter the methods employed, was supposed to succeed. It was natural selection. It was really just an excuse for unbridled greed, but whatever. It sounded good.

Women, clergymen, authors, and bank clerks may have gotten wiped out periodically and regularly, but men like Vanderbilt and Jerome made absolute fortunes. In 1859, Jerome hired a British architect to design him the most opulent home in Manhattan. Sitting on the corner of Madison Avenue and Twenty-Sixth Street, across from Madison Square Park, it was six stories tall, styled after a French palace, and contained a ballroom and a private theater. It was a marked contrast to the staid brownstones that comprised the neighborhood. Jerome wanted it that way. It was completed in 1865, and Jerome and his wife threw lavish parties and were generally the big-spending showoffs they sound like.

New York became a city crammed with miniature palaces like Jerome's, made of brick and stone and marble, with spires and balconies and grand entrances and gardens, stuffed to the rafters with every opulent re-creation of European high culture that could be thought of. Everyone wanted to outdo everyone else. The Astors (whose *paterfamilias* John Jacob made his fortune in everything from the fur trade to real estate to opium) had their castle on Fifth Avenue. Various members of the Vanderbilt family (railroads, shipping, stocks) built several homes on Fifth Avenue between Fifty-First and Fifty-Seventh Streets. Vanderbilt's son Cornelius built a French Renaissance castle at Fifty-Seventh and Fifth. It was the largest private home ever built in the city. J. P. Morgan (banking) bought three opulent brownstones in Murray Hill and mashed them together to form one massive residence. Andrew Carnegie (steel) went uptown and built a gigantic, sixty-four-room mansion on Ninety-First and Fifth. It was the first building in America to have a steel frame, and one of the first to have a working elevator and central heating. And none of those family fortunes matched that of John D. Rockefeller, whose wealth from his Standard Oil company would have been worth more than $400 billion today—putting Bill Gates, Jeff Bezos, and Elon Musk far behind him. Rockefeller built his palace, called Kykuit, in Mount Pleasant, about twenty-five miles north of the city.

It's easy to look at somebody like Rockefeller and see a robber baron. At one point his Standard Oil sold 90 percent of all the oil produced in the country, and he was ruthless to his competition. But Rockefeller himself didn't see it this way. Quite the opposite. Rockefeller operated under almost exactly the kind of impression I've been discussing. According to biographer Ron Chernow, the devout Baptist Rockefeller had an "evangelical certitude about his business plans, such a messianic sense that he represented rationality and order in the oil business and was doing God's work to tame its rough-and-tumble nature, that he disdained those who stood in his way."[17] The Almightier never had a greater proselytizer.

With the French idea of laissez-faire, Smith's completely rational, scientific explanation of how markets function, the work of other economists, and the Constitution of the United States, the groundwork was finally laid for a commercial system that put the individual—especially the wealthy individual—at the top, above governments, above kings, above the church. Men like Leonard Jerome, Andrew Carnegie, Cornelius Vanderbilt, and John D. Rockefeller became some of the richest men this country has ever seen, and they did it by ruthlessly pursuing their own interests. Importantly, none of them came from royalty. Jerome, Vanderbilt, and Rockefeller came from modest families, and Carnegie was a Scottish immigrant. This further emphasized the example set by Cosimo de' Medici centuries beforehand that this new faith could raise up absolutely anybody to the heights of wealth and power. It is at this point we finally see—more than four hundred years after Poggio Bracciolini quietly suggested "avarice, sometimes, is beneficial"—a world that universally paints individual greed as the highest quality.

11

CLASS STRUGGLE

There was a great friction between people, between capital and labor, workers and owners. On both sides of the Atlantic, it was becoming hard to ignore that the new system, like those before it, created only a few winners and many losers. For some that was unacceptable. One radical was determined to destroy the entire system. One politician tried to bend it and make it work better for the little people. And one capitalist tried to give it all back.

In the centuries since Poggio Bracciolini first suggested that greed could be good Europe, Africa, North America, and South America had been transformed. The European powers all became international, dispersed colonial empires; Great Britain's accurate and not-at-all-humble brag was that the sun never set on its empire. The Americas in particular were unrecognizable from their pre-Columbus existence. Native Americans were slowly and methodically wiped out as the European and later American powers spread westward. The newspaper columnist John O'Sullivan argued in 1845, after the United States took Texas from Mexico, that US expansion was God-ordained "manifest destiny."[1] The embrace of the Almightier created vast fortunes. But it also created problems. I showed you some of them, the vast excesses fueled by greed and the disastrous results; the tulip bubble, the Mississippi Bubble, the booms and busts of the nineteenth century. Rousseau was questioning the logic of it all, but others were feeling it viscerally. When the economy went bust and money became scarce, working people suffered the most. By 1848 the stew of issues that had been bubbling around Europe, everything from people being fed up with monarchies to workers' demanding better conditions to a new sense of nationalism in a number of countries, reached a boiling point. The great disparity in wealth between the rich and the poor—which had only grown in the time since the discovery of the Americas and the advent of Calvinism and a real gospel of wealth—a disparity greatly boosted by the ethos of beneficial greed, was a key part of the discontent.

Beginning in Sicily in January of that year, the revolutionary fever spread across the continent. Austria, Belgium, Denmark, France, the various states of the German Confederation, Hungary, Ireland, Poland, Spain, Sweden, and Switzerland all saw severe upheavals. In some cases the governments were sacked. It was the biggest wave of popular revolts in history and it shook power structures that had been in place for centuries. The uprisings also sparked an explosion in ideas. When everything's up in the air, everybody's got an idea about how to fix things (spend time on any social media platform and you'll see nothing has changed). One typical organ of new ideas was a German newspaper called *Neue Rheinische Zeitung*. It advocated for a democratic German republic to replace the confederation of states, and a war with Russia to restore Poland.[2] The paper lasted for only about a year and it likely would be completely forgotten today if not for the name of its editor: Karl Marx. It's almost impossible today to come at Marx fresh. He is intensely polarizing; people who have never read a word of his writings automatically have an image in their head when they hear the word *Marxism*. In the West, his very name is an epithet. But whatever you think of him or his philosophy, you can't argue that he didn't have an impact on the world, even if he didn't seem destined for that. The details of Marx's life are pretty typical, and even sad. He came from a middle-class background. As a student at Bonn University, he was a notorious drinker; indeed, he drank and smoked heavily all his life and it took a toll.[3] He married his childhood sweetheart and had four daughters, all of whom were named Jenny after their mother (isn't that a sweet factoid that humanizes him?) and three sons. Only one lived to adulthood. Poverty followed him most of his life—he was ironically in constant need of money—and he died virtually unknown and unremembered. But he was also, for all of his adult life, an energetic opponent of the capitalist system in which he lived and worked and struggled. He really did want to burn it to the ground.

In 1848, when Europe was coming apart at the seams, Marx was a thirty-year-old living in Cologne with a young wife and three children. He wasn't the old, bald, bearded terror of Western capitalism that we all know today. Hell, he was younger than Taylor Swift when she released *Tortured Poets Department*. But it was in 1848, while he was editing the *Neue Rheinische Zeitung*, that Marx published a work that would make him famous: *The Manifesto of the Communist Party*. "A spectre is haunting Europe—the spectre of communism," it began, sharply and ominously. Like Calvin, one of the things that made Marx's work stick was the fact that he was a clear thinker (regardless of whether you agree with his thinking or not) and a good writer. "The history of all hitherto existing society is the history of class struggle." The system that had emerged in Europe since the end of feudalism had created new classes of people but had retained the basic friction of class struggle. To Marx, you were either bourgeois or proletarian, and . . . well, I'm not going to go too far down this road. It's been done to death a million times over. Some of what he argued for was really radical, like the abolition of private property and state control of all industry and agriculture. But some of what he argued for we actually have today: a progressive income tax, national banks, universal public education. What I want to focus on is how his ideas and their implementation took aim at the Almightier—and failed.

Marx was every bit as radical as his reputation suggests, and it seems he started young. He had seen the potential power of the working class before the great wave of 1848. Four years earlier, Prussian weavers numbering in the thousands broke into the mansions owned by their bosses and trashed them. Eleven died when the military was called in to put down the uprising. Marx called it "a human protest against a dehumanized life."[4] He was an ardent disciple of breaking down the system that had been built up over the previous four hundred some-odd years, ever since Poggio Bracciolini and Cosimo de' Medici turned around the reputation of the merchant class. The commoner kings of Medici's time had become the ruling bourgeoisie of Marx's time, and Marx reviled them. In his mind, the history of society was basically a history of class struggle, patrician and pleb, master and slave, oppressor and oppressed. Some of that might sound vaguely familiar by this point (relax, I'm not trying to turn you into communists). Marx also spent a lot of time getting kicked out of various European cities. He was in Cologne in 1848 because he'd gotten thrown out of

Paris, and after he got tossed from Cologne he landed back in Paris and later London.

While editing the *Neue Rheinische Zeitung,* he wrote a series of columns in which he tried to define, in his own terms, wages and capital and the entire capitalist system. These essays were essentially his take on Adam Smith's work and would form the backbone for Marx's critique of the system and his proposed replacement; they were a first draft of his more epic treatise on the topic, *Capital,* which would be published decades later. These essays, which themselves would later be published under the title *Wage Labor and Capital,* took a decidedly different approach to economics than Smith. It's not that Smith didn't understand the difference between workers and management, he just didn't see anything particularly wrong with the arrangement. But Marx saw the entire structure as inherently unfair. To Marx, "capital" isn't created by capitalists. Capital is the ultimate output of factories and farms and industry. Capital isn't money, it's labor. "Does an operator in a cotton factory produce merely cotton goods? No, he produces capital." What the workers are ultimately making, he argued, isn't just product, it's capital itself. Without the workers, the owners wouldn't have a moneymaking enterprise, they wouldn't have any capital, nothing to reinvest, no business to build around year after year. The whole system was fundamentally predatory because it tried to demean the only commodity that really mattered: labor. It was a key insight, and it colored everything else he said and did and advocated for.

And, well, he's not really *wrong* about that. You can certainly argue about how others interpreted that insight and what they did with it (and I'm looking at you, Lenin, Stalin, and Mao). But the insight itself is the fault line in every single argument between workers and management going back to those pyramid workers in ancient Egypt who were pissed that they weren't getting paid. Nothing gets built without the workers, and in nineteenth-century Europe and America, the workers were not getting paid their fair share. And whether people adopted the rest of the capital-C Communist outlook, that is the way a lot of people saw it on both sides of the Atlantic.

Attacks on capitalism were only growing, especially in America as more and more people recoiled from the excesses of men like Rockefeller and Carnegie. If there was any morality to capitalism and industrialization, it wasn't visible to the laborers in the warehouses. What workers saw was an increasingly unfair bargain; long hours doing dangerous work in hazardous conditions for them, glittering marble palaces for the owners. This divide only got wider as the century went on, with all those stock market crashes, and the first efforts to push back against the system mushroomed up. But while communism had its followers in the United States, it never really took off here, and I'd argue that was because most were already wedded to the church of the Almightier; and Marxism found only limited uptake in western European countries as well, the places where the ethos of beneficial greed was born and first flowered. Indeed, the attacks in the US against the system that made Rockefeller and Carnegie rich never really tried to overthrow the whole system, just to split the pie more equitably.

The tension would at times burst into violence. In 1886, Chicago police descended on a strike and killed several workers. The next day, at another protest at Haymarket Square, the police were attacked by the protesters. Somebody threw some kind of an improvised bomb, and the place literally exploded into violence. Seven policemen and one protester were killed and nobody knows how many were injured.

After the Panic of 1893, and the depression that followed it, workers had finally had enough. They started going right to the heart of the matter. For the first time in forty years, voters put Democrats into the White House and in control of both houses of Congress. Still, that went only so far. The president, Grover Cleveland, supported the gold standard, which many in the labor movement saw as a tool capitalists used to keep them down. And to a certain group of Americans the gold standard represented everything they hated. At the Democratic Convention in 1896, a thirty-six-year-old former representative from Nebraska named William Jennings Bryan delivered an absolutely blistering attack on the gold standard. It's a speech that quite nearly, but not quite nearly enough, changed history.

Once again the battle lines were drawn between the creditor class and the working class, and centered quite specifically on money. The discoveries of gold and silver in the West had upset the balance of the circulation of gold and silver coins; there was, in the opinion of Eastern creditors, too much silver, an already more plentiful metal that could be made into money. More silver put too much money into the hands of the working classes and made it too easy for them to pay their debts, in the view of the Eastern elites. The government ended bimetallism and made gold the only monetary commodity. This infuriated people, especially farmers and laborers in the West. The Free Silver movement pushed for the unlimited coinage of silver.[5]

Bryan took up their cause. He argued in his speech that working-class people were as much businessmen as bankers and financiers, and deserved to be treated as such. Now, Calvin was a good writer, Marx was a good writer, and so were Rousseau and Smith and Bracciolini and even Cotrugli. But Bryan was really something special. I'd highly recommend finding his speech and reading the whole thing.

To this day, it is considered one of the greatest speeches in American history, the "Cross of Gold" speech:

> There are those who believe that if you just legislate to make the well-do-to prosperous, that their prosperity will leak through on those below. The Democratic idea has been that if you legislate to make the masses prosperous their prosperity will find its way up and through every class that rests upon it. You come and tell us that the great cities are in favor of the gold standard. I tell you that the great cities rest upon these broad and fertile prairies. Burn down your cities and leave our farms, and your cities will spring up again as if by magic. But destroy our farms and the grass will grow in the streets of every city in the country.[6]

Before I go any further, read that first sentence again. If you want to know how old the idea of "trickle-down economics" is, well, there you go. Okay, now what Bryan is doing here is basically drawing the same battle lines as Marx. Worker vs. capital. Farmer in the country vs. merchant in the city. But Bryan wasn't advocating for a wholesale overthrow of the economy like Marx. What he wanted was far less radical: the restoration of silver as money. It sounds kind of small today, but it was a big deal at the time. Silver was the money of the little people; gold was the money of the bankers and merchants and robber barons. This was a serious cultural and economic split, and Bryan mined its depths to make his point in his great speech. As he was speaking, the crowd was getting worked into a frenzy. Bryan was both a gifted writer and a gifted orator, and he used all his abilities to whip up the crowd. Here's more from the speech:

> We stand here representing people who are the equals before the law of the largest cities in the state of Massachusetts.

When you come before us and tell us that we shall disturb your business interests, we reply that you have disturbed our business interests by your action. We say to you that you have made too limited in its application the definition of a businessman. The man who is employed for wages is as much a businessman as his employer. The attorney in a country town is as much a businessman as the corporation counsel in a great metropolis. The merchant at the crossroads store is as much a businessman as the merchant of New York. The farmer who goes forth in the morning and toils all day, begins in the spring and toils all summer, and by the application of brain and muscle to the natural resources of this country creates wealth, is as much a businessman as the man who goes upon the Board of Trade and bets upon the price of grain. The miners who go 1,000 feet into the earth or climb 2,000 feet upon the cliffs and bring forth from their hiding places the precious metals to be poured in the channels of trade are as much businessmen as the few financial magnates who in a backroom corner the money of the world. We come to speak for this broader class of businessmen.

Why shouldn't the interests of wage earners or small-town shopkeepers or miners be on an equal footing with bankers and financiers, Bryan was asking. But he aimed to do more than that. He not only sought to elevate the workers in the West and the South, Bryan's true constituents, he cleaved the entire debate neatly in two. You were either for the people and silver or for the robber barons and gold. Bryan forced everybody to make a choice. And as he wound up, he grew increasingly more biblical and prophetic. The words, the imagery—he was really going for it. And then he closed:

If they dare to come out in the open field and defend the gold standard as a good thing, we shall fight them to the uttermost, having behind us the producing masses of the nation and the world. Having behind us the commercial interests and the laboring interests and all the toiling masses, we shall answer their demands for a gold standard by saying to them, you shall not press down upon the brow of labor this crown of thorns. You shall not crucify mankind upon a cross of gold.

The response to his speech was thunderous, like "one great burst of artillery."[7] Delegates threw their coats in the air. The crowd applauded for nearly an hour. Grown men shouted, cheered, and wept. They carried Bryan around on their shoulders like a conquering hero. They hastily scribbled words onto signs: "No Crown of Thorns." "No Cross of Gold." It was manic. "For the first time, I can understand the scenes of the French Revolution," one delegate quipped.[8] Bryan tapped the same fire that Marx lit in Europe, the one that inflamed debtors against creditors.

Bryan's scintillating rhetoric made him a hero at the convention and won him the presidential nomination, but it was a harder sell to the general public, though Bryan wasn't seeking the kind of revolution for which Marx had agitated. "He did not really advocate a revolution," the University of South Carolina professor William Harpine wrote in analyzing the speech. "He sought to rise to power within the American political system, a system in which he firmly believed."[9] The proposal met with a lot of resistance. *The Nation* editorialized at the time that Bryan's Free Silver movement would be an economic calamity were it to actually be adopted. "If the business community supposed that there were any real danger of this dishonest policy being put into practical operation, there would be a panic and crash the like of which has never been seen in this or any other country."[10] The fact that there hadn't been any panic, the paper concluded, was because nobody was taking Bryan or his speech or his movement seriously.

They were right. Bryan lost the election, and the nation's monetary policy remained a source of stress and friction until the creation of the Federal Reserve in 1913 (which I suppose you could argue created a different kind of monetary stress and friction). But the broader labor movement would only grow. The nation was rapidly becoming industrialized, more people were getting drawn into working for ever-growing companies, and the laissez-faire capitalists were getting ever richer. And you had these bitter, decades-long fights over labor conditions and worker pay and things we are still debating and fighting over today. But unlike in eastern Europe and in parts of Asia and Africa and South America, Marxism never got close to seizing the levers of power. Like Bryan, most people here didn't want to overturn the system. They just wanted a better shot at making a living *within* the system. Capitalists and laborers alike were parishioners within the church of the Almightier. We still are.

THE GOSPEL OF WEALTH

Marx and Bryan weren't the only ones decrying the greed of the bourgeois. In 1889, one man went so far as to declare that the rich should just give their money away. The millionaire who gives up his fortune only when death takes him is not to be envied or remembered well, he said, for it's likely such a man would have taken his money with him to the grave if he could have. The wealthy man who hoards his fortune and passes it on to his heirs is doing so for vanity, and his spoiled children will be ruined by the money. No, this speaker reasoned, the only good that could come of a fortune earned was for it to be given away, emphatically and energetically, while the earner was still alive. This, he said, was the only way to restore the social contract between the rich and poor, the workers and the capitalists, the only way to bring about balance in society.

The Marxist who made this declaration was Andrew Carnegie.[11] Carnegie made his money in steel and was one of the richest men in America. In 1889 he laid out his case for giving away his fortune in an essay entitled "Wealth." In it, Carnegie comes out in favor of an aggressive wealth tax, arguing that most fortunes should be taken back for the public via taxation. He also defends what he sees as the natural law of the land, which he characterizes in a single word: *individualism.* He argues against hereditary fortunes and against millionaires holding on to their earnings and only bequeathing them upon their deaths. "The man who dies thus rich dies disgraced," he wrote. "Such, in my opinion, is the true Gospel concerning Wealth." In 1900, a publisher collected a number of his writings and put them out as a book called *The Gospel of Wealth.* Remember when Benedetto Cotrugli argued that the merchant should give away the bulk of his money? Here it is again, nearly four hundred years later, and coming from a *far* more successful merchant.

Carnegie said he was done trying to make money and would spend the rest of his life trying to give it all away.[12] And he did give away a massive chunk of his fortune. He funded retirement trusts for his workers, he financed a string of more than sixteen hundred libraries across the country. He founded a research center, the Carnegie Institution. He started something called the "Hero Fund," which helped the families of people who died in service to others (he said he got the idea reading about a coal mine supervisor who lost his life helping others during an accident). He also bought the land in 1898 to build his mansion on Ninety-First Street and kept enough of his fortune to allow his family to live comfortably in it (his wife Louise lived there until her death in 1946). So, he didn't give it *all* away, but he certainly set a good example for his peers.

There is a trace of self-serving rhetoric in Carnegie's gospel—I think it would be impossible for there to not be. He says that it's beyond the ability of any one person to change how the world is structured, and the best anyone can do is to live within the laws as they exist. He argues that people at that time were overall living better than at any time in history. "The farmer has more luxuries than the landlord had, and is more richly clad and better housed. The landlord has books and pictures rarer, and appointments more artistic, than the King could then obtain." He acknowledges there is a price paid for this progress. The massive enterprises of the day treated workers as mere parts of a machine. The rules of the game put every person into one of several castes, and all of them come to resent the others. "There is friction between the employer and the employed, between capital and labor, between rich and poor. Human society loses homogeneity."

It's possible that men like Carnegie and Rockefeller, who also spent his last years holed up in his palace overseeing the dispersal of his wealth, were trying to assuage their consciences, not dissimilar to Cosimo de' Medici rebuilding a monastery at the behest of a pope. But in the same way that some people loved Cosimo and some hated him, many hated "robber barons" like Carnegie. Carnegie, to at least some degree, implicitly acknowledges his critics' arguments in his gospel. He notes the friction between labor and capital, he realizes his solution is imperfect. He was content to say, in a nutshell, "Here is a system, I don't know why it is set up like this or how it works, but I accept it as it is." Of course, it wasn't hard for him to find the system acceptable. He was one of the richest men in the world. And he tried to make the system seem more acceptable by drawing an implicit connection between money and religion in his gospel. He used the language of religion to defend the embrace of greed and the pursuit of money. Of course, that didn't work for a lot of people. Massive fortunes were created, but only for a few, and the many who weren't getting rich—which is to say, almost everybody—chafed against the unfairness of the system. Carnegie himself acknowledged this in his gospel. He at least proposed a solution, even if ultimately it didn't do anything on a systemic level. But it fell far short of explaining why the system worked the way it did, and why that was a good thing. The job of doing that would come from others.

12

MAKE THE SIGN OF THE DOLLAR

The twentieth century saw the emergence of the Almightier in its full form. The German sociologist and historian Max Weber argued that capitalism was a result of Calvinism and the Protestant Reformation, as previously mentioned. But another writer, a refugee from the oppression of the Soviet Union, rejected that idea and said capitalism was a perfect system that didn't need any morality layered on top of it and people should indulge their own greed for their own profit. Meanwhile, the primacy of religion as an organizing force for society that had existed since before the written word was dying out. People reached for something familiar to replace it with.

𝕿here was another writer around this time, though, who did understand how the system developed and what underpinned it. I mentioned Max Weber briefly earlier but want to come back to him now, because what he wrote perfectly explains how money went from just a thing to the Almightier, and what he wrote is really the capstone of this entire argument I've been making. Weber was a German economist and sociologist who studied the history and development of Western society. He bounced between academia and politics, and also traveled quite a bit. Around the turn of the century, he was trying to address the friction that was at the heart of the newly industrialized West. He published two essays on the topic in 1904 and 1905, later published together under the title *Die protestantische Ethik und der Geist des Kapitalismus.* In English, that's *The Protestant Ethic and the Spirit of Capitalism.*

DE-MAGIC-ATION

What Weber understood that his peers did not was that science, and the burgeoning field of economics that was now within science, wasn't *everything.* It was very good at explaining hows, but it was terrible at explaining whys—at least in explaining whys as they pertained to human beings. As in, why are we here? Why are we doing this? What's the good in it? What's the purpose? In Weber's mind, science had replaced religion as the core principle of society, but it didn't answer questions of meaning the way religion did, and what resulted was a society struggling to find meaning. All around him Weber saw people struggling to provide a "why" to modern society. The economists couldn't do it. The new system was great for Carnegie, Vanderbilt, Jerome, and Rockefeller, but it left most other people with a hollow feeling. People like Bryan and Marx howled about it, but they were missing the mark, too. Nobody seemed to really get it.

The word Weber used to describe this malaise was *Entzauberung,* commonly translated as "disenchantment," which has become the name for Weber's thesis. But the literal translation is "de-magic-ation." Science had taken the magic out of the world and replaced it with nothing. Just science and math and equations and logic and things that were completely irrefutable but emotionally hollow. It tells people how to do something, but not why. So you end up with, for instance, a bureaucratic state that can process amazing amounts of information but strikes every person who comes in contact with it as utterly alien and inhuman.

People don't just surrender to this disenchantment, Weber said. They keep searching for meaning. It's very interesting that in his 1918 talk on the topic, he kept referring to the youth of his time, and their rejection of science and rationality, and how that was leading them to irrational pursuits and mysticism and things like that. And while the references are clearly about a group of people from the World War I era, it's impossible for a reader today not to think he could just as easily be talking about kids from the 1960s, or today. The search, in other words, continues. What Weber tried to do was to explain why the new way of the world could fill that void if only people actually understood it. And what he detailed was precisely religion's embrace of money as a symbol of God's favor. The Protestant Work Ethic, which is what Weber for the first time explained, is a meshing of money and religion, and its offspring is capitalism. In this way, Weber saw capitalism as a moral system, as something that could replace religion and provide the "why" in people's lives.

"We live as did the ancients when their world was not yet disenchanted of its gods and demons, only we live in a different sense. As Hellenic man at times sacrificed to Aphrodite and at other times to Apollo, and, above all, as everybody sacrificed to the gods of his city, so do we still nowadays, only the bearing of man has been disenchanted and denuded of its mystical but inwardly genuine plasticity." The explanations that worked for the Greeks and medieval Europeans don't work for us, but that doesn't mean we don't keep searching. And what you end up with, Weber said, is a tremendous polytheism of competing "truths." For some it is science. For some it is religion. We still have our little household gods, our totems we turn to for meaning and reason, and we still pray to them. And we have this new incentive system, and these new ways of powering society. What Weber tried to do was combine the two.

What you see from the time of Adam Smith until, well, until this very minute, is a field that *thinks* it's a science, and *acts* like it's a science, and is very taken with matters of probabilities and formulas and equations and outcomes, but is not actually a science at all. At least, not a "hard" science. Smith, Malthus, Say, and the rest saw the entire world in terms of math equations, and shoved every single relationship, business, and trade they could find into a math equation, and then assumed that the math equations were the primary reality and that all you needed to do was run the equations and you'd be running the economy. And really, just about every economist from Irving Fisher to Alan Greenspan to Ben Bernanke to Jerome Powell has made this same mistake. What they've almost consciously ignored is that the primary reality of economics is not math at all. It's people. Economics is the study of people. Harriet Martineau understood this. Economics is a humanities course, not a science course. And the thing that motivated people for ten thousand years or longer had been the concept of the supernatural, a god. And *that* thing was no longer the primary driving force in society. Max Weber was an economist who actually understood this.

To Weber, this was the entire argument, that religion was transferred to a system of economics, that system became capitalism, and that system was just and moral, because it was coming from a religious background. This is the Protestant Work Ethic. Money, economics, and religion kitbashed together into a system that did become the primary driving force in society. And Weber's argument is a *defense* of this system, especially in the face of the kind of hedonism and rampant inequality that was then choking Europe and the US in the late nineteenth and early twentieth centuries. Weber was in the middle of all this, and he was on the side of capitalism. He was celebrating capitalism, holding it up as the thing that could give meaning to our lives. He was trying to show that capitalism had a moral foundation, and because of that the modern economic system was virtuous.

Here he is making explicit a connection that at the time virtually nobody else saw:

> What the great religious epoch of the seventeenth century bequeathed to its utilitarian successor was, however, above all an amazingly good, we may even say a pharisaically good, conscience in the acquisition of money, so long as it took place legally. Every trace of the *deplacere vix potest* has disappeared.
>
> A specifically bourgeois economic ethic had grown up. With the consciousness of standing in the fullness of God's grace and being visibly blessed by Him, the bourgeois business man, as long as he remained within the bounds of formal correctness, as long as his moral conduct was spotless and the use to which he put his wealth was not objectionable, could follow his pecuniary interests as he would and feel that he was fulfilling a duty in doing so. The power of religious asceticism provided him in addition with sober, conscientious, and unusually industrious workmen, who clung to their work as to a life purpose willed by God.
>
> Finally, it gave him the comforting assurance that the unequal distribution of the goods of this world was a special dispensation of Divine Providence, which in these differences, as in particular grace, pursued secret ends unknown to men.

The phrase in italics, *deplacere vix potest,* isn't strictly Latin. It should be *Deo placere vix potest,* which means "he can scarcely please God." Weber was saying that proper capitalism was not an affront, that it was moral and just and upstanding, that it was a social good. All of this, Weber says, has resulted in the world in which we live: one where capitalism determines the path of society, where it has almost complete power over people's lives. It has replaced religion. It has "escaped its cage," he says. Now, Weber was proud of this connection. He saw it as a positive thing. He was promoting it, at a time when it wasn't generally accepted. Indeed, he had a lot of critics and had a lot of fights over it. The capitalists didn't want to acknowledge the religious roots of their new system. They didn't want it back in that cage, with all its squishy morality and ethics.

"Victorious capitalism, since it rests on mechanical foundations, needs its support no longer. The rosy blush of its laughing heir, the Enlightenment, seems also to be irretrievably fading, and the idea of duty in one's calling prowls about in our lives like the ghost of dead religious beliefs. Where the fulfillment of the calling cannot directly be related to the highest spiritual and cultural values, or when, on the other hand, it need not be felt simply as economic compulsion, the individual generally abandons the attempt to justify it at all." Weber seems to think, or maybe just hope, that illustrating this hidden history and connection will somehow make capitalism more moral again, that the people raging against the robber barons will stop and accept it the way Carnegie did.

What Weber did was to reveal the obscured underpinnings of capitalism and call them the Protestant Work Ethic. That is controversial even today (just Google "Max Weber was wrong"). What he leaves out is that the work ethic in Protestantism itself is derived from the Protestant religion's embrace of the ethos of beneficial greed.

MAKE THE SIGN OF THE DOLLAR

Weber found resistance because he was trying to fuse together two different parts, religion and capitalism, and the people who supported each of those parts wanted nothing to do with the other. A different writer took Weber's theory a step further. She wasn't trying to fuse religion and capitalism, she was holding up capitalism *as* religion, the new religion for a modern world. She published a novel in 1957 that proudly laid out her vision of capitalism as a new religion, money as its iconic symbol, and greed as its morality. Her name was Ayn Rand. The novel was *Atlas Shrugged.*

Like Weber's *Spirit of Capitalism,* Rand's *Atlas Shrugged* was and still is controversial (just Google "Ayn Rand was wrong"). It is a massive, overstuffed, melodramatic, twelve-hundred-page opus that includes an astounding sixty-page speech from its hero. The core of her belief system came to be called Objectivism, and in a nutshell it is a belief that nobody owes anybody else anything, that the individual is all that matters, and that each person should be allowed to do anything they please regardless of anybody else's needs or desires. Objectivism is a rejection of Christianity, but also Carnegie's gospel, Bracciolini's ethos of beneficial greed, Calvin's theories, and even Weber's work ethic. Like Marx before her, Rand was trying to burn it all to the ground.

To understand Rand's work, you need to understand a bit about her background. She was Russian, born in 1905. When the Bolsheviks, fueled by Marx's theories, overthrew the czar, they were intent on establishing a new kind of country, one based entirely on communism. Rand's father owned a pharmacy, which was seized. Everything was seized. The new republic was going to remake society: the Union of Soviet Socialist Republics. She fled in 1926, made her way to America, and landed in Hollywood. Can you imagine the cognitive dissonance of going from the dank gray reality of the Soviets to the Technicolor splendor of the Dream Factory? She wrote screenplays and a novel called *The Fountainhead,* moved to New York, and became the leader of a group called the Collective that met in her apartment on Saturdays, where she would read aloud from her new work, *Atlas Shrugged.* But she never forgot what the Soviets had put her through, and her homeland, and she absolutely burned with grievances against them for her whole life. Everything she wrote was shaped by the anger she held for the Soviets and the way of life they forced on Russia.

If you're not old enough to remember the USSR, it's hard to explain just how feared and loathed it was here in the United States. The Reds were the polar opposite of everything the US stood for, and they (so we assumed) were ready at a moment's notice to blow us to smithereens with a million nukes. In the second half of the twentieth century, you had two massive empires squaring off against each other, capitalism versus communism, for the entire world. It felt like everything was at stake, all the time. Now, in retrospect, it's obvious that the Soviet model was a human rights catastrophe destined to fail; Rand, for all her flaws, was correct to stand against it. But I'm not going into this just to give some context to Rand's work. What stands out to me about the USSR in light of the subject of this book is this: even in the godless, anti-capitalist, anti-imperial, anti-bourgeois, communist empire, there was *still* a place for the Almightier. They still had money.

Oh, they wanted to get rid of it, just like Marx did.[1] Marx had predicted that in a society based on communism, money would essentially become superfluous and would just kind of fade away and disappear. Russia's new czars thought that would happen, too. They essentially considered themselves stewards who would dismantle the old Russia and rebuild it in Marx's utopian vision. So after the October Revolution, they planned to take over the monetary system and then abolish it.[2] Only they found it impossible to do that. Between 1917 and 1924 the Soviet Union experienced a classic inflation spiral. The value of the ruble plummeted and prices for everything went haywire. People didn't want to hold currency for even an hour because of how fast it lost value. Barter and exchange became acceptable, even for government taxes.[3] The government printed rubles like mad and ran up enormous deficits trying to keep up. The crisis was solved only in a way that surely would have appalled Karl Marx: In 1922 the state bank created a new currency, the chervonets, backed by gold and bonds and other state assets. They kept the supply low and the price steady, and the new currency balanced out the insanity of the ruble inflation. The engineers of the communist state learned a really important lesson about how modern economies work, how deeply embedded money was in our collective consciousness, and how impossible it was to get rid of money.

By the 1950s, the still-money-based Soviet economy operated in many respects like its American counterpart.[4] The only difference was the oppressive hand of complete state control, a mirror image of Smith's invisible hand. And that led to all sorts of imbalances. I found one study of Soviet income inequality that reported there were about four thousand writers in the country in 1936 who earned up to four hundred rubles a month.[5] There were fourteen who earned more than ten thousand a month. It's obvious why that particular study appealed to me, but the wider point is that far from being a nation where everybody was equal and shared equally in the output of the nation, there were substantial inequalities. In 1980, the USSR's last decade, this inequality was pretty well entrenched. One US-based study[6] used published data to come up with a "Gini coefficient," a standard measure of income inequality, for the Soviet Union. On a scale of 0.00 to 1, where 0.00 is perfect income equality and 1 is the opposite, the USSR as a whole scored a 0.290. Doesn't sound too bad, right? Nowhere near 1. But, consider that in the United States, in 2022, the Gini coefficient was 0.47. Also, the study's authors noted that because the data were incomplete, they couldn't account for state subsidies to the masses and, more importantly, "privileges." Privileges were pretty much what they sounded like—there was a favored class in the USSR that got benefits the masses did not.[7] For the income study's authors, it was impossible to account for the value of these privileges, but it was likely that if they could have it would have driven the Gini coefficient way higher. "We can predict that adding privileges to official income would unambiguously increase inequality," the study's authors wrote. The point, therefore, is that despite its Marxist claims of egalitarianism, Soviet society economically was no more equal than capitalist countries, and with far, far less personal freedom. It never was egalitarian. What I would conclude is that even in the communist, Marxist Soviet Union it was still possible to see the hand of the Almightier at work, and tying to pretend that it didn't exist is what actually created the moral rot that led to the collapse of the USSR.

Back to Rand. Rand's philosophy is the endpoint of a nearly six-hundred-year evolution in the elevation of greed, starting way back with Bracciolini and de' Medici. To Rand, greed is not sometimes, maybe, possibly, beneficial. Greed is the only morality anybody need employ. Selfishness is the whole point of Objectivism, and according to Rand laissez-faire capitalism is the best system for allowing people to pursue their own selfish wants and desires without getting tied down by any icky morality or guilt or responsibility to others. Man, she argued, "is an end in himself, not the means to the ends of others."[8]

Rand's work presented a self-contained religion centered around avarice and the pursuit of wealth. She was similar to Weber in that she assumed she was explaining the key truth about capitalism for the first time ever. She believed that she had unlocked the secret. She kept the temple and the currency, but got rid of the gods and their inconvenient morality. In Rand's world, the only thing that matters, the only virtue, is the complete dedication to one's self. To Rand, the "morality of altruism" is the problem. She was vocally in favor of abandoning altruism altogether, or any form of basic cooperation between people. "Altruism holds that man has no right to exist for his own sake, that service to others is the only justification of his existence, and that self-sacrifice is his highest moral duty, virtue, and value. Capitalism and altruism are incompatible."[9] Rand thought that the only role government should be allowed to play was as a preventer of any violent attack on individual rights, especially property rights. She advocated for a completely pure version of laissez-faire capitalism, which she said had never actually been brought into existence. "I am for an absolute laissez-faire, free, unregulated economy," she said in 1959. "If you separate the government from economics, if you do not regulate production and trade, you will have peaceful cooperation, harmony, and justice among men."[10]

If you're not familiar with *Atlas Shrugged,* or don't have

the patience to wade through twelve hundred pages, it's the story of a massive struggle between two groups. On the one side are the industrialists and capitalists, the people who in Rand's mind are the creators of everything good and valuable. The makers. On the other side is, well, everybody else, people who just want to leech off the creators and bring them down and mire them in some dystopian hell-scape where the individual is beaten and drowned (given her history with the communists this shouldn't be surprising). The takers. The hero is a man named John Galt, who creates a sort of utopia for the makers in the Rocky Mountains called Galt's Gulch. One day, they all decide to leave society and go there and society collapses. As the world burns, Galt harangues them over the radio with a four-hour speech, I guess just to rub it in. Now, I'm not here to argue for or against Rand and her Objectivism. What I am here to do is make the point that Rand painted capitalism as a new religion, and used the iconography of religion to make the point. Galt is pretty clearly a messianic figure, meant to lead the people to the Promised Land. In the middle of Galt's Gulch stands a three-foot-tall solid-gold dollar sign erected on a pedestal. "It hung in space above the town, as its coat-of-arms, its trademark, its beacon—and it caught the sunrays, like some transmitter of energy that sent them in shining blessing to stretch horizontally through the air above the roofs," Rand wrote. The dollar sign in Rand's Shangri-La has replaced the Christian cross, and if there is any doubt about this, she makes it explicit at the very end of the book. John Galt stands at the edge of his town, looking out across the valley and the mountains, contemplating the world beyond, which he has announced they are going back to save. "He raised his hand and over the desolate earth he traced in space the sign of the dollar."

THE NEW RELIGION

By the time Rand came around with her philosophy centered on the individual and the naked pursuit of money, the
nation was more than ready to accept it. I think, and I've
tried to show you this, that money had been moving along
a slow and steady ascending path and religion had been
moving along a slow and steady descending path. During
the Revolutionary Era people like Jefferson and Thomas
Paine were pushing for a sort of nonsectarian deism, while
Madison was enshrining property rights for the individual
as a cornerstone. Religion's primacy was further damaged
during the Civil War: both North and South claimed God's
will favored their side. After four long, bloody, destructive
years, both sides were left to wonder if God favored either
side, or was even there to begin with.[11] "It is clear to my
mind, that the theological and formal part of Christianity
has in great measure lost its power over the minds of men,"
James A. Garfield, who would go on to become president,
wrote in his diary in 1873.

In the first years of the twentieth century, these organizing
principles crossed paths, permanently. On March 26, 1911,
former president Teddy Roosevelt delivered a speech at
the Pacific Theological Seminary in Berkeley, California, in
honor of the three hundredth anniversary of the King James
Bible. The Rough Rider himself was just one of myriad people taking part in celebrations of the most famous version of
the Bible across America and in the UK. The British prime
minister took part in a celebration at Royal Albert Hall on
March 29. The city of Chicago staged events over five days,
including a reading from an actual 1611 Bible and a speech
from William Jennings Bryan. Woodrow Wilson, whose star
was rising and who a few years later would become president
himself, addressed a crowd of twelve thousand in Denver.[12]

It was a celebration of something that had already peaked, though. About eight years earlier, in 1903, a pair of bicycle-manufacturing brothers named Orville and Wilbur Wright built and launched a contraption they called the Wright Flyer. When their plane left the ground and took to the air, the brothers achieved a first in human history: powered flight. Soon enough, mortal men were flying in the clouds, eye to eye with where for millennia we *thought* the gods, and God, lived. We got up there and found . . . nothing. It's hard to maintain the belief in a supernatural being when virtually any of us can get on a plane and see for ourselves that there is no Valhalla, no Olympus, no heaven up above the clouds. I don't think there was any turning back after that. World War I, World War II, the atom bomb, these things only amplified the trend.

Religion's central place as a driving force in society faded. Five thousand years ago, the first city-states literally revolved around the temple, the home of the gods. Everything people did was done to curry the gods' favor. Five hundred years ago, people were motivated by trying to do enough good things to ensure their entry to heaven after they died. That's not the case today. Now, obviously there are still billions of people who do believe in a religion, not just Christianity but Islam and Judaism and Buddhism and Taoism and Hinduism and even less prominent religions. There are billions of people who define their lives and their values by the morals they get from religion. I'm not trying to argue that point. I'm saying that religion is no longer an organizing principle on a society-wide level, but as Weber pointed out, people still need something to believe in. I suppose it could've been science; that's essentially what Paine wanted, and indeed science has been a driving force over the past few centuries. But science also strives by its very nature to be amoral. Science doesn't try to nurture the soul. Money doesn't either, but it had been a fellow traveler with religion for five thousand years. It had the sheen of the Almighty going all the way back to Mesopotamia. No, if it wasn't going to be religion, and it wasn't going to be science, the next thing that made sense was money. We'd already been worshipping it for centuries.

What Cosimo de' Medici and Poggio Bracciolini started six hundred years ago has today brought money full circle. It was nurtured by the Catholic popes and the Protestant reformers. It was adopted by the economists. It was championed by the capitalists. It was turned into its own mythology and mission by Ayn Rand. And people flocked to it. For whatever reason, we seem to need some *thing* in the middle of our societies, and we found it in Bracciolini's suggestion that "avarice, sometimes, is beneficial." We embraced greed as an organizing principle, we embraced the myth of the Magnificent Man. And that is why in the movie *Wall Street* when Gordon Gekko says "greed, for lack of a better word, is good," it just completely lands. Even the cadence is similar to Bracciolini's statement. It is the culmination of a six-hundred-year odyssey for greed, from the bane of existence to the essence of individual virtue. There weren't any solid-gold dollar statues built in the '80s, at least none that I know of, but we did get a giant bronze bull on Wall Street. A Sicilian artist named Arturo Di Modica created it and just dropped it there one morning in 1989. If you ever visit Wall Street, you're sure to see throngs around it. It's very popular.

Now it's important to keep in mind that this isn't just about excess. That money engenders greed is just a fact of human frailty. No, what I want you to think about is the fact that money has become the primary driving force in our lives. Unlike in Mesopotamia or even medieval Europe, today we use money for *everything*. It sits in the middle of virtually every single transaction people make. If you want food, shelter, heat, clothing, education, or healthcare, you need money. There is nothing you do that doesn't involve money. It is the way just about every working person is rewarded, and rated, and valued. If money abruptly disappeared from the world today, the world would collapse. Whether you're greedy, miserly, or altruistic, we've reached the point where we can't live without money. That doesn't mean, though, that we can't live with it better. It's time to talk about some things we can do to restore our control over money.

13

UTOPIA,
FOR LACK OF A BETTER WORD

It's time to start talking concretely about what we do next. There are a lot of options, some easy, some hard, some radical. But in a rapidly changing world, the unthinkable can become thinkable. So let's starting thinking about how we can restructure our world and restore balance.

𝕵acob S. Coxey stepped out of his home outside Massillon, Ohio, and walked east. It was a cold, damp day, and elsewhere people dressed in their finest headed for church. It was Easter Sunday, 1894. Coxey, dressed in a tattered Union Army uniform that was a relic of his service during the war, was not bound for church. He was joined by about fifty other men, all unemployed. As parishioners celebrated the resurrection of their Lord, the ragtag group marched eastward, out of town. They had a long journey in front of them.

A depression the previous year had ravaged the nation's economy. Banks failed, businesses closed, and people hoarded gold amid widespread fears of currency shortages. The depression hit Coxey differently. By the contours of

his life, Coxey was the very picture of a free-market capitalist.[1] He owned a farm and a sandstone quarry, and a
processing mill that produced silica for the iron and glass
industries. He employed about fifty men and was worth
about $250,000, then a tidy fortune. He owned horse farms
in Kentucky and Ohio and made even more money from
racing, breeding, and selling horses. Coxey was no robber
baron, though. He appeared to care deeply about the plight
of the working man. And that was what had him leading
a group of unemployed men marching in the cold on that
morning rather than sitting in his warm home counting his
money. Coxey wasn't content to just complain about the
hard times. He had a plan.

Coxey dreamed up an audacious proposal to put men
back to work: have the federal government issue $500 mil-
lion worth of debt to fund the building of roads and hire
men to build them. The automobile had just been invented,
and America's roadways were nothing but mud. Coxey envisioned a plan for a nationwide road system, paying workers $1.50 a day for eight-hour shifts. He expected that the
wages paid to the newly employed men would stimulate the
economy and pull the nation out of depression. To drum up
support for this plan, he sent word out across the country:
he would march from his home in Ohio to Washington, DC,
to demand government relief and to demand jobs that paid
decent wages. Coxey's small Massillon band was joined by
men from San Francisco, Los Angeles, Montana, Chicago,
Providence, and elsewhere. When they arrived in the nation's capital, thirty-five days after Coxey walked out his
front door, they numbered almost six thousand men on
horseback, in wagons, and on foot. The capital had never
seen such a throng; it was the city's first organized march.
His proposal was actually introduced as a bill in Congress,
but the resistance to it was fierce. When Coxey and the

other planners staged a rally on the Capitol lawn, they were arrested. His plan went nowhere.

Coxey was amazingly persistent. He ran for president, governor of Ohio, and the Senate as a member of the Populist Party, and lost every election. In the early years of the twentieth century his businesses ran into trouble, and he filed for bankruptcy. But he just kept grinding, as we'd say today; he got his quarry back and acquired ownership interests in gold and silver mines in Nevada and an arsenic mine in Virginia. He started a company making gas turbine engines. By 1913 he was a millionaire. But he never stopped thinking about how to improve conditions for the working man. And he kept pushing his ideas. Decades later, his labor plan got absorbed into plans created by the new administration of Franklin Roosevelt in the early years of the Great Depression. The Works Progress Administration was founded to take America's unemployed masses and put them to work. Coxey even briefed FDR on his plan at one point. More than thirty years after he first proposed it, Coxey's plan became a reality.

Coxey was protesting against the extreme wealth disparity that emerged during his own time, but he also had a lot in common with reformers and protesters who'd come before him, like Enmetena, Agis, Yeshua, Rousseau, Marx, Bryan, and Daniel Shays. Even Andrew Carnegie. They were people from all over the political and the social spectrum who looked at the world around them, saw the inequality, and demanded better. None of them were anarchists. These were kings and farmers, businessmen and carpenters. The question we must answer for ourselves today is the one they all asked themselves: Can't we do better? I hope by now it is clear that there aren't any gods coming to save and protect us. There is no Almighty, there is no Almightier. It's just us. It's always been just us. And as Aristotle pointed out more than two thousand years ago, money is a man-made force, and it is within our power to change it if it creates disharmony. It is, in fact, our moral imperative to change it.

The main point of this book was to draw a detailed map of the trajectory of money, to show where it came from, how it evolved, and how it became the organizing force in the world that it is today. I don't believe anybody has done that, and I think it's important to have that understanding if we are going to keep improving as a little global tribe of people. Unfortunately, doing that leaves little space in this book for a discussion of what we do next, so what follows is a series of incomplete sketches, ideas I've had while writing. There are scores of other ideas, too, from other people, things I haven't even thought of. We need to start talking about them, all of them. If people out there really are ready to blow the system up, and it seems like we are, we're going to need a plan for the next one that gets built. We can't just re-create the old system. We can't.

SUNERGOS

The best way that I can think of to help us start restoring balance in society is to revive the oldest principle we have: the golden rule. Do to others what you'd want them to do to you. The embrace of greed and the uncapped pursuit of wealth that I have traced in this book has taken us away from that commonsense truth. The view that unmitigated greed is good for all is both wrong and deeply pernicious. It has made us forget how much we need each other (and in that sense, even treating others well has a selfish component to it; their prosperity benefits you, too, and if that helps you adopt the golden rule, well, you know what, that's fine). The great thing about the golden rule is that it already exists in basically every religion and ethos known to man. As we've seen, it was even baked into capitalism at one point. You can both pursue your own goals and care about the welfare of your fellow man. There is a word that appears a number of times in the Bible, but you wouldn't see it unless you read it in the original Greek (or found a translation that pointed it out, like I did). "For we are laborers together with God; ye are God's husbandry, ye are God's building," St. Paul writes in Corinthians.[2] The Greek for "labor together" is *sunergos,* and a modern derivation of it is the word *synergy.* The idea in the Bible is that people working together can bring about God's kingdom, but it would have the same meaning in a secular sense: if we all labor together we can build great things. Of course we can.

The idea shows up all over the place. The Swahili word *harambe* appears on Kenya's national seal. It means "pull together," and it represents a tradition of people working together to help one another. "Sisi kwa sisi," they say. "Us for us." If you sit in enough meetings with corporate consultants you are bound to be spoon-fed some version of this as well, and it's also right there on the back of the US dollar bill: *e pluribus unum.* Out of many, one. If we need to have some animating principle around which to build society, something that can effectively replace money and a vengeful god and give people a reason to live and work and contribute their talent to society, this is a good one. Working together. Sunergos. Harambe, e pluribus unum.

And don't get me wrong: I am not talking about communism. I am not suggesting we get rid of private property and subsume the individual into the state. We've seen that tried and it's a mess. All I'm talking about is getting us back to a commonsense place that existed when large-scale societies were first emerging, a place where you understand that the best way for society to prosper is to treat neighbors, countrymen, and strangers the way you'd want them to treat you.

That was the first universal law, it was the animating principle of the Founding Fathers, and I think it could still be a guide for us today. Or, if that's too old-fashioned for you, how about following the time-tested philosophy of William S. Preston and Theodore Logan: be excellent to each other.[3]

That's not a bad rule of thumb, is it? And *then* you go and do the thing that you really want to do that's gonna make you rich and famous. I mean, it's not like I'm giving this book away. We want to keep that motivation for people, we don't want to squelch that. I just want to balance it out. We've gotten so far out of whack that any suggestion of reining in the individual in any way is met with malice, but what I'm talking about is not nearly as insane as it sounds.

CULTIVATE VIRTUE

I opened this chapter with that story about Jacob Coxey because it shows two things: one, that you can pursue your own comfort and success and wealth and at the same time care about others, and also that we progress as a society only through long endurance. Coxey kept at it through the Panic of 1907, World War I, the Roaring Twenties, and the Great Depression. We're going to need Coxey's kind of gumption if we want to make any real changes. Beliefs about money have become deeply ingrained over the course of generations and millennia. If you're still reading this, I imagine you found the stories in here as revealing as I did. Imagine how many more people didn't read past page one. And our economics has not even begun to grapple with the fact that of the two biggest ideas animating it—scarcity and the invisible hand—one isn't a fundamental problem anymore and the other was a myth all along. We have a long road ahead of us.

It's easy to feel like there isn't anything an individual can do to change our money culture. As soon as you start talking about any of this, you will get the side-eye, or be outright berated. I've tried! Even people you think would be sympathetic aren't; like I said, this isn't just about greedy Wall Streeters. We've built our entire society around money, and suggesting any changes to it is so far outside of daily experience that most people can't even grasp the idea. It's like saying the color blue is actually a horse named Stan; it sounds like absolute gibberish. That said, there are things you, as one person sitting here reading this book, can do.

How do you get started? Well, if you are one of the world's twenty-eight hundred or so billionaires, it's easy; just do like Andrew Carnegie and start giving your money away. But virtually all of you reading this (and me, too) do not, nor will you ever have, Andrew Carnegie–level wealth. Still, the ethos he espoused can be made part of most people's lives, and not only at the end when you're staring death in the eye. All of us can cultivate altruism, in big ways and small ways, with money and with deeds. Find a cause, and support it, monetarily if you can. It could be anything, and it could be any amount. Be generous with your money, and the more you have, the more generous you should be. Or maybe you have nothing left after taking care of yourself and your family. Well, it doesn't have to be money. Give your time, give your expertise. I have a cousin who spends one week every summer volunteering at a camp for special-needs youth; he's gotten his children and other cousins involved as well. That's how you make the world a better place from one generation to the next.

We need each other! Ayn Rand was totally wrong in her belief that nobody owed anybody anything. None of us would get very far without help. Without the advantages of a structured society, none of us would amount to anything. Albert Einstein would've been a moderately clever monkey.

I don't care who you are or how much you have, you rely on other people. Think about the house you live in, the car you drive, the food you eat, the clothes you wear, the TV you watch, the education you got. How much of it did you make or grow or discover on your own? We help (or hurt) others in a million ways that we don't even see. Sisi kwa sisi. We do it every day unconsciously anyhow. I'm just saying, embrace it and cultivate it.

"Cultivate virtue in your own person, and it becomes a genuine part of you," Lao Tzu wrote in the *Tao Te Ching*. "Cultivate it in the family, and it will abide. Cultivate it in the community, and it will live and grow. Cultivate it in the state, and it will flourish abundantly. Cultivate it in the world, and it will become universal."[4] That is the proper course, and it's been that way throughout the more than twenty-five hundred years since Lao Tzu's time and probably for eons before that. It's another universal truth. All we need to do today is to redefine what constitutes virtue. Be more altruistic, and less greedy.

Of course, greed is a powerful motivator. Obviously! It's been driving this entire story. The problem today isn't that greed exists—as Bracciolini said, it is an inherent part of us—it is that we have obliterated all the collars on greed and allowed it to run rampant. We convinced ourselves that it is a virtuous thing, a moral thing. So while it's fine to encourage people to make small, personal improvements on their own, that isn't enough. We need to create the conditions that make that kind of action feasible for people. We need to reset the structure of our financial system, which has become badly warped because of this greed-as-virtue school of thought. We can acknowledge that greed exists without venerating it as a virtue. Money should be the reward for performing an action that contributes to society—it should come after the action—but we mashed them together and made money the reward *and* the action. That's the mix-up we need to unwind.

AND WE'RE BACK TO USURY

The most concrete and potentially consequential action we can take today, and one that isn't *too* hard to imagine actually happening, is to enact a big reset on interest rates and what is considered an allowable rate. We don't need to dig some rare mineral out of the earth or invent a new technology to do this. And it's not unnatural or impossible. There are limits on interest rates today, and rulers have capped rates since before Caesar. All we need is the gumption to call excessive interest what it is. This is about correcting a practice that does more to upset social balance than any other single financial transaction; excessive interest tilts the balance too far to a small group of creditors at the expense of everybody else. History shows this conclusively.

To be very clear, I'm not talking about banning lending. I'm talking about capping interest. For a thousand years, the Justinian code capped interest rates at 10 percent. Earlier Roman leaders capped it lower. The Catholic Church claimed *any* rate was usury. What is an acceptable rate for the service of lending today? Is it 5 percent? 10? 15? 30? We have allowed the creditors to set the terms here, and that was a mistake. The average credit card rate is 25 percent, and some charge as much as 35 percent;[5] they were as low as about 12 percent after the financial crisis and were around 16 percent in the 1990s.[6] Private student loan interest rates can go as high as 15 percent. Mortgage rates, by comparison, are relatively affordable. The average thirty-year fixed mortgage interest rate was about 7 percent in January 2025,[7] and had fallen to a decades-long low of about 3 percent during the pandemic. I can't say definitively right here right now what the "proper" rate is. I only know the current world of rates is far too high. These should be called what they are: excessive, predatory, *usurious* interest rates that should not be allowed.

How innovative are lenders, anyway? What are they actually doing to earn that money? If I walk into a pizzeria and order a pie, the pizza maker takes dough, sauce, cheese, maybe some pepperoni and mushrooms, puts them together, and cooks them. He transforms those separate ingredients into something new, and I pay him a modest fee for this service. A lender does absolutely nothing to money. It is no different when he gives it to me than it was when he acquired it. He does not enhance it in any manner. The only thing he's really doing is hoarding great gobs of it specifically to lend out. Sure, there is a demand for that service, and he deserves some compensation for his efforts. But there should be a limit. And if that hurts the banks and lenders, well, that's kind of too bad. JPMorgan made $372 billion in profit from 2008 through 2022.[8] I think they'll be okay. You want to spark economic activity? Put more of the money people pay to interest rates into their own wallets. Capping interest rates would provide huge benefits to the economy as a whole, and morally it's the right thing to do.

Now, there are obviously a whole host of proposed reforms that would be very familiar to everybody, on taxes, housing, education, healthcare that we could discuss here, but I'm not going to do that. They've been debated to death, and I want to spend the time we have left discussing things that haven't been talked about as much, or at all. I want to challenge us to think differently. And to help us do that, let's look at another idea from Jacob Coxey.

In 1913, the same year the Federal Reserve was created, Coxey presented a new plan to Congress at a hearing of the banking and currency committee. In the "Coxey Plan," he proposed establishing a government bank in every town with a population greater than one thousand. In smaller towns, these new banks would operate through the post office. Government-backed money would be printed and engraved just like postage stamps, and issued in enough quantities to support the economy. The money would be loaned out under standard terms, accepting standard collateral—and charging 2 percent interest.

Read that again: 2 percent!

And to Coxey, it wasn't even interest. He called it a tax. He figured half a percent would go toward the operation of this new banking system, and the rest would be government revenue. His flat-out stated goal was to eliminate interest. "Simply because the people have had interest thrust upon them for centuries is no reason why it should be continued," he wrote in a book he printed to explain the plan.[9] He estimated this would save the economy $1.5 billion a year (a lot back then), mostly by eliminating the interest paid to private bankers. It would put the private banking industry out of business, and that was its nearly explicit point. He noted that in his hometown of Massillon there were five banks, five bank presidents, five cashiers, five sets of clerks, and five buildings. They all charged about 8 percent interest. "Under my plan we would have only one bank president, one cashier, one set of clerks, one set of books and one bank building, loaning out $4 million at a tax of 2 percent," he wrote. Liquidity for the people, at rates they could afford. (He seemed uninterested in the spike in the local unemployment rate created by the suddenly unemployed bankers.)

The Coxey Plan as proposed clearly didn't get adopted, but some of the ideas animating it have actually started to float around again recently, in different forms. From the US Post Office's inception through the 1960s, it did offer a variety of banking services, not as a replacement for private banks but as a service to immigrants and others who had trouble getting accounts at private banks.[10] Post offices in some countries like France and the UK still offer banking services. Since the Panic of 2008 there's been a steady drumbeat of people proposing alternative systems as well. Most of them sound a lot like what Coxey proposed. The inspector general of the US Post Office in 2014 endorsed the idea of offering some banking services once again, seeing it as a way to help the so-called unbanked—those who can't qualify for accounts at commercial banks—and generate revenue for the post office at the same time.[11] In 2021, the post office started a very small pilot program in a handful of locations allowing people to buy gift cards with their payroll checks, a roundabout way to cash checks.[12] The gist of the question here is this: can we come up with a different way to provide banking services and provide credit for the public? The answer is almost certainly yes. Like I said, banking isn't magic.

REWIRING MONEY

Another unorthodox idea that's been mentioned a bit in recent years is making bank accounts available to the public at . . . the Federal Reserve, the US central bank. Let me explain. Many commercial banks maintain accounts with the Fed. The benefit to the banks is they can access the Fed's payments system directly and park money there that has no risk of disappearing. The Fed pays banks interest on that money, the same way a commercial bank pays an ordinary depositor. (The benefit to the Fed is that these banks are essentially the conduit between Fed policy and the real economy.)

You and I can't get these accounts, but there's no technical or technological reason for that, and if individuals could have that kind of account, well, it'd be a lot safer and more profitable than a commercial savings bank account; the Fed's rates on deposits are much better than what any commercial bank offers. The Fed's own rules are the only things standing in the way of this, but those could be changed, and in fact some people have suggested doing exactly that. In 2018, a group pitched something called the FedAccount program, which would open up the Fed's books to individuals, businesses, and institutions.[13] "The FedAccount program would bring genuinely transformational change to the monetary-financial system, in ways both obvious and unexpected," they wrote. A public institution like the Fed wouldn't operate on a profit-based motive, and these Fed accounts would be open to any American, which could solve the problem of the "unbanked" (a status that really shouldn't exist in our post-scarcity society). At the very least, this would end the reliance on payday lenders, check-cashing services, and other semi-banking services that prey on people without much money to begin with. It would have wider benefits as well. People and businesses would earn more on their savings than they do in regular banks: the Fed funds rate in January 2025 was 4.3 percent. Most savings accounts pay much less than 1 percent. Users would also save money because the Fed wouldn't impose all the fees private banks do. It would make the entire financial system more secure and less prone to financial crises because the ultimate counterparty in this system, the Fed, can't be forced into default. Forget about bank runs. You wind up with a more open, more sturdy financial system.

And, the paper's authors proposed using . . . *ta da!* . . . the post office as the physical storefront for FedAccounts. They'd house ATMs, and postal clerks would handle deposits and withdrawals as well. Now, the Fed can't just decide to do this unilaterally. It would take a literal act of Congress to make this happen. More importantly, the one very obvious loser in these plans is also one very powerful political player: private, commercial banks.

The Fed and other central banks have been toying with a somewhat similar idea lately: a digital dollar, or to use its formal-but-awkward name, a central bank digital currency (CBDC). This would basically just be a digital version of the US dollar or other currencies, something you could use within a digital wallet, sort of like your Venmo account. Unlike your Venmo account, though, the network would be operated by the central bank and the money would come directly from them. It would cut out all the middlemen. This *could* usher in a sea change in the economy, depending upon how it was structured. The crucial question is, who would host the accounts? Would it be your commercial bank? Or would it be the Fed itself? If it were the latter, it would be very similar to Coxey's plan and the Fed-Account plan, and like Coxey argued, it would represent a huge transfer of money away from interest payments and bank fees and back into people's (figurative, physical, and digital) wallets. Even if savings to consumers didn't lead to an immediate boost in consumption (i.e., people just held on to this found money), the effect of simply having more money in your bank account boosts your mental state and overall well-being, which indirectly improves the economy in so many little ways. But don't hold your breath for any of this to happen. The Fed has talked about it, but only in the most vague manner. They are nowhere near taking it seriously, to say nothing of implementing it. But it would be a really world-changing thing to do.

I do believe that at some point in the future we are going to get some version of these ideas anyhow. The one lasting good thing that bitcoin did was to show that you could construct a currency that could jump borders and operate in an open and transparent network. Central and commercial banks around the world are experimenting with ways to digitize currencies, the systems those currencies move through, and the markets for trading stocks, bonds, commodities, and other assets. Over the next decade or so we will see a fundamental rewiring of the global financial system. Access will become cheaper, the reach will become truly global. Entrepreneurs in Nairobi will be connected to investors in Kansas. The costs of offering people bank accounts and wealth-building opportunities will fall, and more players will get pulled into the formal global economy. It won't solve all our problems, but it will be better than what we have now. Truth be told, this is long overdue. Our current system is just a variation on what the Medici and Italian bankers built in the fourteenth and fifteenth centuries that's been jury-rigged and kitbashed over the eras. We need a fully digitized, internet-based, international, transparent, and open monetary system. What we cannot do, though, is bake into these new systems our antiquated, outdated ideas about money. These systems must be implemented with the ideas of creating tools to help people, not to have a new system where money makes more money.

THE REALLY BIG IDEA

As we've seen, money is not a real, objective thing in and of itself. It is a system devised by people, and because of that it is both fallible and can be manipulated. It also has fatal flaws: credit has a persistent habit of growing out of control until it swamps the debtors, and ultimately destabilizes society itself. And the pursuit of money fuels greed. This was true five thousand years ago and it is true today. We cannot just keep going on like this, spinning plates loaded with debt and hoping nothing collapses. The total public and private US debt is about $71 trillion.[14] Total global debt tops $300 trillion.[15] It is manifestly obvious that it will never all be paid back, and it is choking those least able to bear the burden, both on an individual and on a national level. We need to hit the reset button on the global credit system.

We need a modern, worldwide debt jubilee.

That sound you just heard was the audible gasp of the collective Western economic establishment. I know, I know, but stay with me here for a minute. Now, a debt jubilee is so far outside the mainstream of what anybody is talking about that it seems absurd to say it. Most people have never even heard of a debt jubilee. You'd have to explain the concept before you could even propose it, never mind convince people it was the right thing to do. And that's not even the hard part. Four thousand years ago, a king could unilaterally issue an edict erasing debt, because he was the king. Kings could do those sorts of things. Obviously there is no king of the world today, nor should there be. More importantly, the people and institutions that hold that debt aren't just rapacious payday lenders or predatory mortgagers who deserve to get wiped out. They're pension funds. And sovereign wealth funds. And governments. And central banks, and, yes, commercial banks. Forcing a $300 trillion loss on them would cause an economic crash, and that would be a huge mistake. So how do you wipe out debt without hurting the creditors? Well . . . money isn't real, right? Aristotle said it is within our power to change it if it isn't working for us. The answer therefore is simple: you print new money and give it to the creditors. What I propose is not actually erasing those debts but rather paying them off with newly printed money. Yes, I'm talking about having the world's governments print about $300 trillion worth of new currency to pay off the world's debts in full.

That sound you just heard was the entire Western economic establishment falling off its collective chair. That next sound, horrified and guttural, was them screaming "inflation!" while they try to pick themselves up off the floor. They're not entirely wrong. $300 trillion of freshly printed cash *could* be inflationary, unless the rollout was managed. What really drives inflation isn't money printing or credit creation. What really drives inflation are the beliefs and expectations of the people using a currency—in a word, faith. Let me give you one example of what I mean.

In the wake of the Panic of 2008, the Fed slashed interest rates and bought trillions worth of bonds from banks in order to save the banks and get "liquidity" back into the system. People howled that it would be inflationary, but it never was. During the Covid pandemic, the Fed again flooded the system with trillions worth of liquidity. This time inflation took off. There's no single reason why inflation rises, but consider this: After the financial crisis in 2008, then–Fed chairman Ben Bernanke managed people's expectations, speaking time and time again about how the Fed was going to control inflation, how it wasn't going to let it get out of hand. By contrast, in an August 2020 speech at Jackson Hole, Wyoming, the current Fed chair, Jerome Powell, did something that to my knowledge no other Fed chairman has ever done. He literally came out and said the Fed was going to let inflation rise. And can you guess what happened? Inflation rose. The chairman created a perception, and the people responded to it. Inflation is not, as Milton Friedman claimed, a monetary phenomenon. Like the value of money itself, it is a *psychological* phenomenon.

So, how do we manage expectations and keep inflation from exploding? Two ways. One, the world's central banks do what they always do: manage interest rates to keep the economy steady and be very public about their intention to manage people's expectations. Second, we implement global price controls across the board, temporarily, until the system resets itself. The governments of the world would have to step in and put caps on the prices of everything from commodities like grains and steel to finished products like gallons of milk, iPhones, and cars.

Um, I think the entire Western economic establishment just passed out. Somebody get the smelling salts.

How could you justify doing all this? Well, for one thing, it would correct a historical mistake. Human society has lived with the concept of across-the-board debt relief for longer than we've lived without it. The people who created money understood this; sometimes you need to hit the reset button to restore balance. But even if you're not a history buff, you can still justify a global jubilee both morally and economically. The global debt burden falls heaviest on the countries least able to afford it. Places like Ethiopia, Zambia, Laos, Kenya, Sri Lanka, Chad. In Kenya, for example, just making debt payments comprises 60 percent of all government spending.[16] Nearly two dozen African countries spend more than a quarter of all their government revenue on debt. Ethiopia defaulted in 2023. Sri Lanka defaulted and then their economy collapsed. It is immoral to expect these countries to bear this burden. Those debts should be erased so these countries can get a chance to rebuild themselves and provide proper lives for their citizens. And on an individual country level sometimes debts are restructured or even written off, but wiping all of it out in one grand sweep would be so much more effective. This would also help the millions of Americans who are struggling with debt. You've already seen the movement to write off student loans. I'm just taking that line of reasoning a step further.

And if the historical or moral argument doesn't entice the establishment, how about this: can you imagine the economic boom it would unleash? Trillions of dollars used on debt payments would suddenly become free cash flow. Whatever you pay out a month in mortgages or credit card bills or auto loans or student loans, imagine that all becomes cash in your pocket. There'd be a *huge* wealth effect. It'd be like Christmas Day every day, all over the world. The burst in spending would be unprecedented. It would help companies, too; they could clean up their balance sheets and not having to service their debt would give them an opportunity to use the cash coming in the door to help them expand, surely an economic positive. And it would free up governments all over the world weighed down by debt. For creditors, there might be some tax implications, but we could easily rewrite the tax codes to take care of that. To be clear, I am not talking about erasing debt forever. I'm talking about wiping out the debt we have now. I'm proposing we zero out the global balance sheet and start over (albeit with healthier attitudes toward money). Money is a useful tool, and a debt jubilee would open up a new opportunity to use it. Governments would be freed up to borrow money to do all the public-works projects they currently can't. People and businesses would be freed up to borrow money to start new businesses or expand existing ones.

There is semi-recent precedent for all of this, too. After World War II, the Allied forces forgave the debts of Germany and Japan, allowing those two countries to rebuild their shattered nations. Today Germany is the third largest economy in the world. Japan is fourth. Debt forgiveness is right both morally *and* economically. And really, who'd be hurt by it? The creditors are getting paid. The debtors are being released. As long as you have the Fed and other central banks assuring everybody that the system will go on as it did before, stock markets will remain open, lenders will remain willing to lend, and people would fall in line. Yes, there are a million logistical issues I haven't even begun to address, but those are just details. What causes panics is a surprise. If everybody understood what was going to happen with this plan, it would be the feel-good story of the millennium! And if the historical or moral or economic arguments don't sway you, look at it another way: If we do nothing and just keep going, the collapse of the US government and financial system is virtually guaranteed. And that will be a global catastrophe.

Right now the world loves the United States. How do I know this? They keep buying our debt. In 2024, the federal government collected $4.92 trillion in revenue and spent $6.75 trillion.[17] The difference of $1.8 trillion was made up by the Treasury Department selling bonds. And it has no problem selling bonds. Every treasury offering is "oversubscribed," meaning there are more people bidding for the debt than there is debt to go around. That's because US bonds are the safest asset in the world; indeed, the entire global financial system is built on top of them. This confidence allows us to overspend year after year after year without worrying about the consequences. As a result, we have accrued a total federal debt of about $36 trillion (a number that will definitely be higher when this book is published than it was when it went to the printers). That debt is roughly 120 percent of our GDP ($27 trillion in 2023). The ratio of those two is a key barometer of a nation's solvency. While 120 percent sounds high, it's not worrying anybody in the bond market, at least not enough to scare anybody off buying US bonds. Why?

For all the doomscreaming you hear about unsustainable debts, the fact of the matter is that right now, the US debt is sustainable. The federal government pays its debts and there isn't any real question about its ability to do so. That's because the government not only takes in trillions in revenue, and gets trillions more in bond issuance, but it could quickly tap more sources of revenue if it ever had to: It could raise taxes on the wealthiest country in the world. If that didn't work, it could sell off assets; how much do you think all that federal land out west would bring in? Or an aircraft carrier or two? Or our copy of the Magna Carta? The government has all kinds of ways to make itself whole. Nobody is seriously worried about an imminent collapse of the federal government. However, everybody knows that one day this game will run out. One day paying interest on the debt alone will swamp government revenues, to say nothing of defense spending or public services or even keeping the Lincoln Memorial open. One day, if we don't change course, we will have a debt crisis. It is inevitable. The only question is when.

It's not hard to do the math and come up with a date. Researchers at Penn Wharton in 2023 figured we had about twenty years[18] before the debt-to-GDP ratio reached 200 percent, and at that point no amount of tax increases or spending cuts could keep the government from defaulting on its debt. This wouldn't be some kind of technical default, some political dogfight, this would be a full-fledged default. Others may put the threshold at different levels and come up with their own timelines, but the bottom line is that if we don't alter our public finances a crash and debt crisis is inevitable.

Those are ugly. In 2022, the government in Sri Lanka—after years of overspending, especially during the pandemic[19]—found itself unable to make its bond payments and defaulted.[20] The result was a crisis that engulfed the island nation and cratered its economy. Average people were battered; public anger resulted in protesters storming the president's office and driving him out of the country. The new government negotiated with its creditors, but that wasn't apparent to the people on the street. A nation that already had high levels of poverty was crushed.[21] Just feeding people became a challenge. Prices surged, putting medicine out of reach for some. Schools closed due to fuel shortages. Yes, the United States is a richer country than Sri Lanka. But don't kid yourself; our coming debt crisis will be really painful for millions of Americans. And since the US controls the world's reserve currency, and its bonds are the foundation of the international financial system, a US default would be globally cataclysmic.

The usual scolds argue that we need to either cut spending or raise taxes to address this. And of course our government officials do neither, because both of those actions would involve significant pain. So we sleepwalk into a crisis, and for what? A made-up thing called money. We don't have to do this. We don't have to let countries like Sri Lanka and Kenya and Zambia—and the United States—become consumed by some idea called debt. It is fully within our power to change it. All we need to do is reset the ledger, acknowledging the reality that those debts are never going to be repaid and shouldn't be. Debt isn't supposed to last forever. The people who invented it knew that. We've just forgotten.

So what will it be? Nosebleed taxes or cutting Social Security and Medicare, throwing millions into chaos and endangering their lives? Waiting for an inevitable meltdown and crisis and the global financial panic that would follow? Or simply resetting the ledger, starting over, avoiding calamity, and sparking a new economic boom? I know which one I'd vote for.

The combined goal of all these ideas is to re-create the monetary system in a way that makes it more open and fair so we can take advantage of our ability to provide everybody around the world with all the basics they need to survive. One thing working in favor of rediscovering Bracciolini's original ethos of balancing individual greed against the collective benefits it can bring is this movement into a "post-scarcity" society. For more than five thousand years, our entire lives have been hemmed in by scarcity, how much land we had, how much water we had, how much lumber we had, how much we could grow and build. Those things are not going to be a constraint anymore. There is going to be more than enough for every single person on the planet, and once that reality filters through to the mainstream it will change the way we view everything. It'll be a while before people really get it. We're going to have to help them see it.

Of course, even I don't think we will ever live in some utopia where people lead these completely altruistic lives. Greed is a part of us. Trying to eradicate it would be like trying to eradicate left hands (and I'm left-handed). People will still have wants and desires, there will be a market for those wants and desires, and others will try to make a profit selling goods to fulfill those wants. And that's fine! There's nothing wrong with that, nothing at all. The goal isn't to create a utopia, the goal is to create a society that is in balance between people, providing everybody the maximum freedom to pursue their own individual goals and desires. We don't have to be at each other's throats anymore, imagining we live in a world of limited resources. We can get there. We really can. We just have to focus.

Look, it's hard to argue that money and greed haven't been successful motivating factors, even if they were and are blunt instruments that have caused a lot of harm in the process. Bracciolini wasn't wrong about avarice sometimes being beneficial. In the fourteenth century the bubonic plague wiped out half of Europe; today it is easily cured with antibiotics. There are more people living longer, healthier, more comfortable lives today than at any point in human history. In the nineteenth century it took arduous, dangerous months to cross the North American continent. Today you could drive from New York to Los Angeles on a smooth, paved superhighway in a week, or fly there in five hours, and you even have Wi-Fi access at thirty-three thousand feet. We put a man on the moon. We sent probes out beyond the solar system. The world's farmers grow enough food to feed ten billion people. The internet has made information virtually free. There is no material limit to how much housing could be built. We will eventually figure out clean, limitless energy. We built all that on top of one of our worst impulses. Imagine what we could do if we started from a somewhat higher base.

ACKNOWLEDGMENTS

Writing is a solitary pursuit. Publishing is a group effort. You are reading these words because a lot of people had a hand in ensuring you read them.

My agent, Gillian MacKenzie, first heard the scattershot ideas that would end up being this book in the spring of 2020. She helped straighten out the narrative, fill in the gaps, and hammer together something that could be sold commercially. And of course Gillian made some money from her efforts, but I'm telling you whatever she earned off me wasn't equal to the time and effort she poured into making sure this book found a publisher.

My thanks to the team at St. Martin's, especially my editor, Tim Bartlett, who recognized this book's potential and championed it. This is the third time Tim and I have collaborated, and that familiarity made working on this book a breeze, even when he (correctly) pushed me to rewrite (and rewrite, and rewrite, and rewrite) the parts that weren't working. If this book made sense to you, you can thank Tim for that. Tim's partner in editing, Kevin Reilly, added a number of thoughtful and sharp insights on the early drafts that improved this book. Thanks also to Jonathan Bush, Hannah

Jones, Michelle Cashman, Ginny Perrin, Gail Friedman, Gabrielle Gantz, and Laura Clark.

I first started putting this book together when I was still a reporter at *The Wall Street Journal,* and several editors there were supportive of it, including Jenna Telesca, Charles Forelle, and Karen Pensiero. I spent most of my professional life at the *Journal* and Dow Jones, and all of the ideas that became this book first occurred to me while working there. I am indebted to these editors and others who always indulged my often *seemingly* whacky ideas (I was, of course, always right).

I am also indebted to a number of people who supported me in various ways while writing this book, including Sam Favate, Randy Williams, Jeremiah Owyang, Francesco Rulli, my coauthor, Michael Casey, Mark McClusky, Tara Wellema, Spencer Jakab, John Shipman, Simon Constable, and as always, my mother, Michele, and sister, Jeanne-Michele.

Most importantly, I want to thank my wife and son. Robert has been my motivation ever since he came into our lives, and this entire book can be read as a father trying to understand the world around him and make it better for his son. Elizabeth has been not only my best friend but also the biggest supporter of my writing going all the way back to Montclair High in 1986 when she literally dragged me by the hand into a meeting of the literary magazine to force me to share my writing. And she is still my biggest booster, through the years of trying to pull this story together and taking care of things around the house while I squirreled myself away and wrote. As much as anybody, she is responsible for this book existing.

Lastly, if you've read this far, I want to thank *you.* Words are just words; if this book has any currency in this world, it will be because of people such as you who value it. Molto grazie.

NOTES

Introduction

1. John Searle, *The Construction of Social Reality* (Free Press, 1995).
2. Paola Zaninotto, et al., "Socioeconomic Inequalities in Disability-Free Life Expectancy in Older People from England and the United States: A Cross-National Population-Based Study," *The Journals of Gerontology,* Jan. 15, 2020.
3. A. N. Wilson, "What the 20th Century Did to Christianity," *Catholic Herald,* July 12, 2018, https://catholicherald.co.uk/what-the-20th-century-did-to-christianity/.
4. Jeffrey M. Jones, "Belief in God in U.S. Dips to 81%, a New Low," Gallup, June 17, 2022, https://news.gallup.com/poll/393737/belief-god-dips-new-low.aspx.
5. Aaron Zitner, "America Pulls Back from Values That Once Defined It, WSJ-NORC Poll Finds," *The Wall Street Journal,* March 27, 2023, https://www.wsj.com/articles/americans-pull-back-from-values-that-once-defined-u-s-wsj-norc-poll-finds-df8534cd.
6. Eric Holtz-Giminez, Miguel A. Altieri, et al., "We Already Grow Enough Food for 10 Billion People . . . and Still Can't End Hunger," *Journal of Sustainable Agriculture,* July 2012.
7. Casey Crownhart, "Yes, We Have Enough Materials to Power the World with Renewable Energy," *MIT Technology Review,* Jan. 31, 2023, https://www.technologyreview.com/2023/01/31/1067444/we-have-enough-materials-to-power-world-with-renewables.
8. Mehran Moalem, "We Could Power the Entire World by Harnessing Solar Energy from 1% of the Sahara," *Forbes,* Sept. 22,

2016, https://www.forbes.com/sites/quora/2016/09/22/we-could
-power-the-entire-world-by-harnessing-solar-energy-from-1-of
-the-sahara.

9. John Burn-Murdoch, "Repeat After Me: Building Any New
Housing Reduces Housing Costs for All," *Financial Times,* Sept.
15, 2023.

10. "How Many Houses Are in the World?" *Architecture & Design,* Nov.
11, 2021, https://www.architectureanddesign.com.au/features/list
/how-many-houses-are-in-the-world.

11. Simon Patten, *The New Basis of Civilization* (Macmillan Company, 1907), 10–11.

1. In God We Trust

1. Yuval Noah Harari, *Sapiens: A Brief History of Humankind* (Harper,
2015).

2. Madain Project, Encyclopedia of Abrahamic History & Archaeol-
ogy, https://madainproject.com/uruk.

3. William B. Hafford, "Mesopotamian City Life Four Thousand
Years Ago," *Expedition Magazine* 60, no. 1, May 2018, https://
www.penn.museum/sites/expedition/mesopotamian-city-life/.

4. Dr. Senta German, "Sumer: An Introduction," LibreText Humanities, https://human.libretexts.org/Bookshelves/Art/SmartHistory
_of_Art/02%3A_Ancient_Mediterranean/2.02%3A_Ancient
_Near_East.

5. Joshua J. Mark, "Daily Life in Ancient Mesopotamia," *World History Encyclopedia,* April 15, 2014, https://www.worldhistory.org
/article/680/daily-life-in-ancient-mesopotamia/.

6. Marvin A. Powell, "Money in Mesopotamia," *Journal of the Economic and Society History of the Orient* 39, no. 3 (1996).

7. Michael Hudson, "Origins of Money and Interest: Palatial Credit,
Not Barter," *Handbook of the History of Money and Currency,* Nov.
8, 2018.

8. Marty E. Stevens, *Temples, Tithes, and Taxes* (Baker Academic,
2006).

9. Ibid., 152.

10. Michael Hudson, "The Lost Tradition of Biblical Debt Cancellations," Henry George School of Social Science, 1993,
https://michael-hudson.com/wp-content/uploads/2010/03
/HudsonLostTradition.pdf.

11. Ibid.

12. Michael Hudson and Charles Goodhart, "Could/Should Jubilee

Debt Cancellations Be Reintroduced Today?" Center for Economic Policy Research, Jan. 16, 2018.

13. The story is contained in the Book of Nehemiah.
14. Kabir Seghal, *Coined: The Rich Life of Money and How Its History Has Shaped Us* (Grand Central Publishing, 2015), 109.
15. Aristotle, *Nicomachean Ethics*, book IV, chapter 4, in *Aristotle: On Man in the Universe* (Walter J. Black Inc., 1943).
16. Aristotle, *Nicomachean Ethics*, book IV, chapter 5.
17. Aristotle, *Nicomachean Ethics*, book V, chapter 8.
18. Aristotle, *Politics*, book I, chapter 10, in *Aristotle: On Man in the Universe* (Walter J. Black Inc., 1943).
19. Aristotle, *Nicomachean Ethics*, book IV, chapter 3.
20. In book VIII of the *Republic*, Plato describes these rulers as people who took wealth from the rich and gave it to the poor.
21. Plutarch, *The Parallel Lives*, vol. X.

2. The Last Jubilee

1. Luke 4:14–30.
2. Isaiah 61.
3. Will Durant, *Caesar and Christ* (Simon & Schuster, 1935), 330–333.
4. Worker revolts were not unheard of in the ancient world. The first one ever recorded occurred around 1170 BCE in Egypt when workers building the pyramids went on strike because they weren't getting paid.
5. Tacitus, *Annals*, book VI, chapter 15.
6. There is a small but persistent corner of academia that argues Jesus never even existed, that the entire story portrayed in the Gospels is a mash-up of existing myths. We're not going to get bogged down in that debate here.
7. Josephus, *Antiquities of the Jews*, books 18 and 20.
8. Tacitus, *Annals*, book XV, chapter 44.
9. Colin J. Humphreys and W. G. Waddington, "Dating the Crucifixion," *Nature* 306, Dec. 22, 1983, https://www.nature.com/articles /306743a0.
10. Marty E. Stevens, *Temples, Tithes, and Taxes* (Baker Academic, 2006).
11. Micah 3:11.
12. Kaufmann Kohler and Emil G. Hirsch, "Crucifixion," *Jewish Encyclopedia*, https://www.jewishencyclopedia.com/articles/4782 -crucifixion.

3. Everything Is Done for Money

1. Joshua Vincent, "Historical, Religious and Scholastic Prohibition of Usury: The Common Origins of Western and Islamic Financial Practices," 2014, Law School Student Scholarship, 600, Seton Hall Law, https://scholarship.shu.edu/student_scholarship /600.
2. Dr. Ludwig Pastor, *The History of the Popes from the Close of the Middle Ages,* vol. 1 (Kegan Paul, Trench, Trubner & Co., 1906).
3. Michael Creighton, *A History of the Papacy During the Time of the Reformation,* vol. 1 (Houghton, Mifflin & Co., 1882).
4. A. D. Fraser Jenkins, "Cosimo de' Medici's Patronage of Architecture and the Theory of Magnificence," *Journal of the Warburg and Courtauld Institutes* 33 (1970), https://www.jstor.org/stable /750894.
5. Robert S. Lopez, *The Commercial Revolution of the Middle Ages* (Prentice Hall, 1971), 60.
6. Ibid., 57.
7. Arthur White, *Plague and Pleasure* (The Catholic University of America Press, 2014).
8. Phyllis Walter Goodhart Gordan, *Two Renaissance Book Hunters: The Letter of Poggius Bracciolini and Nicolaus de Niccolis* (Columbia University Press, 1974), 129.
9. Benjamin G. Kohl and Ronald G. Witt, *The Earthly Republic, Italian Humanists on Government and Society* (University of Pennsylvania Press, 1978), 237.
10. Gordan, *Two Renaissance Book Hunters,* 131.
11. Kohl and Witt, *The Earthly Republic,* 237.
12. B. L. Ullman, *The Origin and Development of Humanistic Script* (Edizioni di Storia e Letteratura, 1960).
13. Stephen Greenblatt, *The Swerve* (W. W. Norton & Co., 2012).
14. Peter Howard, "Creating Magnificence in Renaissance Florence," presentation at The Power of Luxury: Art and Culture at the Italian Courts in Machiavelli's Lifetime Symposium, Feb. 19–20, 2013.
15. Peter Howard, *Creating Magnificence in Renaissance Florence* (Center for Reformation and Renaissance Studies, 2012), 57.

4. The Magnificent Man

1. Many of these details come from Vespasiano da Bisticci, who wrote biographies of de' Medici and other famous Italians, many of whom he knew personally. His *Lives of Illustrious Men of the*

XVth Century, written in the fifteenth century, was not published until 1839; the modern translation I consulted is titled *Renaissance Princes, Popes, and Prelates* (Harper Torchbooks, 1963).

2. Raymond de Roover, *The Rise and Decline of the Medici Bank, 1397–1494* (W. W. Norton, 1966), 35.

3. Phyllis Walter Goodhart Gordan, *Two Renaissance Book Hunters: The Letters of Poggius Bracciolini to Nicolaus de Niccolis*, letter LXVI (Columbia University Press, 1974), 137.

4. Raymond de Roover, *The Medici Bank, Its Organization, Management, Operations, and Decline* (New York University Press, 1948).

5. Ibid.

6. Ibid.

7. Ibid.

8. "New York Public Library Unveils $1 Billion Transformation Plan," New York Public Library, March 11, 2008, https://www.nypl.org/audiovideo/new-york-public-library-unveils-1-billion-transformation-plan.

9. Colin Moynihan, "To Honor Gift, Public Library Will Add Donor's Name a 6th Time," *The New York Times*, Feb. 28, 2019, https://www.nytimes.com/2019/02/28/arts/design/to-honor-gift-public-library-will-add-donors-name-a-6th-time.html.

10. "Saint Barnabas Medical Center Receives $100 Million from Cooperman Family," RWJBarnabas Health, Sept. 30, 2021, https://www.rwjbh.org/blog/2021/september/saint-barnabas-medical-center-receives-100-milli/.

11. https://www.opensecrets.org/search?q=leon+cooperman&type=donors.

12. https://www.opensecrets.org/search?order=desc&q=stephen+schwarzman&sort=D&type=donors.

13. https://www.forbes.com/sites/phoebeliu/2023/10/03/the-forbes-philanthropy-score-2023-how-charitable-are-the-richest-americans/.

14. https://www.opensecrets.org/elections-overview/biggest-donors?cycle=2022&view=om.

15. Benjamin G. Kohl and Ronald G. Witt, *The Earthly Republic: Italian Humanists on Government and Society* (University of Pennsylvania Press, 1978), 256.

16. Ibid., 260.

17. Ibid., 262.

18. Ibid., 264.

19. Janet Ross, *Lives of the Early Medici, as Told in Their Correspondence* (Gorham Press, 1911), 24.
20. Ibid., 22.
21. Peter Howard, "'A Paradise Where Devils Dwell': Francis William Kent and Renaissance Florence," in *Studies on Florence and the Italian Renaissance in Honour of F.W. Kent*, ed. Cecilia Hewlett and Peter Howard (Turnhout: Brepols, 2016), 1–32.
22. Patricia Rubin, "Magnificence and the Medici," in *The Early Medici and Their Artists*, ed. Francis Ames-Lewis (University of London, 1995), 41.
23. Vespasiano da Bisticci, *Renaissance Princes, Popes, and Prelates* (Harper Torchbooks, 1963), 228–229.

5. The Bishop of Rome

1. Janet Ross, *Lives of the Early Medici, as Told in Their Correspondence* (Gorham Press, 1911), 47.
2. Arthur White, *Plague and Pleasure, The Renaissance World of Pius II* (The Catholic University of America Press, 2014), 95. .
3. Lila Yawn, "Culiseo: The Roman Colosseum in Early Modern Jest," *California Italian Studies* 6, no. 1, 2016, https://escholarship.org/uc/item/40s8d6sq.
4. Mandell Creighton, *A History of the Papacy*, vol. 1 (Houghton, Mifflin & Co., 1882), 12.
5. Bartolomeo Platina, *The Lives of the Popes* (Griffith, Farran, Okeden & Welsh), 235.
6. Mandell Creighton, *A History of the Papacy*, vol. 3 (Longmans, Green and Co., 1903), 98.
7. Vespasiano da Bisticci, *Renaissance Princes, Popes, and Prelates* (Harper Torchbooks, 1963), 31.
8. Creighton, *A History of the Papacy*, vol. 3, 99.
9. da Bisticci, *Renaissance Princes, Popes, and Prelates*, 32.
10. Creighton, *A History of the Papacy*, vol. 3, 100.
11. Ibid., 102.
12. da Bisticci, *Renaissance Princes, Popes, and Prelates*.
13. Dr. Ludwig Pastor, *The History of the Popes from the Close of the Middle Ages*, vol.1 (Kegan Paul, Trench, Trubner & Co., 1906), 165.
14. Ibid., 171.
15. Ibid., 193.
16. Ibid., 194.
17. Erica Kinias, "Trevi Fountain," *The Theater That Was Rome*,

Brown University, https://library.brown.edu/projects/rome/essays/NuovoTeatro85/.

18. Flavia Cantatore, *A Renaissance Architecture of Power: Princely Palaces in the Italian Quattrocento* (Brill, 2015).
19. B. Platina, *The Lives of the Popes* (Griffith, Farran, Okeden & Welsh), 249.
20. Pastor, *History of the Popes,* vol. 1 (1855), 161.
21. Ibid., 155.

6. The Balance Sheet

1. Most of the details concerning Cotrugli and his book come from a 2017 English-language translation of *The Book of the Art of the Trade,* edited by Carlo Carraro and Giovanni Favero and published by Palgrave Macmillan.
2. Benedetto Cotrugli, *The Book of the Art of the Trade,* edited by Carlo Carraro and Giovanni Favero (Palgrave Macmillan, 2017), 95.
3. Ibid., 78.
4. Ibid., 150.
5. Ibid., 88.
6. Ibid., 10.
7. James Aho, *Confession and Bookkeeping* (State University of New York Press, 2005), 37.
8. Ibid., 23.
9. Raymond de Roover, *The Rise and Decline of the Medici Bank, 1397–1494* (W. W. Norton, 1966), 12.
10. Revelation 20:11–15.
11. Aho, *Confession and Bookkeeping,* 28.
12. Ibid., 28.
13. de Roover, *The Rise and Decline of the Medici Bank,* 18.
14. John Dyment, *Meet the Men Who Sailed the Seas* (Random House, 1966).
15. The Treaty of Tordesillas, 1494.

7. The Medici Pope

1. E. R. Chamberlin, *The Bad Popes* (Dorset Press, 1969), 212.
2. Ibid., 223.
3. Ibid., 214–217.
4. Ibid., 239.
5. Paul F. Pavao, "John Tetzel," *Christian History for Everyman,* https://www.christian-history.org/john-tetzel.html.

6. Ludwig Pastor, *The History of the Popes from the Close of the Middle Ages,* vol. 3 (Kegan, Trench, Paul, Trubner & Co., 1908), 294–297.
7. Martin Luther, *95 Theses,* 1517.
8. Pastor, *History of the Popes,* vol. 3, 362.
9. John Calvin, *A Compend of Calvin's Institutes* (Board of Christian Education of the Presbyterian Church in the United States of America, 1939), iv.
10. Ibid., 34–35.
11. Ibid., 114.
12. Ibid.
13. Ibid., 112.
14. Steven Wedgeworth, "John Calvin on the Use of Goods and Money," *The Calvinist International,* Aug. 10, 2017, https://calvinistinter national.com/2017/08/10/john-calvin-on-the-use-of-goods-and -money/.
15. John Calvin, "Commentary on Corinthians," vol. 2, 2 Corinthians 8:15, ccel.org/ccel/calvin/calcom40.xiv.iii.html.
16. John Calvin, *The Institutes of the Christian Religion* (Presbyterian Board of Publication, 1813), Book III, chapter 8.
17. Ibid.
18. Max Weber, *The Protestant Ethic and the Spirit of Capitalism* (Pantianos Classics, 1930), 87.
19. Richard Baxter, *A Christian Directory,* vol. 1, 1664–1665, chapter X, part I, monergism.com/christian-directory-4-ebook-set.
20. Ibid., vol. 1, chapter X, part I.
21. Weber, *The Protestant Ethic,* 165.
22. Baxter, *A Christian Directory,* vol. 1, chapter IV, part VI, moner gism.com/christian-directory-4-ebook-set.
23. Weber, *The Protestant Ethic,* 88.
24. Ibid., 168.
25. Ibid., 95.
26. Ibid., 93.
27. Ibid., 94.
28. Timothy D. Terrell, "What Calvinism Did for Economics," *Chalcedon Magazine,* Jan. 1, 2014, https://chalcedon.edu/magazine /what-calvinism-did-for-economics.

8. The Age of Avarice

1. Mandell Creighton, *A History of the Papacy,* vol. III (Longmans, Green & Co., 1903), 146.

2. Philip D. Curtin, *The Rise and Fall of the Plantation Complex* (Cambridge University Press, 1990), 25.

3. Mark Gollom, "Why Pope Francis May Be Hesitant to Rescind the Doctrine of Discovery," *CBC News*, July 30, 2022, https://www.cbc.ca/news/canada/pope-francis-doctrine-discovery-indigenous-1.6536174.

4. Gonzalo Fernández de Oviedo y Valdés, "Historia general y natural de las Indias," chapter 6, https://earlyfloridalit.net/rodrigo-ranjel-from-%E2%80%9Caccount-of-de-soto-from-gonzalo-fernandez-de-oviedo-y-valdes-historia-general-y-natural-de-las-indias/.

5. Curtin, *The Rise and Fall of the Plantation Complex*, 3.

6. Robin Blackburn, *The Making of New World Slavery: From the Baroque to the Modern, 1492–1800* (Verso, 1997), 127.

7. Ibid., 132.

8. Eric Williams, *Capitalism and Slavery* (University of North Carolina Press, 1944), 3.

9. Blackburn, *The Making of New World Slavery,* 133.

10. Ibid.

11. Williams, *Capitalism and Slavery,* 6.

12. Ibid., 7.

13. Ibid., 26.

14. Blackburn, *The Making of New World Slavery,* 137.

15. Edward Gibbon Wakefield, *A View of the Art of Colonization* (1830), https://historyofeconomicthought.mcmaster.ca/wakefield/colonize.pdf.

16. Williams, *Capitalism and Slavery,* 39.

17. Paul Finkelman, "Thomas R.R. Cobb and the Law of Negro Slavery," *Roger Williams University Law Review* 5, no. 1 (Fall 1999), https://docs.rwu.edu/cgi/viewcontent.cgi?article=1170&context=rwu_LR.

18. Alexander H. Stephens, "Cornerstone Address," March 21, 1861, learningforjustice.org/classroom-resources/texts/hard-history/cornerstone-speech.

19. Thomas Read Rootes Cobb, *An Inquiry into the Law of Negro Slavery in the United States of America* (W. Thorne Williams, 1858). If you really want to try and read the thing for yourself, just to see, you can find a copy at the Internet Archive's Open Library: https://archive.org/details/inquiryintolawof01cobbiala/page/n7/mode/2up.

20. Martin Luther King Jr., "MLK's Forgotten Call for Economic Justice," *The Nation*, March 14, 1966.

9. Talk to the (Invisible) Hand

1. Charles Mackay, *Extraordinary Popular Delusions* (Dover Publications, 2003), based on the original 1841 text.
2. John Flynn, *Men of Wealth* (Simon & Schuster, 1941).
3. Mackay, *Extraordinary Popular Delusions*.
4. Janet Gleeson, *Millionaire: The Philanderer, Gambler, and Duelist Who Invented Modern Finance* (Simon & Schuster, 2000).
5. "Our History," London Stock Exchange, https://www.londonstockexchange.com/discover/lseg/our-history.
6. Lodewijk Petram, *The World's First Stock Exchange* (Columbia University Press, 2014).
7. Anne Goldgar, *Tulipmania: Money, Honor, and Knowledge in the Dutch Golden Age* (University of Chicago Press, 2008).
8. Adam Smith, *An Inquiry into the Nature and Causes of the Wealth of Nations* (Encyclopedia Britannica, 1952), v.
9. *Great Books of the Western World* (Encyclopedia Britannica, 1952).
10. Smith, *The Wealth of Nations*, 348.
11. Adam Smith, *The Theory of Moral Sentiments* (Wells and Lilly, 1817), 245.

10. A More Perfect Union

1. Sean Condon, *Shays's Rebellion: Authority and Distress in Post-Revolutionary America* (Johns Hopkins University Press, 2015), 90.
2. Leonard Richards, *Shays's Rebellion: The American Revolution's Final Battle* (University of Pennsylvania Press, 2002).
3. Charles Beard, *An Economic Interpretation of the Constitution of the United States* (The Macmillan Company, 1913), 27.
4. Ibid., 24.
5. Edward H. Davidson and William J. Scheick, *Paine, Scripture, and Authority* (Associated University Press, 1988), 88.
6. Robert Thomas Malthus, *An Essay on the Principle of Population* (Penguin Books, 1976), 119.
7. Ibid., 118.
8. Ibid., 72.
9. Ibid., 270.
10. Nicki Lisa Cole, "Biography of Harriet Martineau," ThoughtCo., https://www.thoughtco.com/harriet-martineau-3026476.

11. Ted Hovet, "Harriet Martineau's Exceptional American Narratives: Harriet Beecher Stowe, John Brown, and the 'Redemption of Your National Soul,'" *American Studies* 48, no. 1 (Spring 2007): 63–76.
12. Cole, "Biography of Harriet Martineau."
13. Charles Darwin, letter to Caroline Darwin, Nov. 9, 1836, Darwin Correspondence Project, https://www.darwinproject.ac.uk/letter/DCP-LETT-321.xml.
14. Peter Vorzimmer, "Darwin, Malthus, and the Theory of Natural Selection," *Journal of the History of Ideas* 30, no. 4 (Oct.–Dec. 1969), https://www.jstor.org/stable/2708609.
15. Paul Vigna, "Is Bitcoin the Future, or an Echo of a Failed Past?" *The Wall Street Journal,* June 19, 2018.
16. James Medbery, *Men and Mysteries of Wall Street* (Fields, Osgood and Co., 1870), 174.
17. Ron Chernow, *Titan: The Life of John D. Rockefeller, Sr.* (Vintage, 2004).

11. Class Struggle

1. John O'Sullivan, "Annexation," *The United States Magazine and Democratic Review,* vol. 17, 1845.
2. David McLellan, *Karl Marx* (Penguin Books, 1975), 8.
3. Francis Wheelan, *Karl Marx* (Fourth Estate, 1999), 14.
4. Ryan Moore, "How Young Karl Marx Got Radicalized," *Jacobin,* Dec. 26, 2023, https://jacobin.com/2023/12/young-karl-marx-hegel-liberalism-social-democracy.
5. William D. Harpine, "Bryan's 'A Cross of Gold': The Rhetoric of Polarization at the 1896 Democratic Convention," *Quarterly Journal of Speech* 87 (2001): 291–304.
6. This transcript includes an audio recording of Bryan delivering a portion of the speech, made twenty-five years after he first delivered it: https://historymatters.gmu.edu/d/5354/.
7. Ibid.
8. Paul F. Boller, *Presidential Campaigns: From George Washington to George W. Bush* (Oxford University Press, 2004), 168.
9. Harpine, "Bryan's 'A Cross of Gold.'"
10. *The Nation* 63, no. 1620 (July 16, 1896), available at https://www.thenation.com/article/archive/july-9-1896-william-jennings-bryan-delivers-cross-of-gold-speech/.
11. Andrew Carnegie, "Wealth," *North American Review* 148 (June 1889).

12. Andrew Carnegie, *Autobiography of Andrew Carnegie* (Houghton Mifflin Co., 1920).

12. Make the Sign of the Dollar

1. Adam Buick, "Karl Marx and the Abolition of Money," *The Socialist Standard*, April 1980, https://www.worldsocialism.org/spgb /socialist-standard/1980/1980s/no-908-april-1980/karl-marx-and -the-abolition-of-money/.
2. Harry Schwartz, *Russia's Soviet Economy* (Prentice Hall, 1961), 468.
3. Ibid., 470–471.
4. Ibid., 468.
5. Abram Bergson, "On Inequality of Incomes in the USSR," *American Slavic and Eastern European Review* 10, no. 2 (April 1951): 95–99.
6. Michael Alexeev and Clifford Gaddy, "Income Distribution in the USSR in the 1980s," The National Council for Soviet and Eastern European Research, Nov. 27, 1992.
7. Olev Liivik, "The Elite and Their Privileges in the Soviet Union," *Communist Crimes*, Oct. 28, 2020, https://communistcrimes.org /en/elite-and-their-privileges-soviet-union.
8. Ayn Rand, "Introducing Objectivism," *Los Angeles Times*, June 17, 1962, https://courses.aynrand.org/works/introducing-objectivism/.
9. Ayn Rand, "Conservatism: An Obituary," 1960, https://www .libertarianism.org/publications/essays/excursions/ayn-rand -altruism-part-4.
10. Ayn Rand, "The Mike Wallace Interview," Feb. 25, 1959, http://www.youtube.com/watch?v=7ukJiBZ8_4k.
11. Mark A. Noll, *America's Book: The Rise and Decline of a Bible Civilization, 1794–1911* (Oxford University Press, 2022), 471.
12. Ibid., 587.

13. Utopia, for Lack of a Better Word

1. Details about Coxey come from the Massillon Museum, https://www.massillonmuseum.org/documents/massillon-museum -archival-holdings-jacob-coxey.
2. 1 Corinthians 3:9.
3. If you didn't get the reference, it's Bill and Ted; you know, from the movie. Here's Keanu Reeves and Alex Winter explaining what it means to them: https://www.youtube.com/watch?v=gv0i8 YasmEM. Party on.

4. Lao Tzu, translated by John C.H. Wu, *Tao Te Ching* (Shambala Publications, 2006), chapter 54.
5. According to LendingTree: https://www.lendingtree.com/credit-cards/study/average-credit-card-interest-rate-in-america/; according to WalletHub: https://wallethub.com/answers/cc/highest-credit-card-interest-rate-2140660307/.
6. "Commercial Bank Interest Rate on Credit Card Plans, All Accounts," Federal Reserve Bank of St. Louis, fred.stlouisfed.org/series/TERMCBCCALLNS.
7. Bankrate.com: https://www.bankrate.com/mortgages/30-year-mortgage-rates/.
8. JPMorgan financial statements for the years mentioned; I did the math to get the total.
9. Jacob S. Coxey, *The Coxey Plan* (Jacob S. Coxey, 1914).
10. Dylan Miettinen, "USPS Pilots a Public Banking Program," *Marketplace*, Oct. 15, 2021 https://www.marketplace.org/2021/10/15/usps-pilots-a-public-banking-program/.
11. Brian Naylor, "Post Office Could Rack Up Billions by Offering Banking Services," NPR, Feb. 7, 2014, https://www.npr.org/2014/02/07/272652648/post-office-could-rack-up-billions-by-offering-money-services.
12. Miettinen, "USPS Pilots a Public Banking Program."
13. Morgan Ricks, John Crawford, and Lev Menand, "Central Banking for All: A Public Option for Bank Accounts," The Great Democracy Initiative, June 2018, https://rooseveltinstitute.org/wp-content/uploads/2021/08/GDI_Central-Banking-For-All_201806.pdf.
14. This total comes from four sources. Total household debt is about $18 trillion, as per the New York Federal Reserve: https://www.newyorkfed.org/microeconomics/hhdc. Corporate debt is about $14 trillion, as per the St. Louis Federal Reserve: https://fred.stlouisfed.org/series/BCNSDODNS. US federal debt is $36 trillion (and rising rapidly), according to the US Treasury Department: https://fiscaldata.treasury.gov/americas-finance-guide/national-debt/; total state and local debt is about $3.4 trillion, as per the St. Louis Fed: https://fred.stlouisfed.org/series/SLGSDODNS.
15. Terry Chan and Alexandra Dimitrijevic, "Global Debt Leverage: Is a Great Reset Coming?," S&P Global, Jan. 13, 2023, https://www.spglobal.com/en/research-insights/special-reports/look-forward/global-debt-leverage-is-a-great-reset-coming.

16. Masood Ahmed, "Defaulting on Africa's Future," Project Syndicate, June 21, 2023.
17. The source for these numbers is the US Treasury Department.
18. Jagadeesh Gokhale and Kent Smetters, "When Does the Federal Debt Reach Unsustainable Levels?," Penn Wharton Budget Model, Oct. 6, 2023.
19. Lalith P. Samarakoon, "What Broke the Pearl of the Indian Ocean? The Causes of the Sri Lankan Economic Crisis and Its Policy Implications," *Journal of Financial Stability* 70 (February 2024).
20. "Sri Lanka's Economic Crisis and Debt Restructuring Efforts," Reuters, April 16, 2024.
21. "Sri Lanka: Economic Crisis Puts Rights in Peril," Human Rights Watch, Aug. 16, 2022.

INDEX

ABOUT THE AUTHOR

Jeff Bush

Paul Vigna worked as a reporter and editor for Dow Jones Newswires and *The Wall Street Journal* for twenty-five years. He is the author of *Guts* and coauthor of *The Age of Cryptocurrency* and *The Truth Machine*. He has appeared on CNN, CNBC, MSNBC, Fox, and PBS.